AF751013

Research and Applications of Digital Signal Processing

Edited by Joceli Mayer, Malek Karaim and Aboelmagd Noureldin

Published in London, United Kingdom

Research and Applications of Digital Signal Processing
http://dx.doi.org/10.5772/intechopen.1005988
Edited by Joceli Mayer, Malek Karaim and Aboelmagd Noureldin

Contributors
Arturo Hernández-Méndez, Azadeh Mehrabian, Boualem Boashash, Cesar Arriaga-Arriaga, Christopher Mhlongo, Dídac Diego-Tortosa, Gerardo Mino-Aguilar, Germán Ardul Muñoz Hernández, Ha H. Cao, Ibidun Christiana Obagbuwa, Jesús Linares-Flores, José Antonio Juárez-Abad, José Fermi Guerrero-Castellanos, Marian Ghenescu, María Campo-Valera, Md. Sarwar Hosain, Mertcan Özdemir, Mohammad Al-Sa'd, Osman Eroğul, Rafael Asorey-Cacheda, Roxana Elena Mihaescu, Roya Seifipour, Seemeen Wookey, Serban Carata, Siyu Zhang, Tetsuya Shimamura, Tlotlo Fanuel Sebati, Unarine Mukwevho, Wendong Mao, Zhongfeng Wang

© The Editor(s) and the Author(s) 2025

The rights of the editor(s) and the author(s) have been asserted in accordance with the Copyright, Designs and Patents Act 1988. All rights to the book as a whole are reserved by INTECHOPEN LIMITED. The book as a whole (compilation) cannot be reproduced, distributed or used for commercial or non-commercial purposes without INTECHOPEN LIMITED's written permission. Enquiries concerning the use of the book should be directed to INTECHOPEN LIMITED rights and permissions department (permissions@intechopen.com).

Violations are liable to prosecution under the governing Copyright Law.

Individual chapters of this publication are distributed under the terms of the Creative Commons Attribution 4.0 License which permits commercial use, distribution and reproduction of the individual chapters, provided the original author(s) and source publication are appropriately acknowledged. If so indicated, certain images may not be included under the Creative Commons license. In such cases users will need to obtain permission from the license holder to reproduce the material. More details and guidelines concerning content reuse and adaptation can be found at http://www.intechopen.com/copyright-policy.html.

Notice

Statements and opinions expressed in the chapters are these of the individual contributors and not necessarily those of the editors or publisher. No responsibility is accepted for the accuracy of information contained in the published chapters. The publisher assumes no responsibility for any damage or injury to persons or property arising out of the use of any materials, instructions, methods or ideas contained in the book.

First published in London, United Kingdom, 2025 by IntechOpen
IntechOpen is the global imprint of INTECHOPEN LIMITED, registered in England and Wales, registration number: 11086078, 167-169 Great Portland Street, London, W1W 5PF, United Kingdom

For EU product safety concerns: IN TECH d.o.o., Prolaz Marije Krucifikse Kozulić 3, 51000 Rijeka, Croatia, info@intechopen.com or visit our website at intechopen.com.

British Library Cataloguing-in-Publication Data
A catalogue record for this book is available from the British Library

Research and Applications of Digital Signal Processing
Edited by Joceli Mayer, Malek Karaim and Aboelmagd Noureldin
p. cm.
Print ISBN 978-1-83634-497-1
Online ISBN 978-1-83634-496-4
eBook (PDF) ISBN 978-1-83634-498-8

If disposing of this product, please recycle the paper responsibly.

IntechOpen
intechopen.com

Built by scientists, for scientists

Explore all IntechOpen books

Meet the editors

Dr. Joceli Mayer graduated with a degree in electrical engineering from the Universidade Federal de Santa Catarina (UFSC), Brazil, in 1998. He received a master's degree in Electrical Engineering from UFSC in 1991 and a master's degree in Computer Engineering, as well as a DPhil, from the University of California, Santa Cruz (UCSC), USA, in 1998 and 1999, respectively. He received the Best Student Paper Award from the IEEE International Conference on Image Processing and IBM in 2006 and became an IEEE senior member in 2012. Currently, Dr. Mayer is a Full Professor of Electrical Engineering at UFSC. He has published more than 100 articles in conferences and periodicals, authored two books and two chapters, and advised undergraduate and graduate students on research projects. He has developed and supervised projects in super-resolution, speech compression, VOIP systems, image processing, computational vision, digital watermarking, hardcopy document authentication, and assistive technology applications for individuals with hearing, speech, and mobility disabilities, utilizing the Internet of Things and speech recognition technologies. His research has been supported by industry and government agencies, including FINEP, CNPq, Hewlett-Packard, and Intelbras, among others.

Dr. Aboelmagd Noureldin is a Professor and Tier-I Canada Research Chair (CRC) in Resilient High-Precision Positioning and Navigation at the Department of Electrical and Computer Engineering, Royal Military College of Canada (RMC), with Cross-Appointment at both the School of Computing and the Department of Electrical and Computer Engineering, Queen's University. He is also the founding director of the Navigation and Instrumentation (NavINST) research group at RMC, a unique world-class research facility in GNSS, LEO-based Satellite Positioning and Navigation, mmWave wireless positioning, inertial navigation, remote sensing and multi-sensory fusion for navigation and guidance. He published two books, four book chapters, and numerous papers in academic journals, conferences, and workshop proceedings, for which he received several awards. Dr. Noureldin's research led to 13 patents and several technologies licensed to industry.

Malek Karaim holds dual master's degrees and a Ph.D. in Electrical and Computer Engineering, specializing in GNSS, INS, and multi-sensor fusion for vehicular navigation. His work spans Bayesian estimation, Kalman and Particle filtering, Fast Orthogonal Search, and AI-driven algorithms for robust positioning in challenging environments. Recently, he has focused on leveraging LEO satellite signals as an augmentation and alternative to GNSS, advancing navigation resilience under interference and denial scenarios. Malek serves as Head of the Scientific Research and Consultation Office at the Faculty of Engineering and is a member of the International Rankings Committee at the University of Zawia. He is also a Research Associate with the Navigation and Instrumentation Group at the Royal Military College of Canada and Queen's University, where he collaborates on projects involving smart IMU fault detection, GNSS jamming mitigation, and AI-enhanced navigation systems. His contributions include extensive industry collaborations and leadership in applied research and development.

Contents

Preface

Digital Signal Processing (DSP) has emerged as one of the most transformative and influential fields in modern engineering and technology. As we navigate an increasingly interconnected and data-driven world, the ability to efficiently acquire, analyze, manipulate, and interpret digital signals has become fundamental to virtually every aspect of our technological infrastructure. From the smartphones in our pockets to the medical imaging systems that save lives, from autonomous vehicles navigating our streets to the financial algorithms that power global markets, DSP techniques form the invisible backbone that enables these remarkable capabilities.

The rapid evolution of computational power, coupled with advances in machine learning and artificial intelligence, has opened unprecedented opportunities for DSP research and applications. Today's signal processing challenges extend far beyond traditional domains, encompassing complex multidimensional data, real-time processing requirements, and the integration of intelligent algorithms that can adapt and learn from the signals they process. This convergence of classical signal processing theory with modern computational methods has created a rich landscape of research opportunities and practical applications that continue to push the boundaries of what is possible.

The importance of DSP research lies not only in its theoretical foundations but also in its profound impact on society. Whether it's enabling early detection of medical conditions through advanced imaging techniques, improving communication systems to connect remote communities, or developing more efficient energy conversion systems, DSP research directly contributes to solving some of humanity's most pressing challenges. As we face an era of exponential data growth and increasing computational demands, the development of efficient, robust, and intelligent signal processing algorithms becomes more critical than ever.

This book presents a comprehensive exploration of contemporary DSP research and applications, organized into four distinct sections that reflect the diverse and interconnected nature of the field. Each section addresses different aspects of signal processing, from fundamental image analysis techniques to cutting-edge neural network implementations, providing readers with both theoretical insights and practical applications.

The section on "Signal Processing Analysis" focuses on highly specialized signal processing applications that address unique challenges in biological and acoustic signal analysis. The chapter "Time-Frequency Functional Brain Networks: Application to Newborn Seizure Analysis" presents groundbreaking research in time-frequency functional brain network analysis, specifically applied to the detection of newborn seizures. This chapter showcases advanced time-frequency analysis techniques and multiplex network approaches for processing electroencephalogram signals, demonstrating how sophisticated DSP methods can contribute to early medical intervention and improved patient outcomes.

The chapter "Signal Processing for Estimating the Time of Arrival and Amplitude of Nonlinear Underwater Acoustic Waves" addresses the complex challenges of underwater acoustic signal processing, with a focus on estimating the time of arrival and amplitude of nonlinear acoustic waves. This research is crucial for underwater communication systems, marine exploration, and naval applications, as it illustrates how DSP techniques must be adapted to handle the unique propagation characteristics and nonlinear effects present in underwater acoustic environments.

The section on "Image Processing and Computer Vision" focuses on the foundational aspects of visual signal processing and computer vision applications. This section begins with the chapter "Analysis of the Characteristics of the Formation of Multispectral Television Component Signals", which examines the characteristics of multispectral television component signal formation. This chapter explores the technical aspects of color filter systems, adaptive demosaicing techniques, and image recovery methods, offering essential insights into how multispectral imaging systems process and reconstruct visual information across multiple spectral bands.

The chapter "Kimberley Road Degradation Detection Using Digital Image Processing" continues the image processing theme by addressing practical applications in infrastructure monitoring through the Kimberley Road Degradation Detection project. This chapter demonstrates how digital image processing techniques, combined with deep learning approaches, can be effectively applied to real-world problems such as automated road defect detection and infrastructure maintenance, showcasing the practical impact of DSP in civil engineering and urban planning.

The section concludes with the chapter "GDPR Compliance in Video Surveillance Systems and Applications", which explores the critical intersection of technology and privacy through GDPR compliance in video surveillance systems. This chapter addresses the growing importance of ethical considerations in signal processing applications, examining how modern object detection algorithms, such as YOLO, can be implemented while maintaining compliance with data protection regulations, and highlighting the responsibility that comes with powerful signal processing capabilities.

The section on "Deep Learning and Neural Networks" represents the cutting edge of signal processing research, where traditional DSP techniques meet artificial intelligence and machine learning. The chapter "Efficient DNN Algorithm Design and Hardware Acceleration for Low-Level Vision" opens this section with an exploration of efficient Deep Neural Network (DNN) algorithm design tailored explicitly for low-level vision tasks. This chapter addresses the critical challenge of balancing computational efficiency with performance in image and video processing applications, providing insights into hardware acceleration strategies that make real-time deep learning applications feasible.

The chapter "Deep Learning Methods for Accelerated Cardiac MRI Reconstruction" presents a specialized application of deep learning in medical imaging, focusing on accelerated cardiac MRI reconstruction. This chapter demonstrates how advanced techniques such as Generative Adversarial Networks and diffusion models can significantly reduce MRI acquisition times while maintaining diagnostic image quality, representing a perfect example of how DSP research directly impacts healthcare outcomes.

The chapter "Enhancing Speech Emotion Recognition through Bone-Conducted Speech" explores the emerging field of speech emotion recognition through bone-conducted speech processing. By combining BiLSTM networks with attention mechanisms, this research opens new possibilities for human-computer interaction and assistive technologies, demonstrating how novel signal acquisition methods can be enhanced through sophisticated processing algorithms.

The section concludes with the chapter "Application of Artificial Neural Networks in Economic and Financial Sciences", which examines the application of artificial neural networks in economic and financial sciences. This chapter illustrates the versatility of neural network approaches in signal processing, showing how these techniques can be adapted for economic trend prediction, resource allocation optimization, and investment strategy development, thereby extending DSP applications beyond traditional engineering domains.

The final section bridges the gap between theoretical signal processing concepts and their practical implementation in hardware and control systems. The chapter "Robust Flat Filtering DSP-Based Control of the Buck-Boost Power Converter" presents research on robust flat filtering DSP-based control of buck-boost power converters. This chapter demonstrates the application of advanced control theory and DSP implementation techniques in power electronics, showing how digital signal processing can improve the efficiency and reliability of energy conversion systems.

The chapter "How Open-Source Wireless Networking Frameworks Can Contribute to Advances in Adaptive Filtering: Theory and Application" concludes the book by exploring how open-source wireless networking frameworks can contribute to advances in adaptive filtering theory and applications. This chapter addresses the growing importance of open-source development in DSP research and highlights the potential for collaborative approaches to solve complex signal processing challenges in 5G networks and software-defined networking environments.

Together, these chapters represent the current state of digital signal processing research and applications, demonstrating both the maturity of established techniques and the exciting potential of emerging approaches. The diversity of applications—from medical imaging to financial analysis, from infrastructure monitoring to underwater acoustics—illustrates the universal applicability of DSP principles while highlighting the need for specialized solutions to domain-specific challenges.

As we look toward the future, the integration of artificial intelligence with traditional signal processing methods promises to unlock even greater capabilities, while the increasing emphasis on ethical considerations and privacy protection ensures that these powerful techniques will be developed and deployed responsibly. This book serves as both a comprehensive reference for current practitioners and an inspiration for the next generation of researchers who will continue to push the boundaries of what is possible in digital signal processing.

We hope that readers will find in these pages not only technical knowledge but also inspiration for their own research and applications, thereby contributing to the continued evolution of this dynamic field.

Joceli Mayer
Department of Electrical and Electronics Engineering (EEL),
Federal University of Santa Catarina (UFSC),
Florianopolis, Brazil

Malek Karaim
Queen's University,
Kingston, Canada

Aboelmagd Noureldin
Royal Military College of Canada,
Kingston, Canada

Section 1

Signal Processing Analysis

Chapter 1

Time-Frequency Functional Brain Networks: Application to Newborn Seizure Analysis

Mohammad Al-Sa'd and Boualem Boashash

Abstract

This chapter describes a time-frequency (TF) signal processing framework for constructing functional brain networks (FBNs) from multichannel electroencephalogram (EEG) recordings. Standard methods often rely on time- or frequency-domain connectivity measures, assuming local stationarity and thereby failing to capture the dynamic and frequency-specific nature of brain interactions. To address this limitation, we introduce TF-based extensions of amplitude and phase connectivity by leveraging multi-sensor time-frequency distributions. These extensions preserve the joint temporal and spectral structure of EEG signals, enabling localized analysis of energy coupling and phase synchrony. The novelty of this framework lies in its ability to compute connectivity directly from the TF domain using cross-sensor tempo-spectral representations, thus revealing transient interactions and avoiding distortions from temporal or spectral averaging. This unified approach allows for improved spatial resolution, better handling of non-stationarity, and reduced sensitivity to spurious correlations arising from volume conduction or sample bias. We demonstrate the practical utility of the proposed framework through an application to neonatal EEG, where pathological seizure networks are analyzed and contrasted with healthy and seizure-free brain states. The results show that TF-based networks can more reliably differentiate between clinical conditions, including disturbances during non-seizure periods that are not captured by traditional methods. Overall, this chapter offers a general, high-resolution methodology for functional connectivity analysis in nonstationary multichannel signals, based on advances in signal processing theory and clinical diagnostics.

Keywords: time-frequency analysis, functional brain network, electroencephalogram, multiplex networks, coherence processing, synchrony, connectivity analysis, seizure detection

1. Introduction

The analysis of nonstationary, multi-sensor signals is a central problem in modern signal processing, with broad applications in communications, radar, and biomedical engineering where precise localization of events and patterns is required [1–3]. Among biomedical signals, the electroencephalography (EEG) presents unique

IntechOpen

challenges due to its multichannel, nonstationary nature and the need to extract meaningful structure from highly dynamic brain activity [4, 5]. EEG signals exhibit strong temporal and spectral variability, motivating the use of time-frequency (TF) analysis techniques to capture their evolving oscillatory content [5, 6]. In many applications, the goal of EEG analysis extends beyond analyzing individual sensor activity to understanding how brain regions interact, giving rise to the computational model of functional brain networks (FBNs) [4, 7]. These networks model statistical dependencies between pairs of EEG channels, revealing the large-scale coordination underlying cognitive function or neurological disorders [4, 8]. Nevertheless, most traditional methods construct FBNs using time- or frequency-domain measures that assume local stationarity and often fail to capture rapid, transient interactions crucial for real-time analysis or clinical interpretation [9].

This chapter provides a general framework for constructing TF functional brain networks (TF-FBNs) by extending widely used amplitude-based and phase-based connectivity measures into the TF domain [4, 8]. The approach leverages multi-sensor time-frequency distributions (MTFDs) to enable fine-grained, localized analysis of brain connectivity across time, frequency, and space [3]. Specifically, we define TF extensions of pairwise correlation and generalize various phase synchrony measures to compute TF-localized connectivity from inter-sensor tempo-spectral representations [10]. These extensions address key limitations of conventional FBN methods: (1) they preserve the nonstationary signal structure, (2) reduce reliance on temporal averaging, and (3) mitigate the effects of volume conduction. As a demonstration of the practical value of this framework, we apply it to the analysis of seizures from neonatal EEG recordings, a clinically critical task where conventional measures often fail to identify subtle or early-stage network disruptions [6]. This application highlights the framework's capacity to detect both overt and latent patterns of abnormal synchronization, particularly in dynamic and frequency-specific regimes.

A wide range of methods for FBN construction have been proposed, generally categorized into amplitude-based and phase-based measures [9, 11, 12]. Amplitude-based methods, such as pairwise correlation, quantify linear or monotonic dependencies between EEG signal envelopes and have been applied to track developmental changes or global synchrony fluctuations [9]. Phase-based methods, such as phase locking value and phase lag index, exploit phase synchrony to reveal directional or coherent oscillatory coupling [3, 4, 11, 12]. More advanced versions address common issues such as volume conduction and sample-size bias. Despite their utility, these measures are typically computed in the time domain or within predefined frequency bands, relying on windowed averaging and assumptions of signal stationarity [9]. This, however, restricts their ability to capture fast, localized changes in connectivity, which are especially relevant in dynamic neurological conditions such as epilepsy [7]. Time-frequency analysis, by contrast, enables simultaneous temporal and spectral resolution, making it well suited for analyzing transient or task-related brain connectivity [1, 5]. In signal processing terms, a time-frequency representation (TFR) characterizes how a signal's spectral content evolves, using tools such as the short-time Fourier transform, wavelets, or bilinear distributions [1, 13]. This joint representation allows nonstationary features, like bursts, shifts in oscillatory content, or brief synchrony changes, to be captured without assuming global stationarity [2]. While some early efforts have attempted TF-based coherence or synchrony measures using spectrogram, wavelet, and Rihaczek distributions, they often lack adaptability or spatial generality [9, 11]. In other words, there is a need for a signal processing framework that enables robust, high-resolution FBN construction using multivariate TF signal representations.

The remainder of this chapter describes the proposed approach and is structured as follows. Section 2 reviews conventional functional brain network analysis methods, including amplitude- and phase-based connectivity metrics, and discusses their limitations in nonstationary environments. Section 3 introduces the proposed TF framework, detailing the basis of multi-sensor TF signal processing and the extensions of amplitude- and phase-based connectivity measures. Section 4 presents the application to neonatal seizure EEG analysis, including clinical context, data processing, and dynamic network construction. Section 5 discusses the results, contrasting traditional and TF-based connectivity measures across clinical groups. Finally, Section 6 concludes the chapter by summarizing the key contributions, discussing their novelty, and outlining future research directions for improving and applying TF-based brain network analysis in general signal processing and neuroscience.

2. Conventional functional brain networks

Functional brain network analysis characterizes neural interactions by examining the relationships between signals recorded from multiple EEG sensors [4]. These interactions can be quantified using different connectivity measures, broadly categorized into amplitude-based and phase-based networks [9]. Amplitude-based networks capture dependencies in the signal-level fluctuations, while phase-based networks measure the synchronization of neural oscillations across brain regions [9]. By constructing connectivity matrices from these measures, we can model large-scale brain networks and analyze their topological properties to investigate the differences between network configurations [4, 8].

2.1 Multi-sensor signal processing

EEG signals are inherently multicomponent and nonstationary, reflecting the dynamic interplay of neural activity across distributed brain networks [5]. Analyzing these signals requires a mathematical framework that effectively captures their time-varying structure while accounting for both spectral and spatial complexities. In multi-sensor EEG recordings, each electrode measures a merger of overlapping neural sources, making it essential to model the signal as a combination of distinct components with varying amplitude and frequency. A well-defined signal representation not only facilitates the extraction of meaningful neural features but also enhances the interpretation of functional connectivity and transient oscillatory patterns. In the following, we formulate a multi-sensor signal model that provides a structured basis for EEG analysis, enabling the precise characterization of neural dynamics across time and space.

Let $\boldsymbol{s}(t) = [s_1(t), s_2(t), \cdots, s_P(t)]^T$ be a multi-sensor signal collected from P sensors, such that $s_p(t)$ is a multicomponent waveform defined as:

$$s_p(t) = \sum_{k=1}^{K_p} s_{p,k}(t) = \sum_{k=1}^{K_p} A_{p,k}(t) \cos\left(\phi_{p,k}(t)\right) \Pi\left(\frac{t - C_{p,k}}{T_{p,k}}\right), \tag{1}$$

$$\phi_{p,k}(t) = 2\pi \int f_{p,k}(t)\, \mathrm{d}t, \tag{2}$$

$$\Pi(t) = \begin{cases} 1 & : -1/2 \leq t \leq 1/2 \\ 0 & : \text{otherwise} \end{cases}, \tag{3}$$

where K_p is the number of components in $s_p(t)$, $A_{p,k}(t)$, $\phi_{p,k}(t)$, and $f_{p,k}(t)$ are the instantaneous amplitude (IA), instantaneous phase (IP), and instantaneous frequency (IF) of the kth component, respectively, $T_{p,k}$ is the component's duration, $C_{p,k} = t_{p,k}^{\text{start}} + T_{p,k}/2$ is its center time, and $t_{p,k}^{\text{start}}$ is the start time. This multi-sensor signal model provides a structured representation of EEG signals by decomposing each recorded waveform into time-localized components. Each component is defined by its IA and IF, capturing the nonstationary nature of neural oscillations [5]. The rectangular window function ensures temporal localization, allowing for precise modeling of transient neural activity. By summing these components, the model effectively describes the multifrequency composition of EEG signals, facilitating functional connectivity analysis and distinguishing between normal and pathological brain dynamics.

Now, let $\boldsymbol{z}(t) = [z_1(t), z_2(t), \cdots, z_P(t)]^T$ be the analytic associate of the multi-sensor signal $\boldsymbol{s}(t)$ obtained via the Hilbert transform as follows:

$$\boldsymbol{z}(t) = \boldsymbol{s}(t) + j\int \frac{\boldsymbol{s}(t-\xi)}{\pi\xi}\, d\xi, \tag{4}$$

where $j = \sqrt{-1}$ and ξ is an integration dummy variable. This analytic signal representation $\boldsymbol{z}(t)$ provides a complex-valued version of the original multi-sensor signal $\boldsymbol{s}(t)$, enabling a detailed characterization of its IP law [13]. For instance, one can simply compute the relative phases between two signals $z_p(t)$ and $z_q(t)$ as follows:

$$\phi_{pq}(t) = \phi_p(t) - \phi_q(t) = \arg\left(\frac{z_p(t) z_q^*(t)}{|z_p(t)|\,|z_q(t)|}\right), \tag{5}$$

where $p, q \in [1, P]$ and $z_p^*(t)$ is the complex conjugate of $z_p(t)$.

2.2 Amplitude-based networks

Amplitude-based functional connectivity quantifies the statistical relationships between the amplitude of the EEG signals [9]. In this chapter, Pearson's correlation and Spearman's correlation are used to estimate amplitude-based connectivity. These correlation measures describe how neural activity fluctuates in amplitude across brain regions and provide insights into large-scale neuronal coordination, aiding in identifying functionally coupled areas. The Pearson's correlation captures linear amplitude relationships and is suitable under the assumption of normally distributed data, while the Spearman's correlation measures monotonic associations and remains robust in the presence of non-Gaussian distributions and outliers. Using both measures ensures that amplitude-based connectivity can be reliably assessed across varying statistical properties of EEG signals, enhancing the generalization of the analysis.

2.2.1 Pearson's correlation

It is a parametric measure that quantifies the linear relationship between two continuous variables. It is most appropriate when the amplitude values are normally distributed, and it assumes a bivariate normal distribution in the population [14]. Pearson's correlation is highly sensitive to outliers and may be inflated or distorted when the data contains extreme values. Moreover, Pearson's correlation is sensitive to the scale of measurement and its settings, meaning that correlation values computed from one dataset may not be directly comparable to those from another if the underlying signal amplitudes differ, even when the strength of association is similar [14].

2.2.2 Spearman's correlation

It is a rank-based, nonparametric measure that assesses monotonic relationships, whether linear or nonlinear [15]. By ranking the amplitude values before computing the correlation, the Spearman's method reduces the impact of outliers and non-Gaussian distributions, making it more robust for real data where amplitude distributions may exhibit heavy tails or skewness [15]. It is instrumental when the data exhibit nonlinear but monotonic trends, ensuring that functional connectivity can still be detected in the presence of nonlinearity.

2.3 Phase-based networks

Phase-based functional connectivity focuses on the synchronization of oscillatory neural activity across EEG sensors [4, 8, 11, 12]. This chapter used multiple single-trial phase-synchronization measures, including the phase locking value (PLV), imaginary PLV (iPLV), corrected imaginary PLV (ciPLV), phase lag index (PLI), weighted PLI (wPLI), and debiased weighted PLI (dwPLI). These phase-based measures provide complementary insights into neural synchronization, with PLV capturing general phase consistency and others minimizing spurious connections due to volume conduction and measurement biases.

The problem of volume conduction refers to the instantaneous spread of electrical activity across the scalp due to the conductive properties of brain tissue and the skull. This can create artificial zero-lag correlations between signals recorded at different electrodes, leading to spurious indications of synchrony that do not reflect true neural interactions [11, 12]. To address this, one must discount or suppress zero-lag components, thereby focusing on non-instantaneous, physiologically meaningful interactions [11, 12].

2.3.1 Phase locking value

The PLV measure quantifies the consistency of IP differences between two signals over time, i.e., [12]:

$$\mathrm{PLV}(p,q,t) = \left|\mathbb{E}_t\left[e^{j\phi_{pq}(t)}\right]\right|, \tag{6}$$

where $\mathbb{E}_t[.]$ is the expectation operator over a short moving window centered around t, ensuring a localized estimate. A PLV value close to 1 indicates strong phase synchronization, while a value near 0 suggests no phase relationship. The PLV is highly sensitive to volume conduction, which can lead to overestimating connectivity, even when no functional interaction exists [12].

2.3.2 Imaginary phase locking value

To reduce the effect of volume conduction, iPLV extends PLV by considering only the imaginary component of the phase difference, such that [12]:

$$\mathrm{iPLV}(p,q,t) = \left|\mathbb{E}_t\left[\Im\left(e^{j\phi_{pq}(t)}\right)\right]\right|, \tag{7}$$

where $\Im(x)$ is the imaginary part of a complex number x. Since volume conduction typically causes zero-lag synchronization, iPLV helps remove spurious connections. Specifically, the imaginary part mitigates the issue by isolating non-zero-lag components of the phase difference, which are less likely to result from volume conduction and more indicative of genuine functional connectivity. However, iPLV suffers from biases related to signal duration, potentially leading to inconsistent estimates in shorter recordings [12].

2.3.3 Corrected imaginary phase locking value

The ciPLV improves upon the iPLV by normalizing the imaginary component, reducing bias from variations in data length, and improving robustness across different EEG recordings as follows [12]:

$$\mathrm{ciPLV}(p,q,t) = \frac{\left|\mathbb{E}_t\left[\Im\left(e^{j\phi_{pq}(t)}\right)\right]\right|}{\sqrt{1-\left(\left|\mathbb{E}_t\left[\Re\left(e^{j\phi_{pq}(t)}\right)\right]\right|\right)^2}}, \tag{8}$$

where $\Re(x)$ is the real part of a complex number x. The denominator in Eq. (8) serves as a normalization factor. Specifically, it reflects the residual variance in the unit phasor after removing the influence of the real part (zero-lag contribution). When the real component has a high magnitude, indicative of strong zero-lag coupling, the denominator becomes small, thereby emphasizing deviations from zero-lag effects. Conversely, when the real component is negligible, the denominator approaches one, allowing the imaginary part (non-zero-lag interactions) to dominate. This correction ensures that ciPLV equals 0 when there is no consistent phase lag and approaches 1 when there is strong and consistent non-zero-lag phase synchronization.

2.3.4 Phase lag index

The PLI improves connectivity estimation by ignoring phase differences that are too close to zero [11]. It focuses only on phase lags that are consistently positive or negative, making it more resistant to volume conduction errors, i.e.:

$$\mathrm{PLI}(p,q,t) = \left|\mathbb{E}_t\left[\mathrm{sign}\left(\Im\left(e^{j\phi_{pq}(t)}\right)\right)\right]\right|. \tag{9}$$

Unfortunately, the PLI does not account for the magnitude of phase differences. In other words, it only considers whether a phase lead or lag exists, which causes it to discard valuable information [11].

2.3.5 Weighted phase lag index

The wPLI mitigates the PLI's pitfalls using the cross-spectral density formulation and by weighting the phase differences with their magnitude, i.e., [8]:

$$\mathrm{wPLI}(p,q,t) = \left|\frac{\int \Im\left(Z_p(f)Z_q^*(f)\right)\,df}{\int\left|\Im\left(Z_p(f)Z_q^*(f)\right)\right|\,df}\right|, \tag{10}$$

where $Z_p(f)$ is the frequency representation of $z_p(t)$ obtained via the Fourier transform over a short moving window around t to ensure a localized connectivity estimate and f denotes frequency. Unfortunately, the wPLI is still affected by small sample sizes and can become unreliable due to statistical biases.

2.3.6 Debiased weighted phase lag index

The dwPLI corrects for the small-sample bias in wPLI, making it more robust while preserving its advantages [4]. It provides the most refined measure of phase synchronization, minimizing false connections while maintaining sensitivity to genuine neural interactions as follows [4]:

$$\mathrm{dwPLI}(p,q,t) = \left| \frac{\left[\int \Im\left(Z_p(f) Z_q^*(f)\right) \mathrm{d}f\right]^2 - \int \left[\Im\left(Z_p(f) Z_q^*(f)\right)\right]^2 \mathrm{d}f}{\left[\int \left|\Im\left(Z_p(f) Z_q^*(f)\right)\right| \mathrm{d}f\right]^2 - \int \left[\Im\left(Z_p(f) Z_q^*(f)\right)\right]^2 \mathrm{d}f} \right|. \tag{11}$$

3. Advanced time-frequency functional brain networks

Functional connectivity analysis in EEG is traditionally performed in either the time domain or in the frequency domain, often assuming that neural interactions remain stable over time. However, as previously mentioned, brain connectivity patterns are inherently nonstationary, meaning that interactions between neural regions evolve dynamically in response to task demands, cognitive states, and pathological conditions [4, 6, 9]. To address these limitations, we introduce a novel TF functional brain networks model by extending conventional time- or frequency-based connectivity measures to the TF domain. This TF extension provides several advantages over traditional approaches:

1. Capturing transient connectivity dynamics—Conventional connectivity measures assume stable interactions across time, making them insensitive to short-lived or event-related connectivity shifts. TF-based measures allow for the detection of momentary synchronization and desynchronization events that might otherwise be overlooked [9].

2. Providing frequency-resolved connectivity insights—Many brain functions rely on frequency-specific oscillations that coordinate information flow within and between neural networks. TF-based connectivity allows for the precise identification of which frequency bands contribute to functional interactions over time [4].

3. Tracking task-related and event-related connectivity changes—Unlike static connectivity methods, TF-based measures allow analyzing the dynamic evolution of neural interactions in response to cognitive tasks, sensory stimuli, or pathological conditions. This is especially useful for studying working memory, attention shifts, and seizure propagation [9].

4. Improving robustness against spurious broadband correlations—Conventional measures often aggregate connectivity over broad time windows or frequency bands, which can lead to misleading estimates. TF-based measures avoid

artificial connectivity inflation by evaluating localized connectivity dynamics in specific time-frequency regions [11].

5. Enhancing multi-scale network analysis—TF functional connectivity enables the study of connectivity patterns across multiple temporal and spectral resolutions. This is particularly important for investigating slow (e.g., delta-band) and fast (e.g., gamma-band) oscillatory interactions, which play distinct roles in cognition and neural processing [6].

3.1 Multi-sensor time-frequency signal processing

Time-frequency analysis is fundamental for characterizing nonstationary signals, such as EEG, where spectral content varies over time [2, 5]. A time-frequency representation (TFR), generated by a time-frequency distribution (TFD), is designed to describe the signal's temporal and spectral evolution, enabling the analysis of transient oscillatory activity [1]. Multi-sensor TF analysis extends this notion by accounting for spatial correlations across multiple channels to capture individual sensor dynamics and interchannel relationships [3, 10]. The formulation of multi-sensor time-frequency distributions (MTFDs) is structured to incorporate both intra- and inter-sensor relationships. This formulation provides a comprehensive means of analyzing the spectral and phase interactions across EEG sensors, supporting functional connectivity and brain network studies.

The MTFD of the multi-sensor signal $\boldsymbol{s}(t)$ utilizes the analytic associate representation in Eq. (4) and is expressed in this general matrix form [3]:

$$\boldsymbol{\rho}_{\boldsymbol{z}}(t,f) = \begin{bmatrix} \rho_{z_1z_1}(t,f) & \rho_{z_1z_2}(t,f) & \cdots & \rho_{z_1z_P}(t,f) \\ \rho_{z_2z_1}(t,f) & \rho_{z_2z_2}(t,f) & \cdots & \rho_{z_2z_P}(t,f) \\ \vdots & \vdots & \ddots & \vdots \\ \rho_{z_Pz_1}(t,f) & \rho_{z_Pz_2}(t,f) & \cdots & \rho_{z_Pz_P}(t,f) \end{bmatrix}, \tag{12}$$

$$\rho_{z_pz_q}(t,f) = \iint G(t-\xi,\tau) z_p\left(\xi + \frac{\tau}{2}\right) z_q^*\left(\xi - \frac{\tau}{2}\right) e^{-j2\pi\tau f}\, \mathrm{d}\xi\, \mathrm{d}\tau, \tag{13}$$

where $\boldsymbol{\rho}_{\boldsymbol{z}}(t,f)$ is the MTFD matrix, $\rho_{z_pz_q}(t,f)$ is the cross-TFD of the analytic signals $z_p(t)$ and $z_q(t)$, $G(t,\tau)$ is the time-lag kernel, and τ denotes lag. The MTFD matrix in Eq. (12) organizes the auto- and cross-TFDs of the analytic signals across different sensors. The diagonal elements represent auto-TFDs, which describe the tempo-spectral energy distribution of individual sensor waveforms, while the off-diagonal elements correspond to cross-TFDs, capturing the tempo-spectral interactions across different sensors [3]. These cross-TFDs quantify how spectral energy is shared across EEG channels over time, which is key for assessing functional connectivity and neural synchronization. Moreover, Eq. (13) provides an explicit formulation of the cross-TFD, where the time-lag kernel $G(t,\tau)$ acts as a smoothing function to suppress interference patterns, named cross-terms, that emerge because of the TFD's bilinear nature [1, 13]. However, there is a more convenient space, called the Doppler-lag domain, that simplifies this formulation by converting convolutions to multiplications, i.e., [1]:

$$\rho_{z_pz_q}(t,f) = \iiint g(\nu,\tau)\, z_p\left(\xi + \frac{\tau}{2}\right) z_q^*\left(\xi - \frac{\tau}{2}\right) e^{-j2\pi(\xi\nu + \tau f - \nu t)}\, \mathrm{d}\xi\, \mathrm{d}\nu\, \mathrm{d}\tau, \tag{14}$$

$$g(\nu,\tau) = \int G(t,\tau)e^{-j2\pi t\nu}\, dt, \tag{15}$$

where ν denotes Doppler and $g(\nu,\tau)$ is the Doppler-lag kernel. This alternative formulation allows the design of high-performing TFDs that exhibit excellent energy concentration with minimal blurring. For instance, the compact support kernel (CSK) has been identified as the most effective approach for generating high-resolution and accurate TFRs [13]. It is well suited for analyzing various signal types in different applications [5].

The CSK is a separable Doppler-lag kernel comprised of two independent smoothing functions operating on the Doppler and lag axes, i.e., [1, 16]:

$$g(\nu,\tau) = e^{\left(c+\frac{cD^2}{\nu^2-D^2}\right)} e^{\left(c+\frac{cE^2}{\tau^2-E^2}\right)} : |\nu| < D, |\tau| < E, \tag{16}$$

where $D \in [0{,}0.5]$ and $E \in [0{,}0.5]$ are normalized cut-offs along the Doppler and lag axes, respectively, and $c > 0$ defines the CSK shape. The CSK's efficient implementation and design flexibility make it the best choice for accurately representing EEG dynamics, enhancing connectivity analysis, and supporting TF feature extraction for both cognitive and clinical applications [5, 16].

3.2 Time-frequency energy-based networks

Amplitude-based functional connectivity quantifies the statistical dependencies between EEG signal amplitudes. However, raw EEG waveforms are noisy and can exhibit rapid fluctuations, which can introduce instability in connectivity estimation and obscure meaningful interactions [2]. Since neural activity is structured across both time and frequency, its energy representation in the TF domain provides a smoother and more stable characterization of the signal dynamics. To better capture these properties, we extend traditional correlation measures to the TF domain, introducing TF-Pearson's correlation (TF-Pearson) and TF-Spearman's correlation (TF-Spearman). Using both of these measures provides complementary insights: While TF-Pearson is effective for detecting linear dependencies in energy fluctuations, TF-Spearman captures broader, possibly nonlinear monotonic relationships. This dual approach ensures robust energy-based connectivity estimation across different signal dynamics.

3.2.1 Time-frequency Pearson's correlation

Pearson's correlation measures the linear association between two signals but does not account for frequency-specific energy dependencies. In conventional EEG analysis, amplitude fluctuations can exhibit rapid variations, leading to highly dynamic correlation values that may obscure stable connectivity patterns. TF-Pearson resolves this by computing the correlation between TFRs instead of raw amplitudes. Since the energy in the TF domain is a smoother representation of signal dynamics, TF-Pearson provides a more stable measure of connectivity while preserving spectral specificity. Moreover, it captures frequency-dependent energy correlations, allowing for a refined analysis of how neural interactions evolve across oscillatory components. This is particularly useful for analyzing event-related connectivity and task-specific energy coupling, where interactions within specific frequency bands may drive network activity.

3.2.2 Time-frequency Spearman's correlation

Spearman's correlation quantifies monotonic relationships between signals, offering robustness against non-Gaussian-type distributions and outliers. It is applied in the time domain to raw amplitudes, but the rapid fluctuations can introduce instability in connectivity estimation. TF-Spearman extends this concept, similar to TF-Pearson, by computing the correlation between TFRs rather than raw amplitudes. This extension improves the detection of nonlinear dependencies in energy coupling, making it particularly useful for analyzing dynamic functional connectivity in EEG, including interactions influenced by cross-frequency coupling and nonstationary neural dynamics.

3.3 Time-frequency phase-based networks

Phase-based functional connectivity quantifies the synchronization of EEG signals. Traditional phase-based measures assume that synchronization remains stable over a given time window, averaging connectivity values, sometimes, over long durations [9]. However, brain connectivity is inherently nonstationary, meaning that phase synchronization fluctuates dynamically over time and across frequency bands [4]. To capture these transient connectivity dynamics, we extend phase-based functional connectivity measures to the TF domain, ensuring a localized, frequency-specific analysis of phase interactions. Specifically, instead of relying on the time-domain analytic signals alone, we extract phase information directly from the cross-TFD. By leveraging this formulation, we define a set of TF-based phase connectivity measures that offer continuous tracking of time- and frequency-dependent phase synchronization patterns.

3.3.1 Time-frequency phase locking value

The TF-PLV quantifies how consistently the relative phase difference between two signals remains stable at each TF point. It is computed as:

$$\text{TF-PLV}(p,q,t,f) = \left| \mathbb{E}_f \left[e^{j\arg\left[\rho_{z_p z_q}(t,f)\right]} \right] \right|, \tag{17}$$

where $\mathbb{E}_f[.]$ is the expectation operator over a spectral moving window around f, ensuring localized spectral estimates. The use of the expectation requires an important assumption. Since the operator is mathematically defined over a statistical ensemble, its application to a finite set of TF samples is only valid under the assumption of local ergodicity, i.e., the statistical properties of the underlying process can be estimated from its TF realizations within that window. The expectation operator, by definition, acts on an ensemble of realizations. In TF signal analysis, where only a single realization is typically available, one assumes local ergodicity to treat samples within a TF region as a surrogate ensemble. This assumption allows practical computation of statistical averages over short spectral neighborhoods. For an in-depth discussion, see Chapter I of Ref. [1].

Unlike conventional PLV, which provides a single connectivity value over a time window, TF-PLV enables a fine-grained, time-resolved analysis of synchronization. This makes it ideal for continuously tracking task-related changes in neural synchronization, particularly in studies where phase coupling emerges and disappears within short time intervals. Additionally, the ability to compute PLV at specific frequency points reduces the risk of masking frequency-specific phase-locking effects, which often occur in traditional implementations where different oscillatory components are averaged together.

3.3.2 Time-frequency imaginary phase locking value

Similar to iPLV, TF-iPLV refines TF-PLV by retaining the imaginary component of the phase difference, effectively removing zero-lag synchronization that may arise from volume conduction or common reference effects, i.e.:

$$\text{TF-iPLV}(p,q,t,f) = \left|\mathbb{E}_f\left[\Im\left(e^{j\arg\left[\rho_{z_p z_q}(t,f)\right]}\right)\right]\right|. \tag{18}$$

The TF-iPLV allows the detection of non-instantaneous, frequency-dependent phase interactions, which makes it particularly useful in studies of large-scale brain networks, where true long-range phase interactions are more relevant than spurious local associations.

3.3.3 Time-frequency corrected imaginary phase locking value

The TF-ciPLV builds upon TF-iPLV by normalizing the imaginary component of phase synchronization to address weak phase synchronization biases:

$$\text{TF-ciPLV}(p,q,t,f) = \frac{\left|\mathbb{E}_f\left[\Im\left(e^{j\arg\left[\rho_{z_p z_q}(t,f)\right]}\right)\right]\right|}{\sqrt{1-\left(\left|\mathbb{E}_f\left[\Re\left(e^{j\arg\left[\rho_{z_p z_q}(t,f)\right]}\right)\right]\right|\right)^2}}. \tag{19}$$

The denominator serves to normalize the imaginary part of the phase difference using the real part, which captures potential zero-lag interactions. Since the real part of the unit phasor is bounded between -1 and 1, the absolute value of its local average across the frequency window lies in $[0, 1]$, keeping the denominator well-defined. This normalization reduces the influence of volume conduction artifacts, enabling more reliable detection of delayed, physiologically meaningful phase interactions across time and frequency. Compared to ciPLV, TF-ciPLV ensures that phase synchronization is reliably tracked across both time and frequency, enhancing its stability across different EEG conditions. This is particularly beneficial in clinical EEG applications, where connectivity estimates can be affected by variability in recording length or changes in neural activity.

3.3.4 Time-frequency phase lag index

TF-PLI extends PLI by accounting for the dynamic nature of phase lags, i.e.:

$$\text{TF-PLI}(p,q,t,f) = \left|\mathbb{E}_f\left[\text{sign}\left(\Im\left(\rho_{z_p z_q}(t,f)\right)\right)\right]\right|. \tag{20}$$

This is particularly advantageous for analyzing task-dependent or stimulus-driven phase synchrony, where the directionality and strength of phase lag relationships may change dynamically over time.

3.3.5 Time-frequency weighted phase lag index

The TF-wPLI improves upon TF-PLI by incorporating magnitude-weighted phase difference information, ensuring that small, unreliable phase differences contribute less to connectivity estimates, i.e.:

$$\text{TF-wPLI}(p,q,t,f) = \left| \frac{\int_{\Omega} \Im\left(\rho_{z_p z_q}(t,f)\right) \, \mathrm{d}f}{\int_{\Omega} \left| \Im\left(\rho_{z_p z_q}(t,f)\right) \right| \, \mathrm{d}f} \right|, \tag{21}$$

where Ω is the support of a short-spectral moving window around f. While wPLI provides a single connectivity estimate over a time window, assuming stationarity, TF-wPLI captures transient synchronization patterns, making it ideal for studying dynamic neural interactions. Additionally, it preserves frequency specificity, avoiding the issue of frequency band averaging that can obscure narrow-band phase-locking effects in wPLI. Nonetheless, both methods suppress zero-lag phase synchronization, reducing volume conduction artifacts, but the TF-wPLI further refines this correction across time and frequency, ensuring spurious connectivity does not persist in different spectral regions. This improvement enhances FBN mapping, providing a more detailed view of task-related and event-driven connectivity changes, making TF-wPLI particularly useful for nonstationary EEG analysis and neuroscience applications.

3.3.6 Time-frequency debiased weighted phase lag index

The TF-dwPLI refines TF-wPLI by further correcting for small-sample statistical biases, ensuring that connectivity estimates are reliable, i.e.:

$$\text{TF-dwPLI}(p,q,t,f) = \left| \frac{\left[\int_{\Omega} \Im\left(\rho_{z_p z_q}(t,f)\right) \mathrm{d}f\right]^2 - \int_{\Omega} \left[\Im\left(\rho_{z_p z_q}(t,f)\right)\right]^2 \mathrm{d}f}{\left[\int_{\Omega} \left|\Im\left(\rho_{z_p z_q}(t,f)\right)\right| \mathrm{d}f\right]^2 - \int_{\Omega} \left[\Im\left(\rho_{z_p z_q}(t,f)\right)\right]^2 \mathrm{d}f} \right|. \tag{22}$$

Traditional dwPLI is commonly used in clinical studies where short-duration trials are analyzed, but assumes stationary phase relationships. TF-dwPLI eliminates this, allowing connectivity to be analyzed dynamically across time and frequency, improving its robustness in real-world applications.

The advanced TF-based functional connectivity measures introduced above provide a flexible and localized framework for capturing dynamic brain interactions. In the following section, we demonstrate their practical utility through application to neonatal EEG recordings. By analyzing TF brain networks in a clinically relevant context, we highlight how these measures uncover both overt and subtle neural dynamics that are often missed by traditional approaches.

4. Application to newborn seizure analysis

Abnormal patterns of neural synchronization and connectivity often precede the onset of seizures, reflecting an underlying shift in the brain's functional organization [6]. Seizure activity in the neonatal brain is not merely a localized event but reflects disruptions in the structure and dynamics of large-scale functional networks [4, 7]. Analyzing seizure FBNs through EEG-derived functional connectivity offers a deeper understanding of how seizures initiate, propagate, and evolve [9]. These network-level disruptions are especially prominent in neonates, where seizure activity unfolds within immature and rapidly developing cortical circuits [6]. In this context, seizure networks exhibit highly dynamic and transient connectivity shifts that may not be evident through traditional analysis [9]. Therefore, by characterizing the topological and temporal properties of seizure-related networks, it becomes possible to uncover mechanisms of seizure generation, track their spatial spread, and evaluate their impact on global brain organization [5]. Such analyses have important implications for early diagnosis, targeted interventions, and improving neurodevelopmental outcomes in neonates with early life adversities [4, 6–8]. In this section, we utilize the proposed TF-based FBNs to characterize seizure dynamics in newborns. We investigate their ability to reveal deviations from healthy developmental connectivity patterns and quantify their effectiveness.

4.1 Fundamentals of newborn seizure analysis

The analysis of neonatal EEG provides critical insights into the development and function of the newborn brain. Unlike adult EEG, which follows more stable and well-characterized patterns, newborn EEG is dynamic and evolves rapidly during early life [6]. The detection and interpretation of newborn EEG are essential for diagnosing neurological disorders, particularly seizures, which may not have clear clinical manifestations [6]. Advancements in EEG monitoring and modeling techniques have improved seizure detection, particularly in neonatal intensive care units [2, 5]. While amplitude-integrated EEG has been widely adopted due to its ease of use, it has limitations, including the potential for missing short or low-amplitude seizures [6]. Multichannel continuous EEG, on the other hand, provides a more comprehensive assessment of neural activity, allowing for precise detection of seizure patterns and an assessment of therapeutic responses [6].

4.1.1 Healthy patterns

Neonatal EEG exhibits unique characteristics that evolve with gestational age. The EEG signal transitions from discontinuous to continuous activity as the brain matures, with distinct features emerging at different developmental stages [6]. Healthy EEG activity is expected to be symmetrical across hemispheres, with synchronized patterns between the left and right brain regions [5]. It consists of background rhythms that are generally analyzed in the following bands [5, 7]:

- δ (0.5–4 Hz): Dominant in neonates, particularly during deep sleep.
- θ (4–8 Hz): Prominent in older infants and during transitional sleep states.
- α (8–13 Hz): Appears with increasing postnatal age, associated with alertness and early cognitive processing.
- β (13–30 Hz): Less pronounced in newborns but more evident with neurodevelopment.

Another key consideration in assessing newborn EEG is the presence of sleep cycling, which reflects healthy brain development [6].

4.1.2 Seizure patterns

Neonatal seizures are a critical neurological concern, often associated with hypoxic-ischemic encephalopathy, perinatal stroke, metabolic imbalances, and genetic epileptic syndromes [5–7]. Unlike in older patients, neonatal seizures are frequently electrographic-only, lacking clear clinical manifestations, making EEG essential for detection. They are characterized by rhythmic, evolving EEG patterns that persist for at least 10 seconds with the following features [5, 6]:

- Rhythmic: They often begin as low-amplitude fast activity, then transition to higher-amplitude rhythmic discharges with varying frequency [6].

- Oscillatory frequency: They manifest in the delta and theta bands, though higher frequencies can appear depending on the underlying pathology [5].

- Focal vs. multifocal onset: Seizures are typically focal, originating from regions affected by perinatal injury, though some may become multifocal, especially in metabolic disorders [6].

- Spatial evolution: Seizures may remain localized or spread across the cortex, with propagation influenced by brain maturation and connectivity [5].

4.2 Experimental design

4.2.1 The Helsinki newborn EEG dataset

We utilized the open-access Helsinki EEG dataset to investigate the effectiveness of the proposed TF-based FBNs and contrast them to conventional techniques [17]. The dataset holds multichannel unipolar EEG recordings of 79 neonates collected in the Helsinki University Hospital, Finland. The EEG signals were acquired with 19 electrodes positioned according to the international 10–20 standard and sampled at 256 Hz [17]. Each EEG recording lasted approximately 1 hour and was annotated for seizures by three experts at one-second resolution using the standard longitudinal bipolar layout. In brief, the dataset contains multichannel EEG from 33 healthy controls and 46 neonates with seizures.

4.2.2 Data preprocessing

We filtered the newborn EEG data using a zero-phase band-pass infinite impulse response (IIR) filter to retain neural information within [0.5–30] Hz. After that, we resampled the filtered data to 64 Hz using a finite impulse response antialiasing lowpass filter. Then, we split the resampled data into the standard four frequency bands of interest using zero-phase band-pass IIR filters (δ [0.5–4] Hz, θ [4–8] Hz, α [8–13] Hz, and β [13–30] Hz); see the example EEG signal in **Figure 1**. We segmented the time course of the decomposed signals via a 16-second sliding window with 25% overlap. Moreover, we aggregated the three experts' annotations via majority voting and generated segment-level masks by checking if seizure activity existed for more

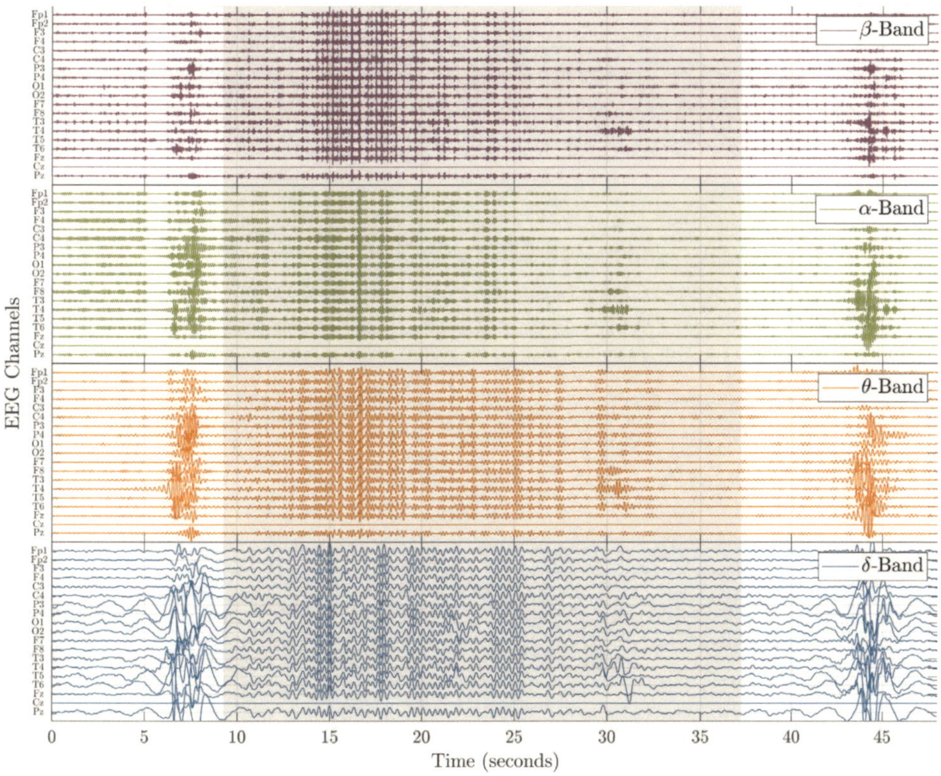

Figure 1.
Example multi-sensor signal from the Helsinki newborn EEG dataset (subject 1, 19.48–20.28 minutes). The EEG signal is decomposed into the four frequency bands of interest (see the legends). The support of the seizure activity is highlighted in gray between 9 and 37 seconds.

than 8 seconds. Finally, we computed the MTFD for each segment in each frequency band using the CSK, with parameters set to $c = 1$, $D = 0.45$, and $E = 0.05$; see the example MTFD in **Figure 2**.

4.2.3 Functional brain network construction

We computed the conventional connectivity measures described in Section 2 for each segment and each frequency band to build a tempo-spectral FBN for each subject. The connectivity measures were calculated using the full segment length and resulted in a 5-way FBN tensor of size $N \times 4 \times 19 \times 19 \times 8$ for each subject, where N corresponds to the number of segments, 4 is the number of frequency bands, 19 is the number of EEG electrodes, and 8 is the number of connectivity measures. Pairwise correlations were calculated at 95% significance, and cross-spectral densities were computed via the FFT algorithm at full resolution.

The proposed TF-based FBNs, described in Section 3, were computed similarly for each subject, each segment, and each frequency band. Specifically, we calculated the TF-extended connectivity measures using the complete support of each frequency band of interest. Moreover, we averaged the time course of the measures within each segment for simplicity, resulting in a 5-way FBN tensor for each subject. Note that this step folds the time-varying nature of the TF-based measures within a segment;

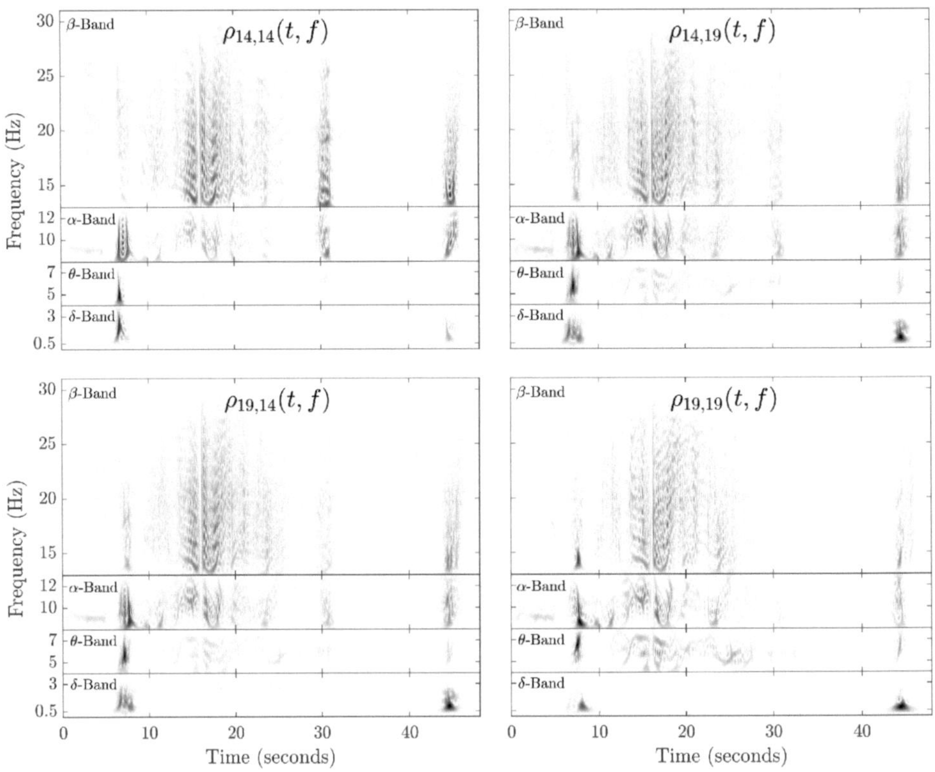

Figure 2.
A subset of the MTFD of the EEG signal presented in ***Figure 1****. The subset is shown for electrodes 14 (T4) and 19 (Pz) to demonstrate the nonstationary behavior of EEG and the CSK's excellent TF readability.*

however, it is necessary to allow associating connectivity with the segment-level seizure annotations. Nonetheless, depending on the objective of the analysis, one may replace the folding operator with other functions, such as temporal deviation, or omit it altogether.

4.3 Comparative analysis and evaluation framework

We categorized the computed FBN segments into healthy, non-seizure, and seizure groups. The healthy group contained segments from the 33 healthy neonates with no seizures. The seizure group included segments from the 46 neonates with seizure diagnoses, annotated as containing seizures, while the non-seizure group included the ones annotated as seizure-free. This grouping was performed because we seek to investigate the differences in FBN organization between healthy controls and neonates diagnosed with seizures. Additionally, we want to examine whether segments that are behaviorally normal but originate from seizure-prone neonates (i.e., non-seizure segments) differ from those of healthy controls. This distinction allows us to explore whether the traditional or proposed TF-based FBN measures are sensitive enough to capture subtle, possibly subclinical, alterations in brain network organization that may persist even during seizure-free intervals. After that, we detected and removed temporal outliers from each subject in each group using the rmoutliers tool in MATLAB. We defined outliers as elements with more than three scaled median absolute deviations from the median. Then, we computed the subject-level tensors by averaging the subjects' FBNs across the segments. This results in a 19 × 19 matrix for each subject, each frequency band, and each connectivity measure in each group. Finally, we constructed the group-level FBNs by averaging across the subjects. We assessed the group-level differences using the Kruskal-Wallis test and corrected for multiple comparisons via the Bonferroni method.

5. Results and discussion

The findings in **Figures 3** and **4** highlight critical differences between the traditional and TF-based FBN measures in distinguishing healthy neonates from those with seizures, including during seizure-free intervals.

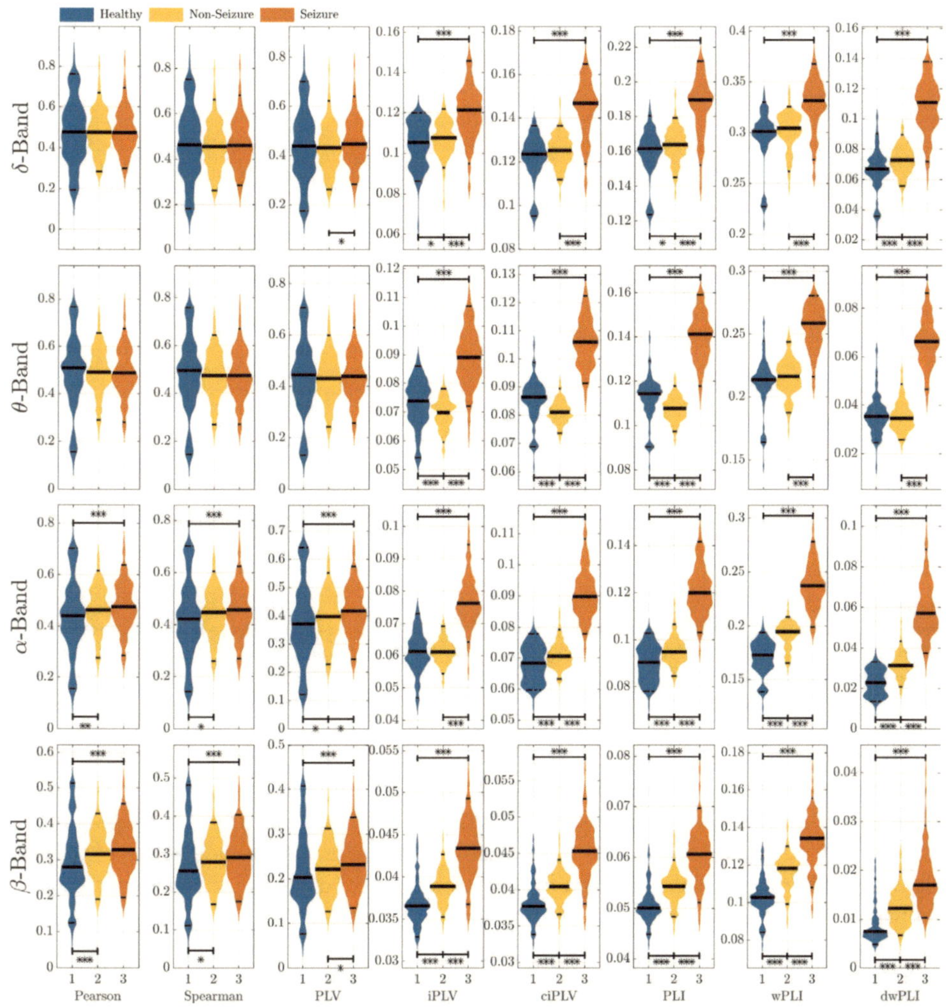

Figure 3.
*Group comparisons using traditional FBN measures. Groups 1, 2, and 3 correspond to the healthy, non-seizure, and seizure categories. Statistically significant differences with p-values below 0.05, 0.01, and 0.001 are indicated by *, **, and ***, respectively. The distributions are smoothed using normal kernels and plotted along with their 25%, 50% (median), and 75% percentiles, indicated by horizontal black lines.*

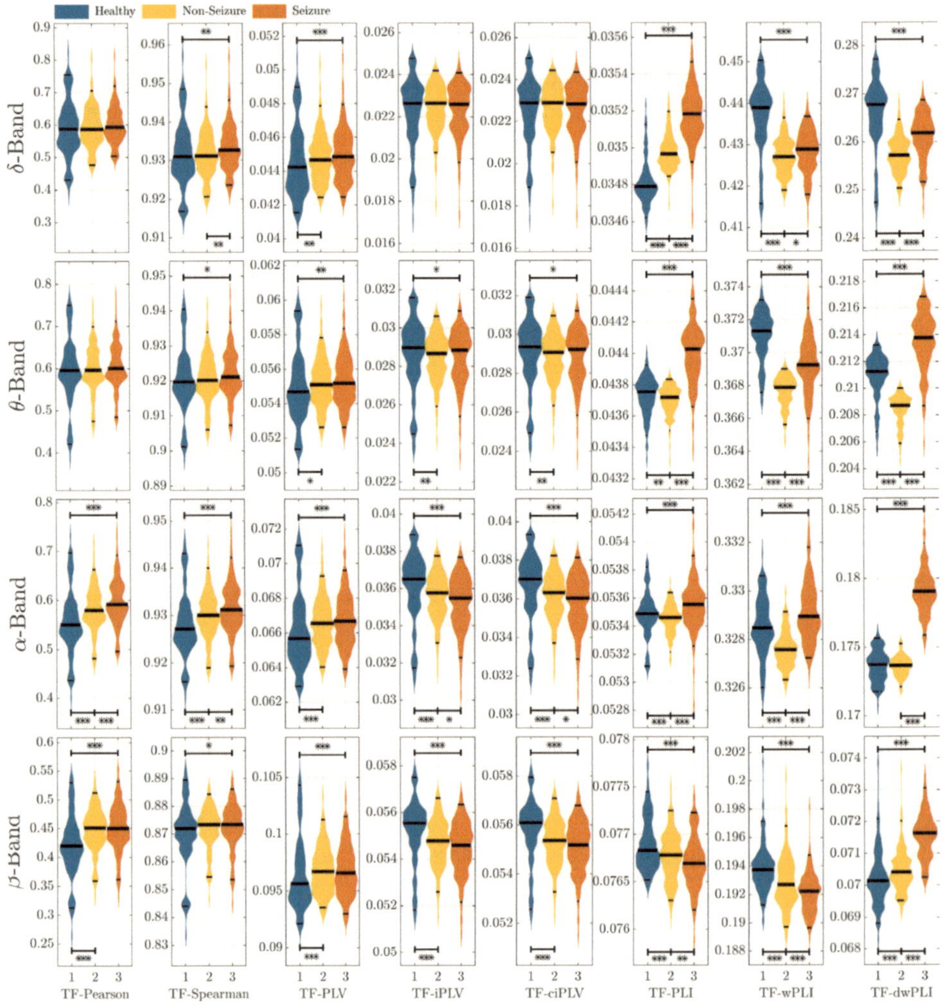

Figure 4.
Group comparisons using the TF-based FBN measures. Groups 1, 2, and 3 correspond to the healthy, non-seizure, and seizure categories. Statistically significant differences with p-values below 0.05, 0.01, and 0.001 are indicated by ∗, ∗∗, and ∗∗∗, respectively. The distributions are smoothed using normal kernels and plotted along with their 25%, 50% (median), and 75% percentiles, indicated by horizontal black lines.

On one hand, the results in **Figure 3** demonstrate that traditional connectivity measures, particularly amplitude-based FBNs, failed to reveal significant group differences in the delta and theta bands. This suggests that amplitude coupling in these bands may be either too subtle or too variable to serve as a reliable marker of pathology in neonatal EEG. Similarly, the PLV networks did not distinguish seizure from healthy networks in the same bands, highlighting the limitations of classical, phase-consistent methods when applied to low-frequency neonatal activity. In contrast, other traditional phase-based metrics were more sensitive and consistently showed higher synchronization in the seizure group, followed by the non-seizure group, and lastly, the healthy group. An exception was observed in the theta band, where the healthy group exhibited higher synchronization than the non-seizure group, suggesting that seizure-free epochs may be characterized by suppressed connectivity, especially in this frequency range. In total, the traditional FBN measures showed

26 (81.25%) and 20 (62.5%) statistically significant differences when comparing the healthy group to the seizure and non-seizure populations, respectively.

On the other hand, the distributions in **Figure 4** illustrate that the proposed TF-based measures provide deeper insight into transient and frequency-specific neural interactions. The TF-Spearman has effectively captured significant differences between the seizure and healthy groups in the delta and theta bands, where its time-domain counterpart failed. This highlights the benefit of incorporating the time-varying spectral structure into energy-based connectivity metrics. Moreover, the TF phase-based measures further emphasized this advantage. Specifically, the TF-PLV preserved the same seizure > non-seizure > healthy ordering as its traditional counterpart. However, the TF-iPLV and TF-ciPLV revealed the reverse trend, suggesting that traditional metrics may overestimate synchronization due to spurious coupling and that corrected measures reveal more physiologically plausible patterns, i.e., stronger phase organization in healthy neonatal networks. Interestingly, while the TF-PLI and TF-wPLI did not exhibit consistent group-level differences, the TF-dwPLI has preserved the expected group ordering across most bands. An exception was noted in the delta band, where all groups showed elevated synchronization, likely reflecting the dominance of early developmental oscillations that can mask pathological network dynamics. Summing up, the TF-FBN measures showed 28 (87.5%) and 24 (75%) statistically significant differences when comparing the healthy group to the seizure and non-seizure groups, respectively.

The findings suggest that TF-based FBNs offer a more sensitive characterization of seizure-related brain dynamics. Specifically, they yield 6.25 and 12.5 percentage-point increases when contrasting healthy subjects to patients with seizure and non-seizure segments, respectively. Moreover, they not only capture heightened synchronization during seizures but also detect subtle alterations in seizure-free segments, potentially indicating latent network dysfunction. The ability to reveal such patterns, particularly through phase-based TF measures that discount artifactual synchrony, underscores their promise for seizure monitoring, early diagnosis, and longitudinal assessment of neurological health.

6. Conclusions

The time-frequency (TF)-based framework for constructing functional brain networks (FBNs) using multi-sensor TF signal representations extends conventional amplitude- and phase-based connectivity measures to the TF domain; it enables a more accurate, temporally localized, and spectrally resolved characterization of neural interactions. These TF-FBNs were constructed by leveraging multi-sensor TF distributions, allowing both energy-based and phase-based coupling to be accounted for and analyzed in a unified, nonstationary framework. The proposed TF approach offers several advantages over standard time- or frequency-domain techniques: (1) it enables the detection of transient connectivity dynamics; (2) it enhances sensitivity to frequency-specific interactions; (3) it mitigates artifacts caused by volume conduction or broadband averaging; and (4) the TF phase-based measures preserve or improve their desirable properties while addressing their known limitation, the stationarity assumption.

The utility of the proposed TF connectivity measures is demonstrated in a neuroscience application that analyzed neonatal seizure FBNs and focused on the measures' ability to differentiate between healthy, non-seizure, and seizure states. The results revealed that TF-FBNs, particularly those based on corrected phase synchrony metrics, were more effective by 12.5 percentage points when compared to their conventional counterparts in capturing both overt and subtle differences in network connectivity. These findings demonstrate that TF-FBNs can uncover latent pathological signatures and improve our understanding of dynamic brain network organization, especially in early life.

These advances in functional brain network analysis define a TF framework grounded in rigorous signal processing theory. They are validated in the clinical application of neonatal seizure analysis, demonstrating that the proposed methods are general and can be applied to a broad range of EEG-based studies in both healthy and pathological contexts, as well as beyond.

The MATLAB package that is needed to reproduce the results of this chapter will be provided freely at https://github.com/Al-Sad/TF-Connectivity.

Acknowledgements

This work was supported by the Jenny and Antti Wihuri Foundation.

Abbreviations

EEG	electroencephalogram
FBN	functional brain network
IA	instantaneous amplitude
IP	instantaneous phase
IF	instantaneous frequency
PLV	phase locking value
iPLV	imaginary phase locking value
ciPLV	corrected imaginary phase locking value
PLI	phase lag index
wPLI	weighted phase lag index
dwPLI	debiased weighted phase lag index
TF	time-frequency
TF-FBN	time-frequency functional brain network
TFR	time-frequency representation
TFD	time-frequency distribution
MTFD	multi-sensor time-frequency distribution
TF-Pearson	time-frequency Pearson's correlation
TF-Spearman	time-frequency Spearman's correlation
TF-PLV	time-frequency phase locking value
TF-iPLV	time-frequency imaginary phase locking value
TF-ciPLV	time-frequency corrected imaginary phase locking value
TF-PLI	time-frequency phase lag index
TF-wPLI	time-frequency weighted phase lag index
TF-dwPLI	time-frequency debiased weighted phase lag index

Author details

Mohammad Al-Sa'd[1,2,3]* and Boualem Boashash[4]

1 Faculty of Medicine, University of Helsinki, Helsinki, Finland

2 Faculty of Information Technology and Communication Sciences, Tampere University, Tampere, Finland

3 BABA Center, Helsinki University Hospital, Helsinki, Finland

4 University of Queensland Centre for Clinical Research, The University of Queensland, Brisbane, Australia

*Address all correspondence to: mohammad.al-sad@helsinki.fi; ext-mohammad.al-sad@hus.fi; mohammad.al-sad@tuni.fi

IntechOpen

© 2025 The Author(s). Licensee IntechOpen. This chapter is distributed under the terms of the Creative Commons Attribution License (http://creativecommons.org/licenses/by/4.0), which permits unrestricted use, distribution, and reproduction in any medium, provided the original work is properly cited.

References

[1] Boashash B. Time-Frequency Signal Analysis and Processing. 2nd ed. London, UK: Academic Press; 2016

[2] Al-Sa'd M. Time-Frequency Analysis: Application to Electroencephalogram Signal Processing. Tampere, Finland: Tampere University; 2022. Available from: https://urn.fi/URN:ISBN:978-952-03-2503-9

[3] Boashash B, Aïssa-El-Bey A. Robust multisensor time–frequency signal processing: A tutorial review with illustrations of performance enhancement in selected application areas. Digital Signal Processing. 2018;**77**:153-186. DOI: 10.1016/j.dsp.2017.11.017

[4] Al-Sa'd M, Vanhatalo S, Tokariev A. Multiplex dynamic networks in the newborn brain disclose latent links with neurobehavioral phenotypes. Human Brain Mapping. 2024;**45**(2):e26610. DOI: 10.1002/hbm.26610

[5] Al-Sa'd MF, Boashash B. Design and implementation of a multi-sensor newborn EEG seizure and background model with inter-channel field characterization. Digital Signal Processing. 2019;**4**(90):71-99. DOI: 10.1016/j.dsp.2019.02.003

[6] Boylan GB, Stevenson NJ, Vanhatalo S. Monitoring neonatal seizures. Seminars in Fetal and Neonatal Medicine. 2013;**18**(4): 202-208. DOI: 10.1016/j.siny.2013.04.004

[7] Abbas AK, Azemi G, Ravanshadi S, Omidvarnia A. An EEG-based methodology for the estimation of functional brain connectivity networks: Application to the analysis of newborn EEG seizure. Biomedical Signal Processing and Control. 2021;**63**:102229. DOI: 10.1016/j.bspc.2020.102229

[8] Yrjölä P, Myers MM, Welch MG, Stevenson NJ, Tokariev A, Vanhatalo S. Facilitating early parent-infant emotional connection improves cortical networks in preterm infants. Science Translational Medicine. 2022;**14**(664):eabq4786. DOI: 10.1126/scitranslmed.abq4786

[9] Hutchison RM, Womelsdorf T, Allen EA, Bandettini PA, Calhoun VD, Corbetta M, et al. Dynamic functional connectivity: Promise, issues, and interpretations. NeuroImage. 2013;**80**: 360-378. DOI: 10.1016/j.neuroimage.2013.05.079

[10] Boashash B, Aïssa-El-Bey A, Al-Sa'd MF. Multisensor time–frequency signal processing MATLAB package: An analysis tool for multichannel non-stationary data. SoftwareX. 2018;**8**:53-58. DOI: 10.1016/j.softx.2017.12.002

[11] Ghanbari Z, Moradi MH. FSIFT-PLV: An emerging phase synchrony index. Biomedical Signal Processing and Control. 2020;**57**:101764. DOI: 10.1016/j.bspc.2019.101764

[12] Bruña R, Maestú F, Pereda E. Phase locking value revisited: Teaching new tricks to an old dog. Journal of Neural Engineering. 2018;**15**(5):56011. DOI: 10.1088/1741-2552/aacfe4

[13] Al-Sa'd M, Boashash B, Gabbouj M. Design of an optimal piece-wise Spline Wigner-Ville distribution for TFD performance evaluation and comparison. IEEE Transactions on Signal Processing. 2021;**69**:3963-3976. DOI: 10.1109/TSP.2021.3089291

[14] Schober P, Boer C, Schwarte LA. Correlation coefficients: Appropriate use

and interpretation. Anesthesia & Analgesia. 2018;**126**(5):1763-1768. DOI: 10.1213/ANE.0000000000002864

[15] De Winter JCF, Gosling SD, Potter J. Comparing the Pearson and Spearman correlation coefficients across distributions and sample sizes: A tutorial using simulations and empirical data. Psychological methods. 2016;**21**(3):273. DOI: 10.1037/met0000079

[16] Abed M, Belouchrani A, Cheriet M, Boashash B. Time-frequency distributions based on compact support kernels: Properties and performance evaluation. IEEE Transactions on Signal Processing. 2012;**60**(6):2814-2827. DOI: 10.1109/TSP.2012.2190065

[17] Stevenson NJ, Tapani K, Lauronen L, Vanhatalo S. A dataset of neonatal EEG recordings with seizure annotations. Scientific Data. 2019;**6**(1):190039. DOI: 10.1038/sdata.2019.39

Chapter 2

Signal Processing for Estimating the Time of Arrival and Amplitude of Nonlinear Underwater Acoustic Waves

María Campo-Valera, Dídac Diego-Tortosa and Rafael Asorey-Cacheda

Abstract

In acoustic environments, many problems arise due to intermodulation distortions that disturb both the timing and amplitude details, and traditional detection methods often do not work well for long-distance communications. This chapter presents an analysis of methods applied to the processing of nonlinear acoustic signals, by means of two approaches, (i) the estimation of the time of arrival (ToA) and (ii) that of the amplitude, two key aspects that usually receive little attention in the literature for this type of signal. This chapter is focused on the nonlinear signals generated by sine-type and sine-sweep modulations, which are characterized by the appearance of low-frequency components due to intermodulation phenomena. These components have a narrow directivity and a high propagation capacity, which is advantageous for long distance transmission and detection applications. Three methods for the ToA estimation are evaluated: threshold, power variance, and cross-correlation. In the amplitude analysis, techniques in the time domain, in the frequency domain, and cross-correlation method are applied. The proposed approaches are validated by a proof of concept with experimental nonlinear signals, demonstrating their robustness, accuracy, and applicability in real scenarios of acoustic propagation.

Keywords: acoustic signal processing, time of arrival estimation, amplitude estimation, underwater acoustics, nonlinear effect

1. Introduction

Underwater acoustic communications represent a highly relevant area of research due to its ability to enable signal interaction in complex underwater environments. Their application is crucial in sectors such as marine ecosystem monitoring [1, 2], maritime traffic management [3], autonomous navigation, and defense and security operations [4]. However, underwater acoustic systems face significant challenges due to the nature of acoustic wave propagation in the marine environment. These challenges include attenuation, background noise and, most importantly, multipath effects, which introduce significant interference and distortion into the received signals. These factors severely degrade the quality and reliability of acoustic transmission, limiting the effectiveness of underwater communication systems.

To overcome these limitations, acoustic signal processing techniques have been developed based on the nonlinear propagation phenomenon known as the parametric effect. This effect was first described theoretically in the 1960s by Westervelt [5] and later by Berktay, who developed a simplified formulation known as Berktay's approximation [6], which is particularly useful for underwater applications.

The parametric effect is produced by the propagation of high-frequency (primary frequencies) at high acoustic intensity. The nonlinear interaction between these waves, along with others, produces low-frequency components (secondary frequency) that were not originally present in the emitted signal. This secondary signal is characterized by a narrow directivity, more specific of high frequencies, which mitigates multipath effects and improves communication quality.

The analysis of underwater acoustic signals has emerged as a crucial area for various applications, such as sound source localization and acoustic environment characterization [7]. In particular, time of arrival (ToA) estimation is presented as an essential tool for accurate source position determination, especially in complex acoustic conditions. Traditionally, ToA and time difference of arrival (TDoA)-based methods have been used to address these challenges. A recent study compared the performance of these approaches in underwater environments with multipath propagation, using a ray-tracing-based propagation model and Bernoulli filters to mitigate adverse effects. The results showed that the choice between ToA and TDoA depends on the specific environmental conditions and application requirements [8].

With the advancement of deep learning techniques, innovative methods for ToA and direction of arrival (DoA) estimation have been developed. For example, a convolutional recurrent neural network (CRNN) that combines convolutional layers for feature extraction and recurrent layers for modeling temporal information has been proposed to improve the accuracy of DoA estimation in complex underwater environments [9].

In addition, denoising algorithms have been explored to improve the quality of underwater acoustic signals, which indirectly benefits ToA estimation by reducing interference from ambient noise. A comprehensive review of these algorithms highlights the importance of developing more robust and adaptive denoising techniques to address the unique challenges of the underwater environment [10].

Knowing the ToA of a received signal enables a more comprehensive analysis of its amplitude. Accurately parameterizing the amplitude of the received signal opens up possibilities for various studies, such as those on the propagation of acoustic signals in the environment, the assessment of noise pollution in surrounding areas, and the characterization of the acoustic properties of the medium, among others.

This chapter focuses on the treatment and analysis of nonlinear acoustic signals, more specifically the phenomenon of the parametric effect. This phenomenon must be carefully analyzed in order to obtain an accurate estimate of the relevant parameters, such as ToA and amplitude. Despite its relevance, the specific analysis of this type of nonlinear signals in underwater environments has been scarcely addressed in the scientific literature, with the authors of this chapter being pioneers in proposing a detailed study framework in [11].

A methodological approach divided into two main stages is proposed. The first approach focuses on the estimation of the ToA using three methods: threshold, power variation (Pvar), and cross-correlation. The selection of the optimal method depends on the propagation environment conditions, signal intensity, and the system's computational cost, as each method offers specific advantages depending on the noise level, the complexity of the acoustic channel, and the processing time requirements.

Once the ToA has been detected, the second approach is applied, which focuses on estimating the signal amplitude. This is done by time and frequency domain analysis, complemented by the use of the cross-correlation method (also used in the time domain). The time domain analysis allows the characterization of the evolution of the signal, providing critical information on the propagation effects. Spectral analysis, based on the Fourier transform, identifies the frequency components of the signal and evaluates their contribution to the observed nonlinear behavior. The cross-correlation method not only contributes to the accurate estimation of the ToA, but also enables the evaluation of the similarity between the expected and received signals, even under adverse conditions with a low signal-to-noise ratio (SNR), thus improving the reliability of the acoustic detection and characterization process.

The use of sine-type and sine-sweep type signals, together with filtering techniques, is key to separating the relevant components from the noise and improving the quality of the ToA estimation. By comparing different processing methods and applying experimental measurements, the aim is not only to characterize the behavior of underwater nonlinear acoustic signals but also to validate the estimation techniques in real-world scenarios where acoustic and environmental conditions can vary significantly.

This integrative approach is advancing the understanding and improvement of underwater communication and sensing technologies, opening new perspectives for applications ranging from ocean exploration to aquatic security communications.

2. Background for nonlinear signals

The parametric underwater acoustic communications take advantage of the nonlinear effects generated in the underwater channel for efficient data transmission. These communications are based on the use of bi-frequency signals, which allow for generating nonlinear interactions that facilitate the propagation of the signal in the medium. A bi-frequency signal of pressure $p'(0,t)$ can be expressed as follows:

$$p'(0,t) = A_a \sin(\omega_a t) + A_b \sin(\omega_b t), \tag{1}$$

where ω_a and ω_b are the high primary frequencies, which should be close to each other, while A_a and A_b are the amplitudes of these frequencies, and they should increase as the distance between the frequencies grows.

When a medium such as water is excited by a bi-frequency signal, as described in Eq. (1), interactions between frequencies are generated due to nonlinear channel effects. These interactions give rise to secondary waves whose frequency corresponds to linear combinations of the primary frequencies, specifically the sums and differences of these, a phenomenon known as beat frequencies. In addition, the medium has dissipative effects that attenuate the higher-frequency waves, causing them to disappear with distance before the produced nonlinear low frequencies. As the signal propagates over long distances from the source, the predominant signal is the one defined as the difference ω_d, the difference between the primary frequencies: $\omega_d = \omega_a - \omega_b$.

This phenomenon is especially important because ω_d, the low-frequency signal, suffers less attenuation and can propagate over longer distances, allowing more efficient communication. This effect, known as the *parametric effect*, not only generates low-frequency signals but also produces narrower radiation patterns, a characteristic of higher primary frequencies [12, 13]. Moreover, a remarkable property of this effect is that it facilitates reliable signal detection and demodulation, which improves the quality and reliability of transmission in underwater environments.

Assuming that $A_a = A_b = A_c/2$, Eq. (1) can be rewritten as follows:

$$p'(0,t) = A_c \cos(\omega_m t)\sin(\omega_c t) = \frac{A_c}{2}\sin\left(\underbrace{(\omega_c + \omega_m)t}_{\omega_a}\right) + \frac{A_c}{2}\sin\left(\underbrace{(\omega_c - \omega_m)t}_{\omega_b}\right), \quad (2)$$

where ω_m is the frequency of the modulating signal (low-frequency signal), ω_c is the frequency of the carrier signal (high primary frequency), and A_c is the amplitude of the carrier signal. In this context, if the envelope $E(t)$ is a harmonic signal, i.e., $E(t) = \sin(\omega_m t)$, the excitation will be reduced to a bi-frequency signal. As a result, the difference frequency $\omega_d = 2\omega_m$ will be twice the frequency of the modulating signal.

Thus, for any signal containing an envelope, the demodulation is related to the second derivative of the time-square envelope, $E^2(t)$, as shown in Eq. (3). This process is fundamental for obtaining the parametric signal, which is defined as p_{param}, and is the way in which the modulated signal can be efficiently recovered from frequency modulation and nonlinear interaction in the channel.

$$p_{param} \sim \frac{\partial^2 E^2(t)}{\partial t^2} \quad (3)$$

The process of obtaining underwater acoustic parametric signals begins with a modulated signal, as shown in Eq. (2). A parametric signal must be designed in such a way that it can be decoded even under the effects of nonlinear propagation [14].

In this chapter, the parametric effect is presented through two different types of amplitude modulated (AM) signals: a sine-type signal and a sine-sweep signal. In the first case, ω_m will remain constant (tone), while in the second case, ω_m will vary. The $E(t)$ of the wideband (sine-sweep) signal is defined as presented in Eq. (4):

$$E(t) = \sin\left(\left(\frac{|\omega_{m2} - \omega_{m1}|}{\tau}t + \omega_{m1}\right)t\right), \quad (4)$$

where ω_{m1} is the initial frequency of the sine-sweep, ω_{m2} is the final frequency of the sine-sweep, τ is the total duration of the sine sweep, and t is time. Define $\omega_d = |\omega_{m2} - \omega_{m1}|$.

The profile of the parametric signal in Eq. (3) can be obtained as:

$$p_{param} \sim 4\frac{\omega_d}{\tau}\sin\left(2\left(\frac{\omega_d}{\tau}t + \omega_{m1}\right)\right) + 2\left(\frac{2\omega_d}{\tau}t + \omega_{m1}\right)^2 \cos\left(2\left(\frac{\omega_d}{\tau}t + \omega_{m1}\right)\right) \quad (5)$$

In Eq. (5), the parametric signal has a frequency twice that of the modulating frequency, and an initial amplitude of zero that increases proportionally to t^2. In this manner, the modulation scheme described in Eq. (4), along with the theories of Westervelt [5] and Berktay [6], models the parametric transmission. For a more detailed analysis of these developments, see [15].

3. Experimental setup and measured signals

To demonstrate the generation of the parametric effect in the measured signals, the experimental setup used consists of a cylindrical tank with a capacity of approximately 19 m^3. The acoustic signal transmitter used was the Airmar P19, which has an emission sensitivity of 167 dB (re 1 μPa/V at 1 m) and a resonance frequency of 200 kHz, making it a very effective device for generating signals in the desired frequency range (carrier frequency, f_c, of 200 kHz).

The used receiver was the hydrophone Reson TC4040, which has a receiver sensitivity of −206 dB (re 1 V/μPa at 1 m) from 2 kHz to 75 kHz. The choice of this hydrophone is particularly suitable for the analysis of the parametric frequencies measurements in the experiments, which are centered in the range from 2 kHz to 20 kHz, making it an ideal choice for obtaining accurate results.

The distance between the transducers, crucial for the analysis of acoustic wave propagation, was set at 42 cm, ensuring the maximum separation without interfering with the recordings due to reflections while considering the characteristics of the tank.

Figure 1 illustrates in detail the experimental setup and the arrangement of the necessary connections for the calibration of the equipment. The E&I 1040 L amplifier, combined with a data generation and acquisition system consisting of a National Instruments PXI-1073 chassis, a PXIe-5433 waveform generator card, and a PXIe-5122 oscilloscope, is operated and controlled via a laptop using the NI PXI ExpressCard-8360. Additionally, to ensure proper signal acquisition, a Testec TT-HV-400 ×100 attenuating probe was incorporated, which allows attenuation of the signal at the amplifier output, facilitating its subsequent recording by the PXI system.

In real-world environments, where the receiver and transmitter operate independently, synchronizing both devices using a common reference, such as the global positioning system (GPS), becomes a critical factor for making accurate ToA measurements. However, in cases where the primary goal is the detection of signals containing information (such as bit strings), strict synchronization may not be as crucial. In such cases, the detected signals can be recorded according to the receiver system's internal clock, whether using universal time coordinated (UTC) or not.

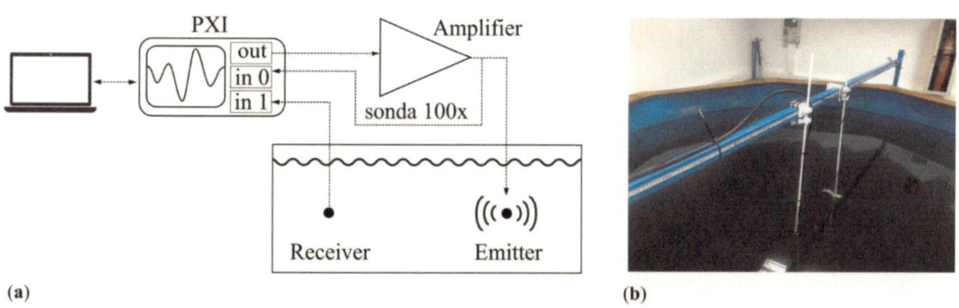

Figure 1.
Experimental setup for measuring nonlinear signals. (a) Equipment used in the experiment, including the computer, amplifier, and PXI system, which allow the generation and acquisition of acoustic signals. (b) View of the tank and the transducers placed at a distance of ∼ 42 cm, setup to study the propagation of acoustic waves.

4. Time of arrival estimation of acoustic signals

Once the measurements have been taken, each recorded signal must be analyzed to examine the parameters of interest. In this case, the recorded waveform will consist of background noise and the signal emitted by the transducer, which will appear at a ToA corresponding to the time of flight (ToF) between the emitter and the receiver. This section will describe three different methods for estimating the ToA for the desired signal.

4.1 Threshold method

The threshold method consists of determining the point at which the signal surpasses a predefined amplitude level (threshold level). This technique demands a good SNR (more than 30 dB) and a detailed evaluation of the emitted signal to set an appropriate threshold in the receiver point, which is defined as the minimum received signal level. Furthermore, this method depends on the time transition of the received signal; that is, if it takes longer to reach a noticeable level relative to the background noise, the calculation of the ToA may not be very accurate. This issue is typically linked to the resonance effect of the transmitter and/or receiver at the frequencies of the emitted signal. In many instances, filtering is essential to capture the signal of interest with greater precision. However, it is important to account for the delay it may introduce to the signal, as this will need to be corrected for an accurate ToA calculation. An example of the threshold method application is shown in **Figure 2**.

4.2 Pvar method (Pvar)

The Pvar method has similar requirements to the threshold method regarding the SNR and the time transition of the received signal and may also require efficient signal filtering. This method includes two variants: "cumulative Pvar" ($Pvar_{cum}$) and "saw Pvar" ($Pvar_{saw}$).

To implement the mathematical formulas $Pvar_{cum}$ and $Pvar_{saw}$, a custom analysis function was created. This function processes the signal using the Pvar-transform

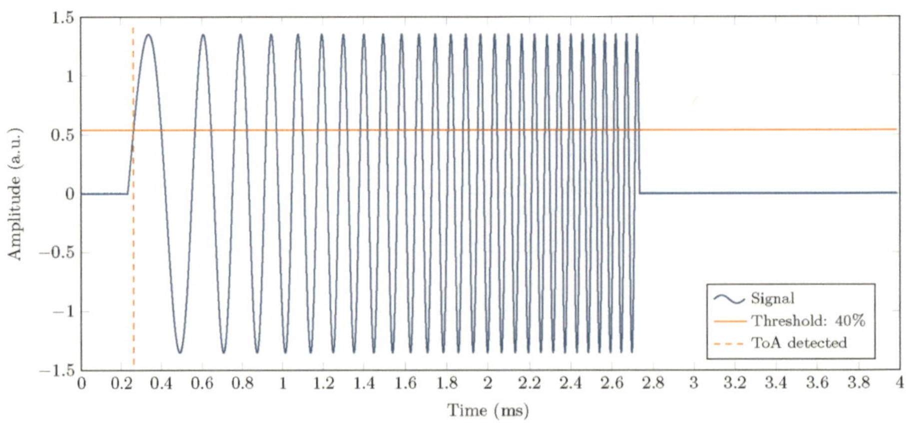

Figure 2.
An example of ToA estimation using the threshold method is shown for a theoretical sine-sweep type signal with a SNR of 90 dB. The threshold level is set at 40% of the signal's maximum amplitude. The estimated ToA is 0.26 ms.

within a defined time window, identifying shifts in the slope of the transformed signal.

The point of intersection between the two first slopes is then computed, which corresponds to the estimated ToA.

4.2.1 Cumulative power variation ($Pvar_{cum}$)

The $Pvar_{cum}$ method computes the cumulative sum of the absolute values of the recorded waveform's amplitude, as represented in Eq. (6) [16]. This approach highlights an increasing trend in the values, with a distinct change in slope when the target signal emerges. By modifying a specific power factor, the slope's steepness can be enhanced, facilitating the identification of the ToA.

$$Pvar_{cum}[n] = \frac{\sum_{i=1}^{n} x_i^k}{\sum x[n]^k}, \quad (6)$$

where k represents the power factor to which each data point x_i is raised, and n represents the total number of data points in the dataset. An example of this method is illustrated in **Figure 3** (orange color). In this case, k is 2.

4.2.2 Saw power variation ($Pvar_{saw}$)

The $Pvar_{saw}$ method involves subtracting the mean value of the recorded waveform from $Pvar_{cum}$ (Eq. (6)), generating a sawtooth-like signal that compensates for background noise contributions, which may reduce the need for extra filtering. The ToA of the signal is identified by the first change in slope observed in $Pvar_{saw}$, as depicted in **Figure 3** (yellow color).

$Pvar_{saw}$ can be obtained as follows [17]:

$$Pvar_{saw}[n] = Pvar_{cum}[n] - Noise[n] \quad (7)$$

$$Noise[n] = a \cdot tn + b, \quad (8)$$

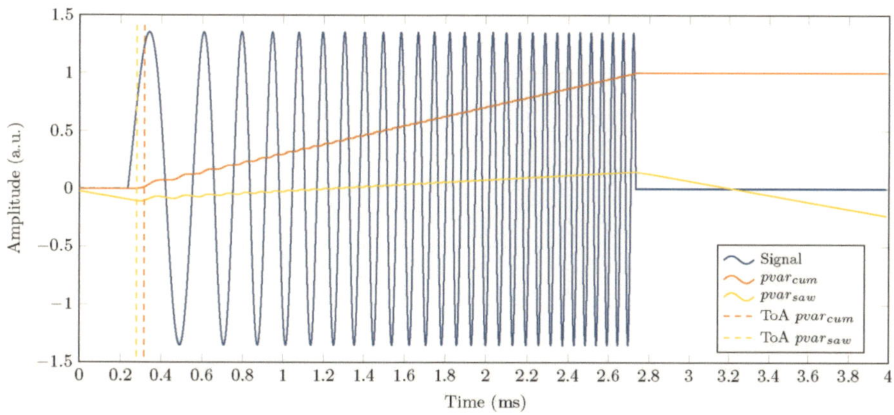

Figure 3.
An example of ToA estimation using the Pvar method is shwon for a theoretical sine-sweep type signal with a SNR of 90 dB. The orange and yellow lines represent the estimated ToA using $Pvar_{cum}$ and $Pvar_{saw}$, respectively. The ToA estimated by $Pvar_{cum}$ is 0.31 ms, while $Pvar_{saw}$ yields an estimate of 0.27 ms.

where, in Eq. (8), a and b represents the coefficients resulting from the linear fit of $Pvar_{cum}$, and $t[n]$ represents the time vector of the discrete-mode signal.

4.3 Cross-correlation method

The cross-correlation method analyzes the similarity between the transmitted signal and the recorded waveform by generating the correlation signal [18]. The amplitude peaks will increase as the two signals align, providing the ToA at its maximum peak. Unlike the previously mentioned methods, this approach is much more effective in noisy conditions without the need for filtering, and yields better results with sine-sweep type signals, since they contain more frequency components to compare.

$$r_{xy}[l] = \sum_{i=1}^{N} x[n]y[n+l] \tag{9}$$

In Eq. (9), $x[n]$ y $y[n]$ denote the signals digitized by the transmitting transducer and the hydrophone, respectively. In this case, $l = 1, 2, \ldots, N$ represents the number of samples by which y is delayed relative to x.

An example of the cross-correlation method application is shown in **Figure 4**.

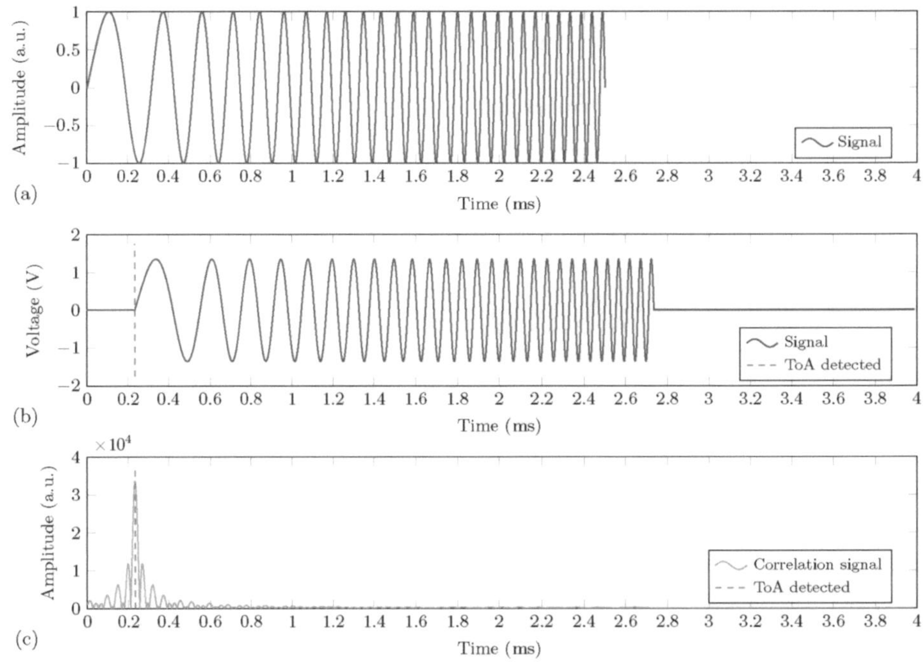

Figure 4.
An example of ToA estimation using the cross-correlation method for a theoretical sine-sweep type signal with an SNR of 90 dB. It shows in (a) the transmitted signal. (b) The received signal. (c) The cross-correlation waveform between them, with a clearly defined peak in the ToA of 0.23 ms.

5. Amplitude estimation of the acoustic signals

Once the ToA is estimated, its amplitude can be studied. To achieve this, three different techniques are analyzed: the time domain, the frequency domain, and the cross-correlation method (also used in the time domain). All these techniques provide the same value for an ideal signal (free of noise). However, depending on the experimental setup and background noise, differences may arise between them, which should be considered. Each technique is described in detail below, highlighting the specific information it provides about the received signal, which is measured in voltage V in this study.

5.1 Amplitude in the time domain

Time domain refers to the detailed description of the behavior of a signal with respect to time, which is the fundamental domain inherent to all acoustic signals. Time is the most basic and universal variable used to characterize the evolution of any dynamic phenomenon. In the case of acoustic signals, its temporal analysis allows for the study of their propagation, attenuation, and variability along their trajectory. Although this parameterization is the most basic, it is crucial for extracting essential information from the signal, such as its amplitude, frequency, and duration, which are necessary for a wide range of applications in acoustic signal processing.

In the discrete-time domain, the signal is observed only at specific moments along the time axis. This means that the signal is represented by discrete values taken at regular intervals. The amplitudes of these values are quantized, meaning they cannot take any continuous real value, but are limited to those defined by the resolution of the quantization, which is determined by the bit depth of the sampling system. This discretization process allows the acoustic signal to be represented in digital form, facilitating its processing with computational tools. The digitalization of the signal involves taking a sequence of N samples at regular intervals, separated by a period $T = 1/f_s$, where f_s is the sampling frequency, a fundamental parameter that must be appropriately selected to capture the characteristics of the signal under study, in accordance with the Nyquist–Shannon theorem, which limits the highest recorded frequency to half of the f_s.

Once the signal has been digitized, it becomes particularly relevant within the context of this study to obtain information about the signal in terms of specific frequencies and/or frequency bands. To extract this information in the time domain, filtering becomes an essential tool. This process is of utmost importance in the analysis of acoustic signals, as it allows for focusing solely on the relevant characteristics of the signal within a determined frequency range, discarding those frequencies outside the range of interest.

In the digital processing of the acoustic signals in this study, filtering primarily serves two functions: (*i*) remove unwanted noise and (*ii*) analyze the signal in specific frequency bands.

In this work, to compare amplitudes between different analysis domains (such as time and frequency domain), the peak value $V_{p,\text{time}}$ is used as a reference parameter. This value provides a measure of the maximum amplitude reached by the signal in the time domain. The choice of the peak value as an amplitude measure is justified by its ability to capture the extreme fluctuations of the signal. For stationary harmonic signals, this peak value can be estimated as [19]:

$$V_{p,\text{time}}\{x[n]\} = V_{rms,\text{time}}\{x[n]\} \cdot \sqrt{2} = \sqrt{\frac{1}{N}\sum_{i=1}^{N}(x_i - \overline{x})^2} \cdot \sqrt{2}, \tag{10}$$

where $x[n]$ is the discretely sampled version of the continuous signal, x_i is the i-th sample of the signal, $\overline{x}$ is the mean (DC component) of the signal, and N is the total number of samples.

5.2 Amplitude in the frequency domain

The Fourier transform $X(f)$ converts a signal from the time domain to the frequency domain. It is a widely used technique for analyzing stationary signals, providing the spectral characteristics of one or more frequencies without altering their content. This representation is fundamental for signal analysis because it allows the study of how energy is distributed across different frequencies.

In the Fourier transform, the signal is interpreted as a superposition of sine waves with periodic amplitude, constant frequency, and phase, that is, harmonic components. The mathematical relationship that describes how the signal transforms from the time domain $x(t)$ to the frequency domain $X(f)$ explains how each frequency component contributes to the overall behavior of the signal in time and is given by the following expressions [20, 21]:

$$X(f) = \frac{1}{\sqrt{2\pi}}\int_{-\infty}^{\infty} x(t) \cdot e^{-j2\pi ft}dt \Leftrightarrow x(t) = \frac{1}{\sqrt{2\pi}}\int_{-\infty}^{\infty} X(f) \cdot e^{+j2\pi ft}df \tag{11}$$

The amplitude of the frequency method is determined by analyzing the energy of the signal within a specified frequency range, defined by f_{low} and f_{high} frequencies. Initially, the signal is transformed from the time domain to the frequency domain using the fast Fourier transform (FFT) which provides information about the frequency components of the signal [21]. Then, the amplitude at a specific frequency is calculated based on the corresponding value in the frequency spectrum. The amplitudes across the specified frequency range are summed to yield a total amplitude value, $V_{p,\text{freq}}$.

$$V_{p,\text{freq}} = [X(f)]_{f_{\text{low}} \le f \le f_{\text{high}}}, \tag{12}$$

where f_{low} and f_{high} are the lower and upper frequency ranges to be analyzed.

5.3 Amplitude in the cross-correlation method

In cross-correlation, the resulting waveform reflects the degree of similarity between two signals: the reference signal and the recorded signal. This process produces a time domain representation in which the amplitude of the peaks provides a characteristic or identification of the signal, showing where these peaks occur in relation to the time origin of the transmitted signal. It is possible to estimate the maximum voltage amplitude, $V_{p,\text{corr}}$, of the received signal using the following expression [22]:

$$V_{p,\text{corr}}[y_{rec}] = \frac{2V_{\text{max,corr}}}{V_{p,\text{send}} \cdot N_{\text{send}}}, \tag{13}$$

where $V_{p,\text{send}}$ is the amplitude of the signal, N_{send} is the number of samples in the emitted signal, and $V_{\text{max,corr}}$ is the maximum value of the correlation waveform between the reference signal and the recorded signal, occurring at the instant of detection.

6. Implementation using the proposed methods

Once the methodology for estimating the ToA and the corresponding signal amplitude is presented, this section analyzes two types of experimental parametric (nonlinear) acoustic signals: (*i*) a sine-type signal and (*ii*) a sine-sweep type signal. For each signal type, five measurements were recorded to ensure repeatability and robustness in the analysis.

As mentioned above, the distance between the transmitter and receiver in the experimental setup is 42 cm. Assuming a sound propagation speed of 1500 m/s in water, the received signal is expected to appear approximately 0.28 ms after the start of the measurement. This value is used as a reference for the experimental ToA estimations.

The transmitted signals have a carrier frequency, f_c, of 200 kHz and are recorded with a sampling frequency, f_s, at 20 MHz. The sine-type signal is created with a modulating frequency, f_m, of 15 kHz, and a duration of 500 μs, which is expected to produce a parametric signal at twice the frequency, i.e., 30 kHz. For the sine-sweep signal, the frequency range is 2 kHz to 20 kHz (f_{m1} and f_{m2}), so the expected parametric signal is 4 kHz to 40 kHz, with a duration of 1000 μs.

The structure used to implement the proposed approaches, which include (*i*) the estimation of the ToA and (*ii*) the estimation of the amplitude of the signals, is developed as follows: first, the recorded signal (already filtered to distinguish the primary and secondary -nonlinear- frequency components) is presented in the time domain. To visualize its spectral content and validate the presence of the parametric effect, the corresponding spectrograms are shown. Once the parametric effect is confirmed, the ToA of the primary signals is estimated. Subsequently, the amplitude of the primary frequencies is determined in order to complete the analysis of the nonlinear signal amplitude. For the amplitude estimation, the ToA is used to clip the received signal in the time domain before the $V_{p,\text{time}}$ and $V_{p,\text{freq}}$ calculation (see Appendix). This step is essential, and care must be taken to cut and isolate the signal accurately, as these methods are sensitive to noise.

The objective is to implement the proposed methods within a representative scenario, thereby establishing a methodological framework that will serve as a benchmark for future analyses of nonlinear acoustic signals.

6.1 Results of the sine-type signals

Once the sine-type signals were recorded, a detailed study of the appearance of the parametric effect was carried out. **Figure 5** shows a normalized comparison between the primary and secondary signals in the time domain. The raw signal is processed using a third-order Butterworth low-pass filter with a cut-off set to 5% above the frequency of interest ($f_c + f_m$ for the primary signal, and $2 \cdot f_m$ for the secondary signal). The peak amplitudes, V_p, of the primary and secondary frequencies are 33.88 $\pm$ 0.00 mV and 25.56 $\pm$ 2.85 μV, respectively. This corresponds to a difference of 33.86 mV, equivalent to -29.41 dB.

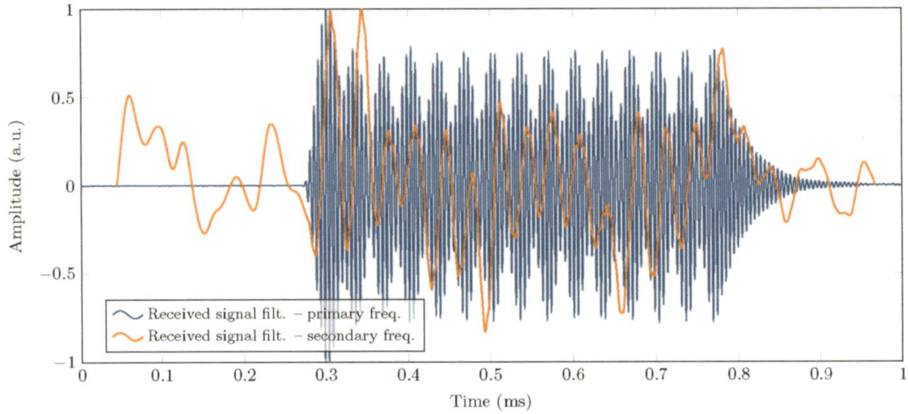

Figure 5.
Received sine-type signal processed through a third-order Butterworth low-pass filter with a cut-off set to 5% above the frequency of interest. The blue signal represents the primary frequency (around f_c) with a $V_p = 33.88\ mV$. The orange signal corresponds to the secondary frequency component (twice the f_m) with a $V_p = 25.56\ \mu V$. Both signals have been normalized to their V_p.

Regarding the SNR, there is a significant difference between the primary and secondary frequencies, with values of 68.09 ± 0.72 dB and 11.91 ± 2.06 dB, respectively. Therefore, the ToA was estimated using the primary signal, since, as shown in the figure, the secondary signal exhibits high temporal fluctuations, making accurate ToA estimation unfeasible in the threshold and Pvar methods.

A spectrogram is a powerful tool that displays the frequency components of a signal over time. It can be used to verify the presence of both the primary and secondary frequency components (i.e., the parametric signal) in the recorded data, in accordance with the characteristics described in Section 2.

For proper display, these signals have been decimated by a factor of 25 for the primary frequency and 50 for the secondary frequency using a second-order Chebyshev filter. **Figure 6** show the resulting spectrograms. An NFFT with 128 samples was applied, using a 75% overlap, resulting in a frequency resolution (F_{bin}) of 1 kHz. This configuration yields a time resolution (T_{bin}) of 40μs for the primary signal

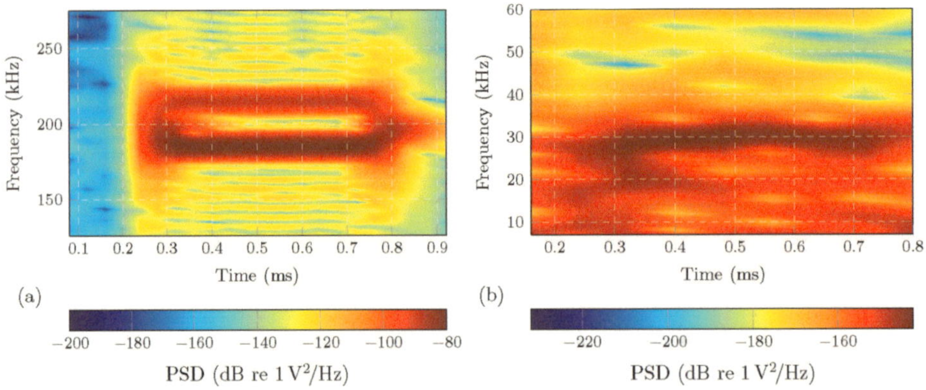

Figure 6.
Spectrogram for the sine-type signal with an NFFT of 128 samples with a 75% overlap and F_{bin} of 1 kHz. (a) The received signal with primary frequency components around the f_c with a T_{bin} of 40 μs. (b) The received signal with a spectral component of the secondary frequency (parametric signal) at 30 kHz with a T_{bin} of 80 μs.

ToA methods	ToA estimation (μs)
Threshold	283.09 ± 0.02
$Pvar_{cum}$	288.51 ± 0.01
$Pvar_{saw}$	288.49 ± 0.01
Cross-correlation	287.37 ± 0.03

Table 1.
Estimation of the ToA of the received sine-type signal by the three methods under analysis of the primary frequency.

and 80 μs for the secondary signal. The minimum valid frequencies (F_{valid}) are 12.5 and 6.25 kHz, respectively, for the primary and secondary signals. A more detailed development of this process can be found in [2].

The first approach proposed in this chapter focuses on the estimation of the ToA for the sine-type signal received and filtered at high frequencies, corresponding to the primary frequency. This choice is justified by the significantly higher SNR of the primary component compared to the secondary one, which enables a more accurate estimation using all the proposed approaches. In this occasion, for the threshold method, a threshold level of 30% over the maximum signal value is used, while for the Pvar method, an order of $k = 2$ is applied.

Table 1 presents the ToA for the threshold method, the Pvar method, and the cross-correlation. In the case of the sine-type signal, it can be seen that the estimated ToA values are consistent in all the methods analyzed.

Once the ToA values are obtained, the amplitudes of the primary frequency are analyzed using the second proposed approach in this chapter: time domain analysis, frequency domain analysis, and the cross-correlation method.

The amplitude of the secondary (parametric) frequency is evaluated using frequency domain analysis and the cross-correlation method. Cross-correlation enables the comparison of the received signals with reference signals, improving the accuracy of amplitude estimation and providing a more robust assessment of their behavior than either time or frequency domain analysis alone. Previous studies, such as those in [11], indicate that amplitude detection in the time domain is unclear due to the low SNR (less than 20 dB), which is why this approach is excluded from the current analysis.

The advantage of the cross-correlation method is that it produces a distinct peak at the location of the received signal, even when applied to the detection of the secondary (parametric, low-frequency) component. The sharpness of this peak may vary, indicating the accuracy of the ToA estimation. However, it also provides a useful indication of the amplitude of the received signal, as shown in **Figure 7**.

Figure 7a shows the transmitted signal correlated with the received signal previously filtered at the primary frequency (blue signal in **Figure 5**). The result is a correlation peak with a detection amplitude of 65.90, shown in **Figure 7b**.

On the other hand, the second derivative of the time-squared envelope of the transmitted signal is shown in **Figure 7c**. This is correlated with the received signal filtered at the secondary frequency (orange signal in **Figure 5**), giving a correlation amplitude of 0.04, as shown in **Figure 7d**.

A summary of the second approach proposed in this chapter, related to the amplitude estimation, for the primary and secondary frequencies is shown in **Table 2**.

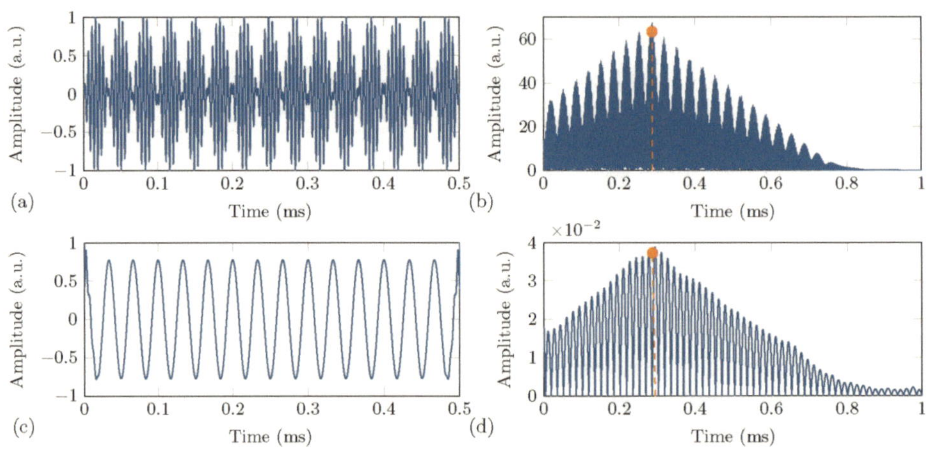

Figure 7.
Cross-correlation of the sine-type signal for the primary and secondary frequencies. (a) Transmitted modulated signal. (b) Cross-correlation between the transmitted modulated signal and the received signal filtered at the primary frequency, with a correlation amplitude of 65.90 in 287.4 μs. (c) Parametric signal corresponding to the second derivative of the time-square envelope of the transmitted signal. (d) Cross-correlation of the parametric signal with the received signal filtered at the secondary frequency, yielding a correlation amplitude of 0.04 in 294.4 μs.

Amp. methods	Estimation of amplitude at primary frequencies (mV)
$V_{p,time}$	20.10 ± 0.00
$V_{p,freq}$	18.28 ± 0.00
$V_{p,corr}$	13.18 ± 0.00
	Estimation of amplitude at secondary frequencies (μV)
$V_{p,freq}$	7.44 ± 0.00
$V_{p,corr}$	7.72 ± 0.46

Table 2.
Amplitude V_p estimation of the received sine-type signal analyzed by time domain, frequency domain, and cross-correlation method, for the primary and secondary frequencies (parametric signal).

6.2 Results of the sine-sweep type signal

As in the previous case, the raw signal is processed using a third-order Butterworth low-pass filter with a cut-off set to 5% above the frequency of interest ($f_c + f_{m2}$ for the primary signal, and $2 \cdot f_{m2}$ for the secondary signal). **Figure 8** shows the normalized comparison of the two signals in the time domain. The peak amplitudes, V_p, of the primary and secondary frequencies are 61.90 ± 0.03 mV and 48.89 ± 2.39 μV, respectively. This corresponds to a difference of 61.82 mV, equivalent to −24.20 dB.

The progressive decrease in the amplitude of the received signal with time can be attributed to the frequency response of the Reson TC4040 hydrophone, whose sensitivity drops significantly after 80 kHz. However, for the parametric frequency range of interest in this study, it is essential to have as flat a sensitivity response as possible, a criterion that this hydrophone adequately satisfies.

In this case, the SNR of the primary frequency is 71.86 ± 1.02 dB, while that of the secondary frequency is 14.73 ± 1.03 dB. As with the sine-type signal, there is a

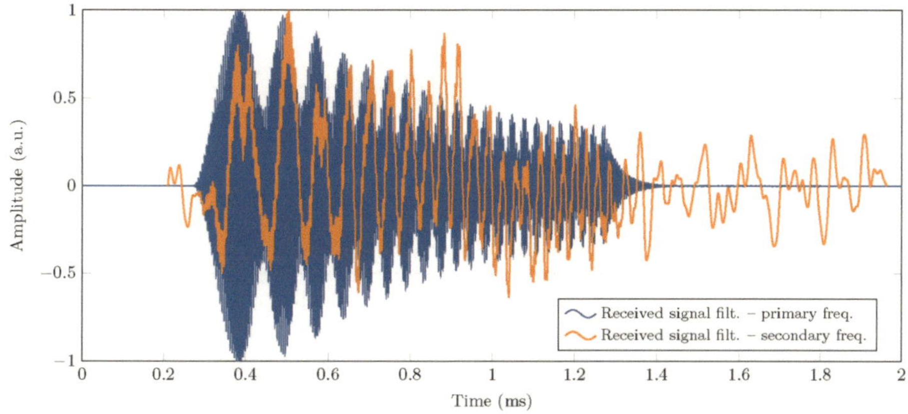

Figure 8.
Received sine-sweep type signal processed through a third-order Butterworth low-pass filter with a cut-off set to 5% above the frequency of interest. The blue signal represents the primary frequency (around f_c) with a $V_p = 61.90$ mV. The orange signal corresponds to the secondary frequency component (twice from f_{m1} to f_{m2}) with a $V_p = 48.89$ μV. Both signals have been normalized to their V_p.

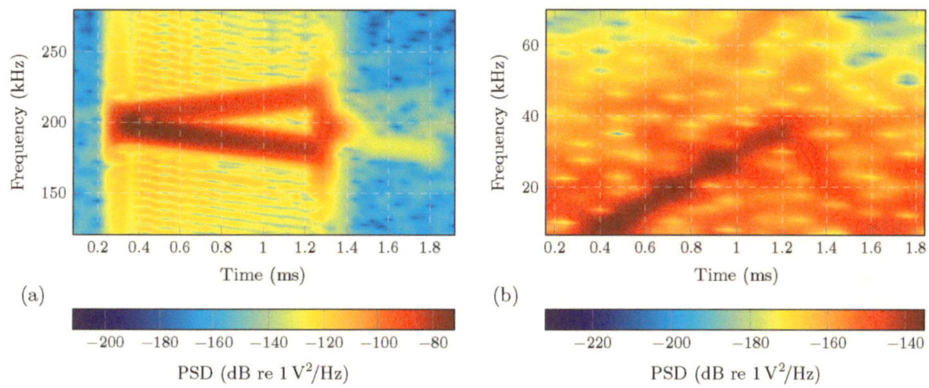

Figure 9.
Spectrogram for the sine-sweep signal with an NFFT of 128 samples with a 75% overlap and F_{bin} of 500 Hz. (a) The received signal with primary frequency components around the f_c with a T_{bin} of 40 μs. (b) The received signal with a spectral component of the secondary frequency (parametric signal) at 4 kHz to 40 kHz with a T_{bin} of 80 μs.

noticeable difference between the two components. Since the primary frequency has a significantly higher SNR, its ToA can be estimated more accurately.

To verify that the parametric effect has been generated in the medium, the sine-sweep type signal is analyzed by a spectrogram with the same NFFT used for the sine-type signal. **Figure 9(a)** shows the content of the primary frequency, around the f_c, while **Figure 9(b)** clearly shows the expected parametric effect, manifested as a frequency between 4 to 40 kHz.

The ToA estimation was performed using the primary received signal. The values corresponding to the proposed methods are summarized in **Table 3**.

As mentioned above, the method that provides the most reliable results is the cross-correlation method, as it demonstrates superior performance under high noise conditions. This time, this effect is more noticeable, as the sine-sweep signal has a longer rise time compared to the sine-type signal.

ToA methods	ToA estimation (μs)
Threshold	313.34 ± 0.02
$Pvar_{cum}$	338.37 ± 0.01
$Pvar_{saw}$	338.36 ± 0.01
Cross-correlation	267.53 ± 0.03

Table 3.
Estimation of the ToA of the received sine-sweep signal by the three methods under analysis of the primary frequency.

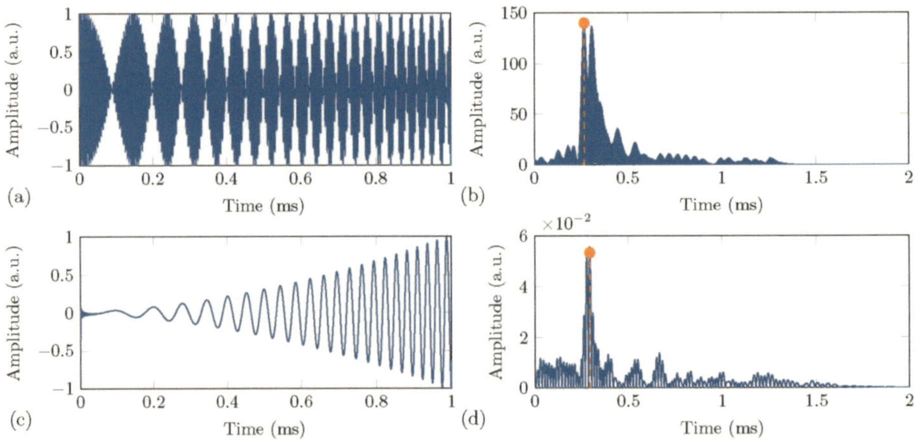

Figure 10.
Cross-correlation of the sine-sweep signal for the primary and secondary frequencies. (a) Transmitted modulated signal. (b) Cross-correlation between the transmitted modulated signal and the received signal filtered at the primary frequency, with a correlation amplitude of 145.71 in 267.55 µs. (c) Parametric signal corresponding to the second derivative of the time-square envelope of the transmitted signal. (d) Cross-correlation of the parametric signal with the received signal filtered at the secondary frequency, yielding a correlation amplitude of ∼ 0.05 in 294.80 µs.

Once the ToA values are determined, the primary frequency amplitudes of the sine-sweep signal are estimated using the second approach proposed in this chapter: time domain, frequency domain, and cross-correlation method.

The secondary frequency amplitude is estimated in the frequency domain and with the cross-correlation method. As in the sine-sweep signal analyzed, the time-domain approach is not considered in the sine-sweep signal.

For the amplitude estimation of the received signal using the cross-correlation method, the results obtained for the primary frequency (high frequency) and the secondary frequency (parametric signal) are presented in **Figure 10**. **Figure 10(a)** shows the sine-sweep transmitted signal correlated with the received signal filtered at high frequencies (**Figure 8**, blue), yielding **Figure 10(b)**. This analysis presents the cross-correlation results with a correlation amplitude value of 145.70 for the primary frequency. On the other hand, **Figure 10(c)** shows the second derivative of the time-squared envelope of the transmitted signal correlated with the received signal filtered at low frequencies (**Figure 8**, orange). The resulting cross-correlation is shown in **Figure 10(d)**, with a correlation amplitude of 0.05 for the secondary frequency.

The correlation peaks in this type of signals are narrower than in a sine-type signal because the sine-sweep has a wider bandwidth. This means that it includes many frequencies, which makes it possible to better locate the exact moment at which the

Amp. methods	Estimation of amplitude at primary frequencies (mV)
$V_{p,time}$	32.59 ± 0.00
$V_{p,freq}$	6.35 ± 0.00
$V_{p,corr}$	14.57 ± 0.00
	Estimation of amplitude at secondary frequencies (μV)
$V_{p,freq}$	3.14 ± 0.00
$V_{p,corr}$	5.39 ± 0.15

Table 4.
Amplitude V_p estimation of the received sine-sweep type signal analyzed by time domain, frequency domain, and cross-correlation method, for the primary and secondary frequencies (parametric signal).

signal arrives. In contrast, a sine-type signal has only one frequency, which might easily be confused with background noise, and its correlation produces a wider and less defined peak, which makes it difficult to precisely identify the time of arrival.

The results of this second approach proposed in this chapter, related to the amplitude estimation, for the primary and secondary frequencies are shown in **Table 4**.

Using this type of parametric signal, it is possible to design a communication system based on binary coding, where bit 1 and bit 0 are represented, e.g., by ascending and descending sine-sweep signals, respectively. It is important to note that other types of modulated signals are also capable of generating this parametric effect, potentially enabling their use in binary transmission schemes [23, 24]. This approach offers a significant advantage by exploiting the properties of low-frequency nonlinear signals, as they can travel much longer distances due to lower absorption by the medium, unlike high-frequency signals that experience greater attenuation. Despite its lower frequency, the nonlinear signal can maintain a narrow directivity similar to that of high frequency signals. This property enables the signal to be focused with high precision on a specific receiver, facilitating communication over long distances without the signal being picked up by other sensors in the same environment. This allows for efficient and targeted transmission, ideal for scenarios where interference minimization and long-range coverage are key factors.

7. Conclusion

In this chapter, the parametric effect of low frequencies has been presented in a controlled environment as a proof of concept. The phenomenon was demonstrated experimentally using both sine-type and sine-sweep signals. Further research is needed to expand the understanding of this type of communication and to evaluate its performance in real environments over longer distances. This would support the optimization of a low-frequency, focused-beam bit transmission system.

The results presented indicate that threshold and Pvar methods for ToA estimation are highly sensitive to the SNR and the temporal slope of the input signal. These methods yield accurate estimates when the signal exhibits abrupt transitions such as in sine signals waveforms, but their performance deteriorates significantly in the presence of gradual transitions, as seen in sine-sweep signals. This strong dependence on signal morphology limits their applicability in scenarios where the temporal profile of the signal cannot be precisely controlled or predicted. By contrast, the cross-correlation method demonstrates superior robustness to temporal variations, delivering more consistent and accurate ToA estimates. Nevertheless, its effectiveness relies on the availability of a reference signal for correlation, which restricts its use in passive detection contexts or in the analysis of acoustic signals of unknown origin, as frequently encountered in bioacoustic applications.

Regarding to amplitude V_p estimation, the nonuniform spectral content of sine-sweep type signals, compounded by the nonlinear frequency response of the sensor, particularly at higher frequencies, poses significant challenges for accurate estimation using conventional time domain methods. Specifically, these methods require both a high SNR and a temporally constant amplitude, conditions that are not fulfilled by weak parametric signals. As a result, alternative approaches based on frequency domain analysis and cross-correlation are employed, offering improved noise resilience and enabling more robust and reproducible amplitude estimation under demanding experimental conditions.

Acknowledgements

This work was a result of the ThinkInAzul and AgroAlNext programmes, funded by Ministerio de Ciencia, Innovación y Universidades (MICIU) with funding from European Union NextGenerationEU/PRTR-C17.I1 and by Fundación Séneca with funding from Comunidad Autónoma Región de Murcia (CARM).

Appendix

This workflow is not suitable for scenarios where the transmitter and receiver are separated by some of kilometers. At these distances, the secondary component of the signal tends to dominate, while the primary component is significantly attenuated, making it difficult, if not impossible, to accurately estimate the ToA. In such cases, although it is recognized that the accuracy of the ToA may be compromised, it is recommended to estimate it using correlation techniques applied to the secondary frequency (**Figure 11**).

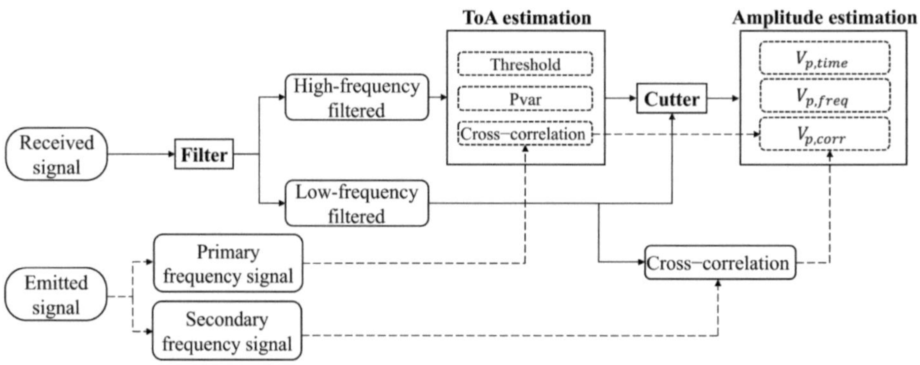

Figure 11.
Workflow summarizing the two proposed approaches: (i) ToA estimation, and (ii) amplitude estimation for nonlinear (parametric) signals, where a controlled system receives both primary (typically good SNR) and secondary (parametric) frequency components.

Author details

María Campo-Valera[1*†], Dídac Diego-Tortosa[2†] and Rafael Asorey-Cacheda[3,4]

1 Telecommunication Research Institute (TELMA), Universidad de Málaga, Málaga, Spain

2 Laboratori Nazionali del Sud (LNS), Istituto Nazionale di Fisica Nucleare (INFN), Catania, Italy

3 Department of Information and Communication Technologies, Universidad Politécnica de Cartagena, Antigones Plaza del Hospital, Cartagena, Spain

4 People Oriented Smart Technologies Laboratory, European University of Technology, European Union

*Address all correspondence to: maria.campo@ic.uma.es

† These authors contributed equally.

IntechOpen

© 2025 The Author(s). Licensee IntechOpen. This chapter is distributed under the terms of the Creative Commons Attribution License (http://creativecommons.org/licenses/by/4.0), which permits unrestricted use, distribution, and reproduction in any medium, provided the original work is properly cited.

References

[1] Mishachandar B, Vairamuthu S. An underwater cognitive acoustic network strategy for efficient spectrum utilization. Applied Acoustics. 2021;**175**: 107861. DOI: 10.1016/j.apacoust.2020.107861

[2] Diego-Tortosa D, Bonanno D, Bou-Cabo M, Di Mauro LS, Idrissi A, Lara G, et al. Effective strategies for automatic analysis of acoustic signals in long-term monitoring. Journal of Marine Science and Engineering. 2025;**13**(3):454. DOI: 10.3390/jmse13030454

[3] Guan S, Brookens T, Vignola J. Use of underwater acoustics in marine conservation and policy: Previous advances, current status, and future needs. Journal of Marine Science and Engineering. 2021;**9**(2):173. DOI: 10.3390/jmse9020173

[4] Aman W, Al-Kuwari S, Muzzammil M, Rahman MMU, Kumar A. Security of underwater and air–water wireless communication: State-of-the-art, challenges and outlook. Ad Hoc Networks. 2023;**142**:103114. DOI: 10.1016/j.adhoc.2023.103114

[5] Westervelt PJ. Parametric acoustic array. The Journal of the Acoustical Society of America. 1963;**35**(4):535-537. DOI: 10.1121/1.1918525

[6] Berktay HO. Possible exploitation of non-linear acoustics in underwater transmitting applications. Journal of Sound and Vibration. 1965;**2**(4):435-461. DOI: 10.1016/0022-460X(65)90122-7

[7] López-Fernández J, Fernández-Plazaola U, Paris JF, Díez L, Martos-Naya E. Wideband ultrasonic acoustic underwater channels: Measurements and characterization. IEEE Transactions on Vehicular Technology. 2020;**69**(4): 4019-4032. DOI: 10.1109/TVT.2020.2973495

[8] Gunes A. Performance comparison of toa and tdoa based tracking in underwater multipath environments using bernoulli filter. Polish Maritime Research. 2023;**30**(1):135-144. DOI: 10.2478/pomr-2023-0014

[9] Li X, Chen J, Bai J, Ayub MS, Zhang D, Wang M, et al. Deep learning-based doa estimation using crnn for underwater acoustic arrays. Frontiers in Marine Science. 2022;**9**:1027830. DOI: 10.3389/fmars.2022.1027830

[10] Gao R, Liang M, Dong H, Luo X, Suganthan PN. Underwater acoustic signal denoising algorithms: A survey of the state-of-the-art. IEEE Transactions on Instrumentation and Measurement. 2025;**74**:6502318

[11] Campo-Valera M, Diego-Tortosa D, Rodríguez-Rodríguez I, Useche-Ramírez J, Asorey-Cacheda R. Signal processing to characterize and evaluate nonlinear acoustic signals applied to underwater communications. Electronics. 2024;**13**(21):4192. DOI: 10.3390/electronics13214192

[12] Tjo/tta JN, Tjo/tta S. Nonlinear equations of acoustics, with application to parametric acoustic arrays. The Journal of the Acoustical Society of America. 1981;**69**(6):1644-1652. DOI: 10.1121/1.385942

[13] Enflo BO, Hedberg CM. Theory of Nonlinear Acoustics in Fluids. Vol. 67. Netherlands: Springer; 2006. ISBN 978-0-306-48419-3

[14] Campo-Valera M, Felis I. Underwater acoustic communication for

the marine enviroment's monitoring. In: MDPI Proceedings, (ECSA-6) 6th International Elecctronic Conference on Sensors and Applications. Vol. 42(51). Switzerland: MDPI; 2019

[15] Campo-Valera M, Villó-Pérez I, Fernández-Garrido A, Rodríguez-Rodríguez I, Asorey-Cacheda R. Exploring the parametric effect in nonlinear acoustic waves. IEEE Access. 2023;**11**:97221-97238. DOI: 10.1109/ACCESS.2023.3311631

[16] Oppenheim AV, Schafer RW. Tratamiento de señales en tiempo discreto. Old Tappan, N.J: Prentice Hall; 2011

[17] Youn D, Mathews V. Adaptive realizations of the maximum likelihood processor for time delay estimation. IEEE Transactions on Acoustics, Speech, and Signal Processing. 1984;**32**(4): 938-940. DOI: 10.1109/TASSP.1984.1164407

[18] Proakis JG. Digital Signal Processing: Principles Algorithms and Applications. Upper Saddle River, NJ, United States: Prentice-Hall, Inc. Division of Simon and Schuster; 1996. ISBN: 978-0-13-373762-2

[19] Cabot R. A note on the application of the hilbert transform to time delay estimation. IEEE Transactions on Acoustics, Speech, and Signal Processing. 1981;**29**(3):607-609. DOI: 10.1109/TASSP.1981.1163564

[20] Choi H-I, Williams WJ. Improved time-frequency representation of multicomponent signals using exponential kernels. IEEE Transactions on Acoustics, Speech, and Signal Processing. 1989;**37**(6):862-871. DOI: 10.1109/assp.1989.28057. ISSN 0096-3518

[21] Serrano EGF, Cardona S, i Foix, and Lluisa Jordi Nebot. Análisis en tiempo y frecuencia de señales de vibración tomadas al pie del carril durante el paso de un tren. Scientia et Technica. 2007; **13**(35):243-247. ISSN 0122-1701

[22] Adrián-Martínez S, Bou-Cabo M, Felis I, Llorens CD, Martínez-Mora JA, Saldaña M, et al. Acoustic Signal Detection through the Cross-Correlation Method in Experiments with Different Signal to Noise Ratio and Reverberation Conditions. Berlin Heidelberg: Springer; 2015. pp. 66-79. DOI: 10.1007/978-3-662-46338-3_7

[23] Campo-Valera M, Felis-Enguix I, Villó-Pérez I. Signal processing for parametric acoustic sources applied to underwater communication. Sensors. 2020;**20**(20):5878. DOI: 10.3390/s20205878. ISSN 1424-8220

[24] Campo-Valera M, Rodríguez-Rodríguez I, Rodríguez J-V, Herrera-Fernández L-J. Proof of concept of the use of the parametric effect in two media with application to underwater acoustic communications. Electronics. 2023;**12**(16):3459. DOI: 10.3390/electronics12163459

Section 2

Image Processing and Computer Vision

Chapter 3

Analysis of the Characteristics of the Formation of Multispectral Television Component Signals

Ha H. Cao

Abstract

In color and multispectral television systems, the formation of a single color component of the image signal as a function of the variables x, y, t (in a two-dimensional rectangular coordinate system (x, y)) is typically performed by limiting the incoming light flux to a specific $i(1, 2, 3, \ldots, n)$ number of fixed wavelength values λ. This necessary limitation of the ith color component signal is achieved using the corresponding ith color filter. If $l(x, y, t, \lambda)$ represents the power of the light flux emitted from objects, and $s(\lambda)$ denotes the sensitivity of the television (TV) system at wavelength λ (which determines the selection of the color component signal corresponding to a specific wavelength λ), then the general signal $l_o(x, y, t)$ at the output of the optical system of the TV system can be obtained by the algebraic summation of all color component signals $l_i(x, y, t, \lambda_i)$. Through the relative mutual weighting of the spectral characteristics of the color filters, the transmission quality of the corresponding color component signals during reproduction can be optimized.

Keywords: multispectral television, color filter, image recovery, adaptive demosaicing, spectrum of video signals

1. Introduction

The development of high-quality single-image sensor (SIS) digital cameras holds significant practical value. Most modern digital cameras employ a single sensor with a color filter array (CFA) to minimize size and cost. Positioned between the lens and sensor, the CFA separates incoming light into red (R), green (G), and blue (B) color channels.

Modern video cameras leverage advanced digital image processing techniques, incorporating the latest innovations in video signal compression to enhance digital television camera systems. A particularly promising research direction involves novel approaches for generating color component signals through interpolation techniques and light flux micro-shifting. Studies demonstrate these methods can potentially improve both resolution and signal-to-noise ratio in digital television (TV) cameras.

This research focuses on developing sophisticated television image restoration methods that utilize spatial, spectral, and temporal characteristics. The primary objective is to analyze and create effective techniques and hardware solutions for

 IntechOpen

enhancing image quality in digital TV cameras through video signal additional sampling. Specific research goals include:

1. developing novel solutions that utilize light flux micro-shifting and additional sampling of optical image signals to address current technological challenges in digital television camera design;

2. examination of video signal processing through additional sampling and subsequent reconstruction with different interpolation techniques;

3. development of a multi-dimensional spatially adaptive (MDSA) algorithm for video signal reconstruction;

4. execution of machine modeling and effectiveness analysis for the novel video signal processing method.

The reference [1] offers a comprehensive summary of color image demosaicing techniques. None of the existing CFA designs [2, 3] can match the image quality of Three-Image Sensor (TIS) cameras when used in SIS systems. To address this limitation, a new CFA structure is introduced to enhance the resolution of SIS cameras. The proposed color filter design enables the capture of full-resolution color signals by employing an MDSA image reconstruction method (adaptive demosaicing) and leveraging the spatial periodic micro-shifts of incoming light flux relative to the CFA [4]. The second section is devoted to the analysis of image sampling in SIS cameras. The third section is devoted to analyzing the recovery of video signal samples in the SIS camera. With additional sampling [5], samples following a constant period of primary sampling F_p are thinned out, forming groups of elements following with a frequency of additional sampling F_p/N. In this section, a method for recovering missing samples of a video signal has been developed.

2. Image sampling in SIS cameras

We consider a monochromatic two-dimensional image, and for clarity, it is assumed that the geometric dimensions of the image along the axes (x, y) are limited. If $l(x, y, t, \lambda)$ is the power of the light flux emitted from objects, $s(\lambda)$ is the sensitivity of the TV system at wavelength λ, then the general signal at the output of the optical system of the TV system is:

$$l_o(x, y, t) = \sum_{i=1}^{n} l_i(x, y, t, \lambda_i) \tag{1}$$

$$l_i(x, y, t, \lambda_i) = s(\lambda_i) l(x, y, t, \lambda) \tag{2}$$

where λ_i and $l_i(x, y, t, \lambda_i)$-fixed wavelength value and corresponding optical image signal of a spectral zone i (i = 1, 2, 3, … , n). If we neglect intermediate integral transformations and changes in the dimensionality of video information in the photodetector (PD), optical image signal $l_i(x, y, t, \lambda_i)$ - > electrical image signal $u_i(x, y, t, \lambda_i)$ then, the sampled video signal $u_i^*(x, y, t, \lambda_i)$ generated at the output of the PD is:

$$u_i^*(x, y, t, \lambda_i) = u_i(x, y, t, \lambda_i) d_i(x, y, t, \lambda_i) \tag{3}$$

where $d_i(x, y, t, \lambda_i)$ is the sampling function corresponding to the disposition of cells of the ith color filter.

Time is fixed $t = t_0$, when using a mosaic color filter, the cells of which are the primary colors—red (R), blue (B), and green (G):

$$u_R^*(x, y, \lambda_R) = u_R(x, y, \lambda_R) d_R(x, y, \lambda_R) \tag{4}$$

$$u_G^*(x, y, \lambda_G) = u_G(x, y, \lambda_G) d_G(x, y, \lambda_G) \tag{5}$$

$$u_B^*(x, y, \lambda_B) = u_B(x, y, \lambda_B) d_B(x, y, \lambda_B) \tag{6}$$

where $d_R(\text{x,y},\lambda_R)$, $d_G(\text{x,y},\lambda_G)$, and $d_B(\text{x,y},\lambda_B)$—sampling functions that take into account the location of the cells of the corresponding primary colors R, G, B of the color filters, $u_R(x, y, \lambda_R), u_G(x, y, \lambda_G), u_B(x, y, \lambda_B)$—the primary color component signals of the TV system.

In multispectral television, $u_1(x, y, \lambda_1), u_2(x, y, \lambda_2), \ldots, u_n(x, y, \lambda_n)$—multispectral image signals in n spectral selection zones.

In the SIS camera (with a CFA filter), by using the additional sampling, signals for one coding color can be transmitted; in place of missing samples, signals for other coding colors can also be transmitted. The following section examines the analysis of one-dimensional additional sampling.

2.1 Analysis of the sampling function under one-dimensional additional sampling

Mathematically, a sampling process can be represented as the multiplication of a continuous-time function by a sampling function, which is defined as follows:

$$d(t, T_p) = T_p \sum_{k=-\infty}^{\infty} \delta(t - kT_p) \tag{7}$$

here $T_p \leq \pi/\omega_{brd}$ represents the primary sampling interval, ω_{brd} denoting the signal's maximum (cutoff) frequency. In the frequency domain:

$$D(\omega, \Omega_p) = \Omega_p \sum_{n=-\infty}^{\infty} \delta(\omega - n\Omega_p) \tag{8}$$

where $\Omega_p = 2\pi/T_p$ denotes the sampling frequency. If $u(t)$ is the original signal with spectrum $U(\omega)$, then the primarily sampled signal can be expressed as:

$$u^*(t, T_p) = u(t) d(t, T_p) = T_p \sum_{k=-\infty}^{\infty} u(kT_p) \delta(t - kT_p) \tag{9}$$

The spectrum of $u^*(t, T_p)$ is given as:

$$U(\omega, \Omega_p) = \frac{1}{2\pi} U(\omega) \otimes D(\omega, \Omega_p) \tag{10}$$

where the symbol $\otimes$ represents the convolution operation.

The additional sampling operation can be mathematically represented by multiplying $u^*(t, T_p)$ with a strobing function $p_s(t, M, N, T_p)$:

$$u^*(t,M,N,T_p) = u^*(t,T_p)p_s(t,M,N,T_p) \tag{11}$$

in this expression, M, N are both positive whole numbers where $M < N$. By applying Eq. (9):

$$u^*(t,M,N,T_p) = u(t)d(t,T_p)p_s(t,M,N,T_p) = u(t)d_s(t,M,N,T_p) \tag{12}$$

where the generalized sampling function $d_s(t,M,N,T_p)$ is given by the multiplication of $d(t,T_p)$ and $p_s(t,M,N,T_p)$.

We will focus specifically on periodic additional sampling. In this scenario, the deterministic functions $p_s(t,M,N,T_p)$, $d_s(t,M,N,T_p)$ can be effectively analyzed *via* the Fourier transform. The strobing function $p_s(t,M,N,T_p)$ is periodic, equaling 1 at allocated sample points and 0 at missed sample points. Its periodicity is defined by the additional sampling period $T_s = NT_p$, and M ($<N$) specifies the number of allocated samples within one such period.

For analysis, it is useful to represent the strobing function $p_s(t,M,N,T_p)$ in the following form:

$$p_s(t,M,N,T_p) = \sum_{m=0}^{M-1}\sum_k \sin c\pi\left(\frac{t}{T_p} - mT_p - kNT_p\right) \tag{13}$$

Figure 1 illustrates the graphical representation of Eq. (13). Its right-hand side represents the convolution of $\text{sinc}\pi(t/T_p)$ with delta functions displaced by $(mT_p + kNT_p)$:

$$\sum_{m=0}^{M-1}\sum_k \sin c\pi\left(\frac{t}{T_p} - mT_p - kNT_p\right) = \sin c\pi\left(\frac{t}{T_p}\right) \otimes \frac{NT_p}{M}\sum_{m=0}^{M-1}\sum_k \delta(t - mT_p - kNT_p) \tag{14}$$

Since $d(t,T_p)\text{sinc}\pi(t/T_p) = \delta(t)$, the expression for $d_s(t,M,N,T_p)$ can be written as:

$$d_s(t,M,N,T_p) = \frac{NT_p}{M}\sum_{m=0}^{M-1}\sum_k \delta(t - mT_p - kNT_p) \tag{15}$$

The spectrum of the generalized sampling function $d_s(t,M,N,T_p)$ can be obtained as:

$$D_s(\omega,\Omega_p) = \Omega_p \sum_{m=0}^{M-1}\sum_{n=-\infty}^{\infty} \delta\left(\omega - n\frac{\Omega_p}{N}\right)e^{-i\omega m T_p} \tag{16}$$

2.2 New mosaic color filter array proposal

In the SIS camera, light flux passes through a CFA before reaching the sensor. When the CFA's mosaic pattern precisely aligns with the sensor's pixel grid during a frame capture, the output generates three color matrices (R, G, and B) representing the coding colors. Since the CFA cell count matches the pixel count, these matrices initially contain zero-valued elements. These missing values can be reconstructed by

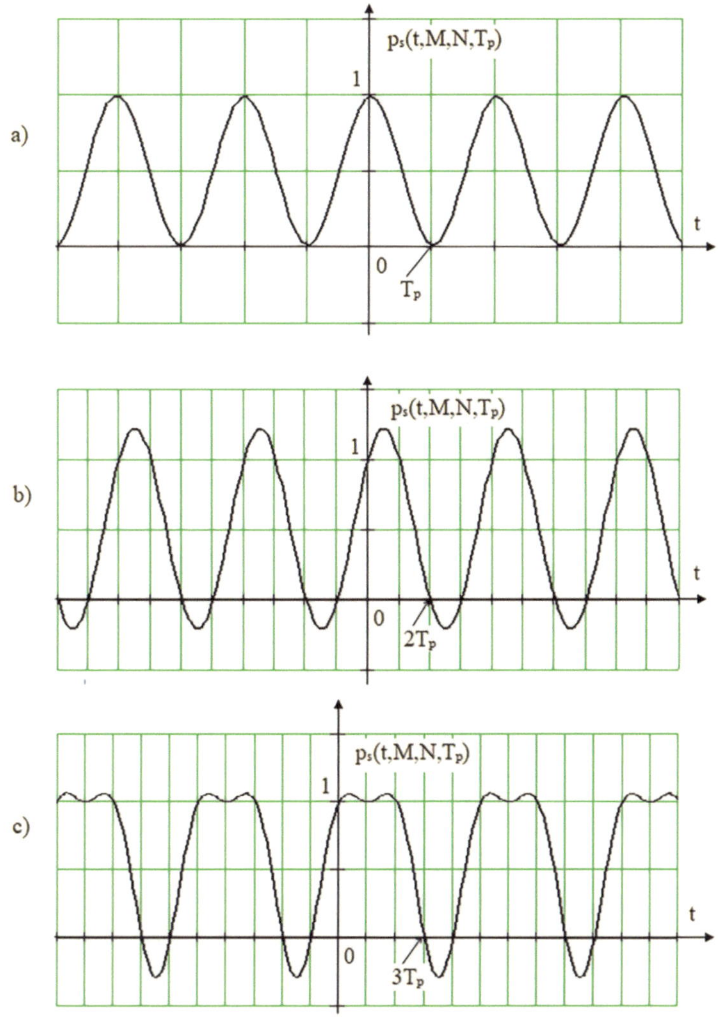

Figure 1.
Strobing function in periodic additional sampling for the case: (a) M = 1, N = 2; (b) M = 2, N = 4; (c) M = 3, N = 5.

analyzing adjacent nonzero elements and leveraging the spatial periodic micro-displacement between the light flux and CFA during frame acquisition. Therefore, the mosaic CFA's cell structure must be chosen considering the following criteria:

i. To optimize hardware implementation for real-time processing and minimize memory requirements, the three color matrices (representing the coding colors) should be partitioned into elementary groups (blocks) of adjacent rows. Within each block, missing pixels must be accurately reconstructed along horizontal, vertical, and diagonal directions. Notably, the pixel-processing algorithms should maintain consistency across all directional interpolations.

ii. The block size must contain a sufficient number of pixels to ensure precise reconstruction of missing values through interpolation.

iii. When needed, the light flux's periodic micro-shift relative to the CFA can provide more reference pixels.

Figure 2 presents the proposed mosaic CFA design, which meets all specified requirements. By implementing a diagonal spatial micro-displacement of 2 pixels through two half-frame captures, we acquire three distinct color matrices (Red, Green, and Black), as illustrated in **Figures 3–5**. This approach necessitates doubling the image sensor's operational speed compared to conventional methods. Missing

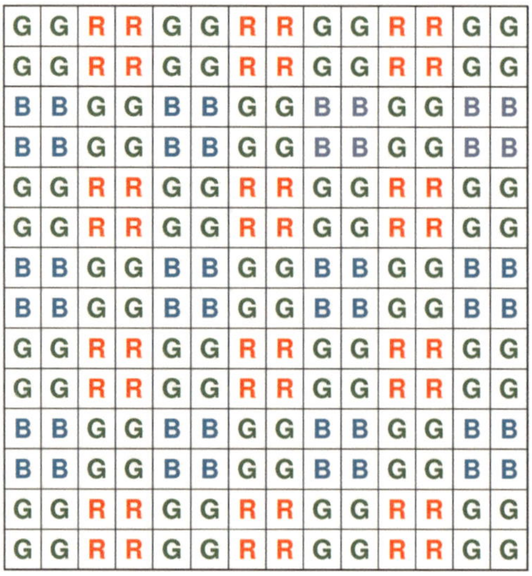

Figure 2.
Structural configuration of the proposed CFA pattern.

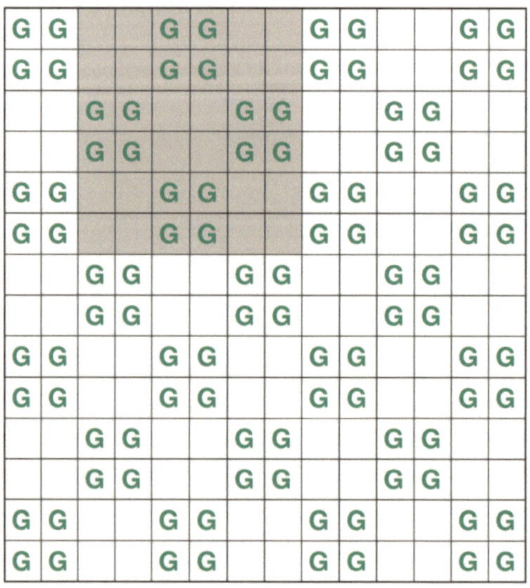

Figure 3.
Location of G-color cells and elementary recovering block.

DOI: http://dx.doi.org/10.5772/intechopen.1010941

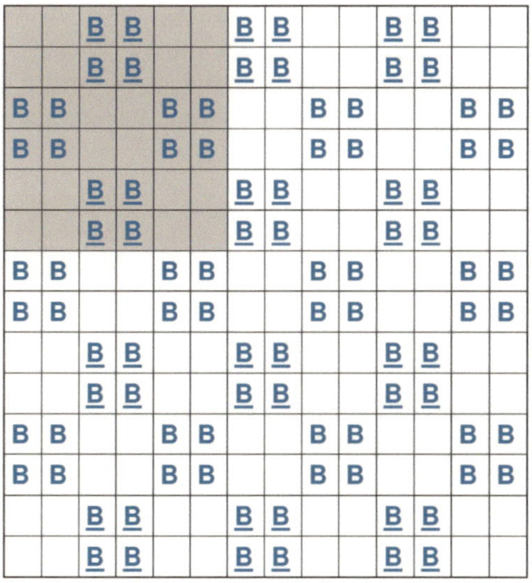

Figure 4.
Combined B-color positions from both half-frames and the reconstruction block. B: first half-frame, $\underline{B}$: second half-frame.

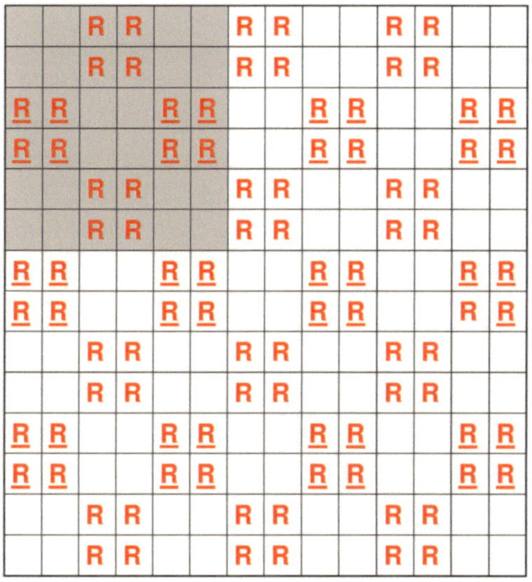

Figure 5.
Combined R-color positions from both half-frames and the reconstruction block. R: first half-frame, $\underline{R}$: second half-frame.

pixels for each color channel are reconstructed within elementary blocks using the MDSA interpolation technique.

The system utilizes a two-cell diagonal micro-displacement of light flux between frames, doubling the reference pixels for B and R channels (**Figures 4** and **5**). During the first half-frame, the image sensor accumulates optical signals aligned with G, B, and R cell positions. The second half-frame captures additional $\underline{B}$ and $\underline{R}$ samples through diagonally offset CFA cells when the light flux shifts downward by two cells. This two-frame cycle repeats continuously. The process effectively performs two-dimensional sampling, with CFA cell count matching the sensor's pixel resolution. To achieve this, the light flux projection frequency must double the frame rate, with pixel readout synchronized to projection intervals. The accumulated frame data is then converted to television signals, effectively exchanging the sensor's temporal resolution for enhanced spatial resolution.

3. Analysis of video signal sample recovery in SIS cameras

Let us consider the sampling structure in **Figure 6**, corresponding to the disposition of the green cells of the color filter in **Figure 3**.

With additional sampling, the samples following a constant period of primary sampling are thinned out, forming groups of elements following with a frequency of additional sampling F_P/N. The use of the proposed structure of the color filter leads to additional sampling with parameters N = 4 and M (the number of elements in the group) = 2.

The recovery of missing samples is a process inverse to the process of additional sampling. The principles of analysis of the process of recovery of missing samples will be considered for the case of ideal recovery.

3.1 Analysis of ideal video signal recovery in additional sampling

3.1.1 Ideal recovery of a signal discretized into groups of adjacent samples

In such a recovery, additional sampling is considered as a case of "recurrent sequential sampling," that is, the case when the sampling points are divided into groups of M points each, with a recurrent period NT_P = N/2F where F is the maximum frequency of a continuous function u(t) with a finite spectrum. It is possible to

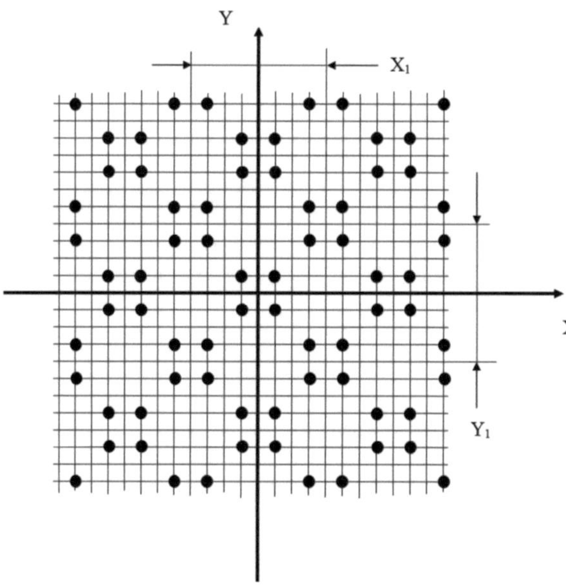

Figure 6.
The sampling structure corresponds to the disposition of green cells of the selected color filter option.

completely recover the function u(t) in the frequency band MF/N, preliminarily limited by the maximum frequency F′ = (M/N)F. This statement is based on Shannon's remark that the function u(t), limited by the band F and the interval T, can be completely determined by its 2FT sampling points; these 2FT sampling points do not necessarily have to be equidistant [6]. In Ref. [7], it is proved that if a signal with a finite spectrum is uniquely determined by its values at the recurrent sampling points t = τ_{mn} = $t_m + nM/(2F)$, m = 1, 2, … ,M; n = …, 0, 1, 2, … the recovery is performed using the formula:

$$u(t) = \sum_{k=-\infty}^{\infty} \sum_{m=1}^{M} u(\tau_{mn}) \psi_{mn}(t) \tag{17}$$

where

$$\psi_{mn}(t) = \frac{\prod_{q=1}^{N} \sin \frac{2\pi F}{M}\left(t - t_q\right)}{\prod_{q=1, q\neq m}^{M} \sin \frac{2\pi F}{M}\left(t_m - t_q\right)} \frac{(-1)^{nM}}{\frac{2\pi F}{M}\left(t - t_m - \frac{nM}{2F}\right)} \tag{18}$$

According to Eq. (17), the recovery of the function u(t) with additional sampling by groups of adjacent samples can be considered as the sum of the responses of filters with impulse responses determined by expression (18) when the corresponding samples arrive at them.

3.1.2 Ideal recovery of missing signal samples

The recovery of missing samples is a process that is the reverse of the process of additional sampling. Its essence lies in the calculation of the specified samples from the known (reference) ones. As a result of such an operation, the signal with additional sampling becomes a signal with primary sampling (equidistant samples). The recovery of missing samples can be carried out using the circuit shown in **Figure 7a**. Here, additional sampling is performed by the discretizer D_1 with the characteristic

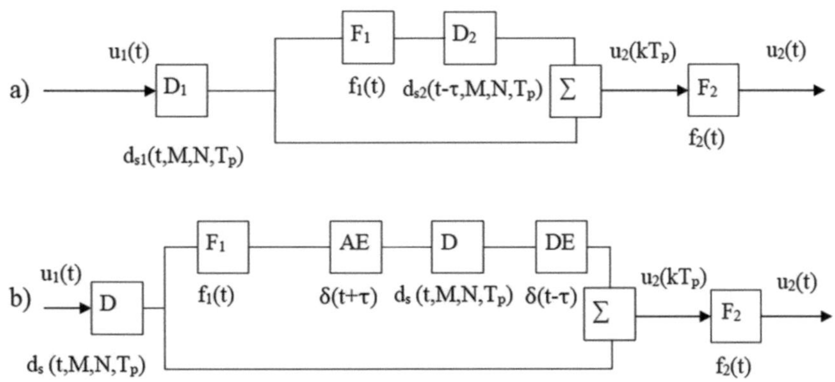

Figure 7.
Recovery of lost samples: (a) with a delay sampler and (b) with in-phase samplers and limiting filters.

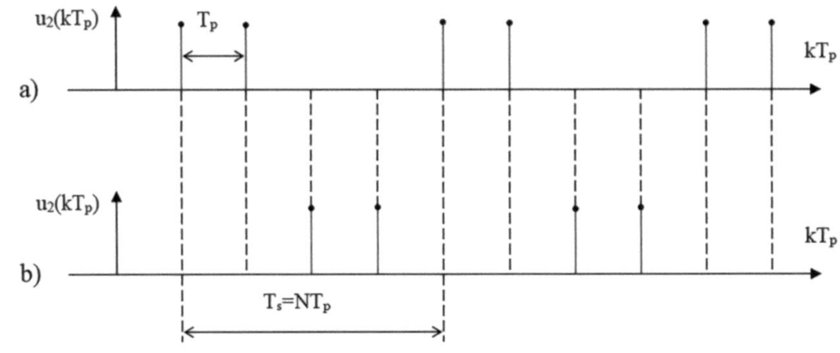

Figure 8.
(a) Reference and (b) recovered samples.

$d_{s1}(t, M, N, T_p)$. The analog signal is recovered from discrete samples by the interpolator filter F_1 with the impulse response $f_1(t)$, determined by the expression (18). The recovered analog signal is secondarily sampled by the sampler D_2 with the response $d_{s2}(t - \tau, M, N, T_p)$—with a delay of the interval τ relative to D_1, where $\tau = MT_p$. The adder adds two discrete sequences, one of which consists of recovered samples and the other of reference samples. The primary signal is finally recovered by filter F_2 with the impulse response $f_2(t)$ (**Figure 8**).

For the analysis, it is more convenient to use a circuit with in-phase samplers (**Figure 7b**), equivalent to the previous circuit, which includes an advance element (AE) with a pulse characteristic: $\delta(t + \tau)$ and a delay element (DE) with a pulse characteristic $\delta(t - \tau)$. The expression for the output signal $u_2(kT_p)$ is written as:

$$
\begin{gathered}
u_2(kT_p) = u_1(t)d_s(t, M, N, T_p) \otimes f_1(t) \otimes \delta(t + \tau)d_s(t, M, N, T_p) \otimes \delta(t - \tau) + u_1(t)d_s(t, M, N, T_p) \\
u_2(t) = (u_1(t)d_s(t, M, N, T_p) \otimes f_1(t) \otimes \delta(t + \tau)d_s(t, M, N, T_p) \otimes \delta(t - \tau) + u_1(t)d_s(t, M, N, T_p)) \otimes f_2(t)
\end{gathered}
\tag{19}
$$

Moving from here to the frequency domain, we get

$$
\begin{gathered}
U_2(\omega, \Omega_p) = U_1(\omega) \otimes D_s(\omega, \Omega_p)F_1(\omega)e^{i\omega\tau} \otimes D_s(\omega, \Omega_p)e^{-i\omega\tau} + U_1(\omega) \otimes D_s(\omega, \Omega_p) \\
U_2(\omega) = (U_1(\omega) \otimes D_s(\omega, \Omega_p)F_1(\omega)e^{i\omega\tau} \otimes D_s(\omega, \Omega_p)e^{-i\omega\tau} + U_1(\omega) \otimes D_s(\omega, \Omega_p))F_2(\omega)
\end{gathered}
\tag{20}
$$

These expressions include the impulse and frequency characteristics of the recovering filters F_1 and F_2, which determine signals $u_1(t)$ and $u_2(t)$ in frequency bands (M/N)F and F. In order to simplify the studies, it is advisable to use the limiting filters F_1 and F_2 with impulse responses $f_1(t)$ and $f_2(t)$ determined not by expression (18) but by the function $sinc2\pi(M/N)Ft$, accordingly, frequency responses $F_1(\omega) = rect(\omega/(M\Omega_p/N))$ and $F_2(\omega) = rect(\omega/(\Omega_p))$ (at M = N, $F_1(\omega)$ -> $F_2(\omega)$). Considering that $D_s(\omega, \Omega_p)$ is determined by expression (16), we finally get:

$$
U_2(\omega) = \sum_{m_2=0}^{N-M-1} \sum_{m_1=0}^{M-1} \sum_{n=-\infty}^{\infty} U_1\left(\omega - n\frac{\Omega_p}{N}\right)\left[rect\left(\frac{\omega - n\frac{\Omega_p}{N}}{\frac{M}{N}\Omega_p}\right)e^{-i2\pi n\left(\frac{m_2+M}{N}\right)} + e^{-i\frac{2\pi}{N}nm_1}\right]
\tag{21}
$$

Calculating the modulus (21) for different M and N allows us to obtain a spectral picture of the distribution of the main and side spectra with ideal recovery of the missing samples. In particular, expression (21) for M = 1, 2; N = 2, 4 has the form:

M = 1,N = 2:

$$U_2(\omega) = \sum_{n=-\infty}^{\infty} U_1\left(\omega - n\frac{\Omega_p}{2}\right)\left[rect\left(\frac{\omega - n\frac{\Omega_p}{2}}{\frac{\Omega_p}{2}}\right)e^{-i\pi n} + 1\right] \tag{22}$$

M = 2, N = 4:

$$U_2(\omega) = \sum_{m=0}^{1}\sum_{n=-\infty}^{\infty} U_1\left(\omega - n\frac{\Omega_p}{4}\right)\left[rect\left(\frac{\omega - n\frac{\Omega_p}{4}}{\frac{\Omega_p}{2}}\right)e^{-i\pi n\left(\frac{m}{2}+1\right)} + e^{-i\pi n\frac{m}{2}}\right] \tag{23}$$

We will assume that the conditional boundaries of the signal spectrum $U_1(\omega)$ are the frequencies $-\omega_{brd}$ and ω_{brd} between which there is the following relationship:

$$U_1(\omega) = 1 - \frac{|\omega|}{|\omega_{brd}|} \tag{24}$$

Figure 9 shows the disposition of spectra $U_2(\omega)$ with additional sampling with the specified M and N, after ideal recovery of missing samples, the analysis of which allows us to make the following comments and conclusions:

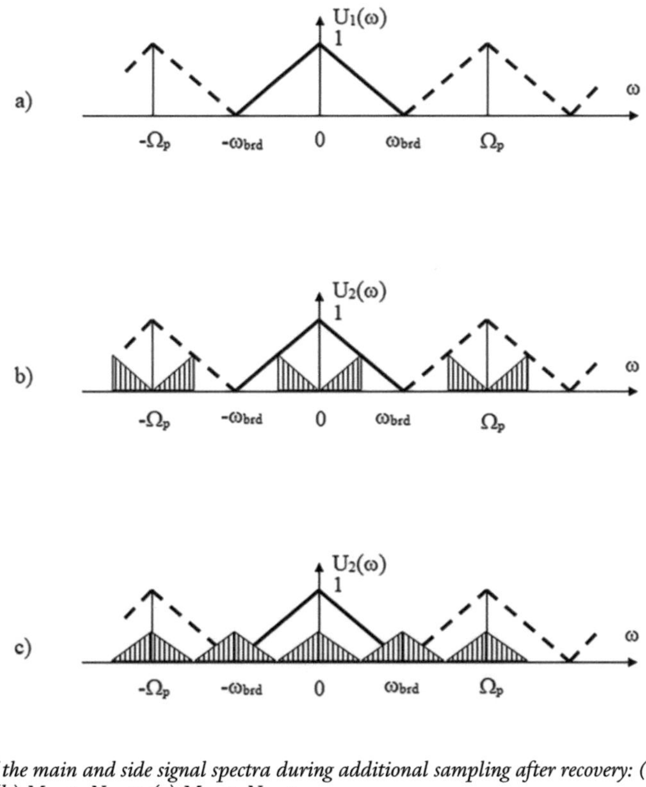

Figure 9.
The disposition of the main and side signal spectra during additional sampling after recovery: (a) the primary signal spectrum; (b) M = 1, N = 2; (c) M = 2, N = 4.

1. With additional sampling with M = 1, N = 2 and ideal recovery of the missing samples, the spectral components of the main and side spectra become comparable and equal in the frequency range of $0.5\omega_{brd}$, which causes Moire distortion to appear in this range. Using formula (21), it can be shown that for M = 3 and N = 2 M, that is, in the case of equality of the number of samples in the group to the number of missing samples, the appearance of Moire distortion will also occur at these frequencies.

2. Only for M = 2, N = 4 there is a shift of the specified frequency range toward the boundary frequency ω_{brd} of the signal spectrum. This range corresponds to frequencies of the order of $0.75\omega_{brd}$.

3.2 Real recovery of missing samples in one-dimensional additional sampling

Perfect reconstruction of missing samples would theoretically require a recovery filter with an infinite impulse response, which is physically unrealizable. In practice, missing samples are estimated using neighboring known values, typically through polynomial interpolation. However, hardware constraints limit the feasible order of interpolation polynomials [8]. This estimation process is commonly executed using a transversal filter. For instance, recovering a target sample u_0 from adjacent samples $u_{-n}, u_{-(n-1)}, \dots, u_{-1}, u_{+1}, \dots, u_{+(n-1)}, u_{+n}$ follows the mathematical relation:

$$u_0 = \sum_{k=1}^{n} (\alpha_k u_k + \alpha_{-k} u_{-k}), \tag{25}$$

where α_k, $k = \pm 1, \pm 2, \dots, \pm n$ are weighting coefficients.

Let us consider some interpolation methods based on the use of expression (25).

3.2.1 Approximation of functions using algebraic interpolation polynomials

Given an unknown function $u(t)$ with known values $u_0, u_1, \dots, u_n$ at discrete points $t_0, t_1, \dots, t_n$ within interval $[a, b]$, we seek to construct an $n - th$ degree polynomial approximation:

$$u_n(t) = \sum_{i=0}^{n} \alpha_i t^i, \quad t \in [a, b], \tag{26}$$

for which the following conditions are satisfied:

$$u_n(t_j) = u_j, \quad j = 0, 1, \dots, n. \tag{27}$$

In practice, Newton's interpolation polynomial is often used to approximate functions. This polynomial is introduced using divided differences of various orders found from the values of the function $u_1, \dots, u_N$ at the points $t_1, \dots, t_N$.

The first-order divided difference is:

$$u(t_i, t_{i-1}) = \frac{u_i - u_{i-1}}{t_i - t_{i-1}}, \quad i = 0, \dots, n. \tag{28}$$

The second-order divided difference is simply the first-order divided difference of $u(t_i, t_{i-1})$, which is:

$$u(t_i, t_{i-1}, t_{i-2}) = \frac{u(t_i, t_{i-1}) - u(t_{i-1}, t_{i-2})}{t_i - t_{i-2}}, \quad i = 0, \dots, n \tag{29}$$

The $n - th$ order-divided difference can be recursively computed using its $(n-1) - th$ order counterpart according to:

$$u(t_{n+i}, t_{n+i-1}, \dots, t_{i+1}, t_i) = \frac{u(t_{n+i}, \dots, t_{i+1}) - u(t_{n+i-1}, t_i)}{t_{n+i} - t_i} \tag{30}$$

the nth-order-divided difference can be represented as:

$$u(t_{n+i}, t_{n+i-1}, \dots, t_{i+1}, t_i) = \sum_{j=1}^{n} \frac{u_{j+i}}{(t_{i+j} - t_i)(t_{i+j} - t_{i+1})\cdots(t_{i+j} - t_{i+n})} \tag{31}$$

It then follows that $u(t)$ can be represented as:

$$\begin{aligned} u(t) &= u_0 + (t - t_0)u(t_0, t_1) + (t - t_0)(t - t_1)u(t_0, t_1, t_2) + \cdots \\ &+ (t - t_0)\cdots(t - t_{n-1})u(t_0, \dots, t_n) + (t - t_0)\cdots(t - t_n)u(t, t_0, \dots, t_n) \end{aligned} \tag{32}$$

which can be rewritten in the following form:

$$u(t) = p_n(t) + r_n(t), \tag{33}$$

where

$$\begin{aligned} p_n(t) &= u_0 + (t - t_0)u(t_0, t_1) + (t - t_0)(t - t_1)u(t_0, t_1, t_2) + \cdots \\ &+ (t - t_0)\cdots(t - t_{n-1})u(t_0, \dots, t_n) \end{aligned} \tag{34}$$

$$r_n(t) = (t - t_0)\cdots(t - t_n)u(t, t_0, \dots, t_n) \tag{35}$$

Polynomial $p_n(t)$ is an interpolation polynomial, since we have the equalities $u(t_j) = p_n(t_j), j = 0, 1, \dots, n$. This polynomial is usually called a Newton interpolation polynomial, whereas $r_n(t)$ is a remainder of the Newton formula.

3.2.2 Using splines to approximate functions

Image interpolation using Newton, Lagrange, and other polynomials is a non-local procedure that requires significant hardware costs for implementation and is therefore unsuitable for real-time image processing. To ensure locality, the initial interval $[t_1, t_n]$ (e.g., one television line) is divided into n subintervals, where it is necessary to recover the intermediate values of the function u(t), then an interpolation polynomial of the first, second, or third degree, respectively, is recovered. Thus, the interpolation procedure becomes local. Such interpolation is called spline interpolation, and a piecewise polynomial interpolating function with a homogeneous structure (composed of polynomials of the same degree) is called a spline function or spline.

To recover the missing samples in the interval (t_j, t_{j+3}) (see **Figure 10**), it is advisable to use an interpolation spline of the fifth degree of defect three, denoted as $\phi_{5,3}(t)$, which ensures both continuity and derivative matching—preserving first and second derivative equality at all interpolation nodes. This approach additionally offers computational efficiency by substantially reducing the required operations.

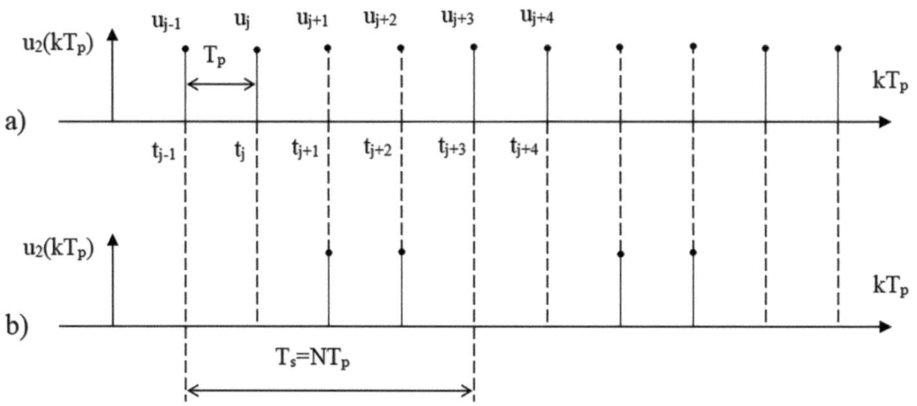

Figure 10.
(a) Reference and (b) recovered samples interpolated using spline interpolation.

The interpolation function $\phi_{5,3}(t)$ satisfies the following conditions:

On each interval (t_j, t_{j+3}), spline $\phi_{5,3}(t)$ is a polynomial of degree 5:

$$\phi_{5,3}(t) = \sum_{i=0}^{5} \alpha_i^{(j)} (t - t_j)^i. \tag{36}$$

Spline $\phi_{5,3}(t)$ belongs to the set of twice continuously differentiable functions on $[a, b]$, denoted by $C^2[a, b]$.

$\phi_{5,3}(t_j) = u(t_j).$

$\phi'_{5,3}(t_j) = u'(t_j).$

$\phi''_{5,3}(t_j) = u''(t_j).$

For brevity, denote $u_j = u(t_j)$. Then, from the above conditions, one obtains a system of equations:

$$\begin{cases} u_j = \alpha_0^{(j)} \\ u'_j = \alpha_1^{(j)} \\ u''_j = 2\alpha_2^{(j)} \\ u_{j+3} = u_j + u'_j(t_{j+3} - t_j) + \frac{u''_j}{2}(t_{j+3} - t_j)^2 + \\ \alpha_3^{(j)}(t_{j+3} - t_j)^3 + \alpha_4^{(j)}(t_{j+3} - t_j)^4 + \alpha_5^{(j)}(t_{j+3} - t_j)^5 \\ u'_{j+3} = u'_j + u''_j(t_{j+3} - t_j) + 3\alpha_3^{(j)}(t_{j+3} - t_j)^2 + \\ 4\alpha_4^{(j)}(t_{j+3} - t_j)^3 + 5\alpha_5^{(j)}(t_{j+3} - t_j)^4 \\ u''_{j+3} = u''_j + 6\alpha_3^{(j)}(t_{j+3} - t_j) + \\ 12\alpha_4^{(j)}(t_{j+3} - t_j)^2 + 20\alpha_5^{(j)}(t_{j+3} - t_j)^3 \end{cases} \tag{37}$$

Solving the above system of equations determines the value $\alpha_3^{(j)}$, $\alpha_4^{(j)}$, and $\alpha_5^{(j)}$. The index j indicates that the j coefficient enters in the interpolation polynomial only on the interval $[t_j, t_{j+1}]$. The system of Eq. (37) has the following solutions:

$$\begin{cases} \alpha_0^{(j)} = u_j \\ \alpha_1^{(j)} = u_j' \\ \alpha_2^{(j)} = \dfrac{u_j''}{2} \\ \alpha_3^{(j)} = \dfrac{1}{(t_{j+3}-t_j)^3}\left[10(u_{j+3}-u_j) - \left(4u_{j+3}' + 6u_j'\right)(t_{j+3}-t_j) + \left(0.5u_{j+3}'' - 1.5u_j''\right)(t_{j+3}-t_j)^2\right] \\ \alpha_4^{(j)} = \dfrac{1}{(t_{j+3}-t_j)^4}\left[-15(u_{j+3}-u_j) + \left(7u_{j+3}' + 8u_j'\right)(t_{j+3}-t_j) - \left(u_{j+3}'' - 1.5u_j''\right)(t_{j+3}-t_j)^2\right] \\ \alpha_5^{(j)} = \dfrac{1}{(t_{j+3}-t_j)^5}\left[6(u_{j+3}-u_j) - \left(3u_{j+3}' + 3u_j'\right)(t_{j+3}-t_j) + 0.5\left(u_{j+3}'' - u_j''\right)(t_{j+3}-t_j)^2\right] \end{cases} \tag{38}$$

Since the exact values of u_j', u_j'' are typically unavailable, this approach proceeds in three stages: (1) approximates the first and second derivatives at interpolation nodes using finite differences, (2) constructs spline $\phi_{5,3}(t)$ using these estimates, and (3) computes intermediate values in $[t_j, t_{j+3}]$ by evaluating (36) with calculated $\alpha_i^{(j)}$ coefficients across the interval.

The recovery interval is shown in **Figure 10** (dotted lines = recovered samples). As previously established, optimal interpolation within (t_j, t_{j+3}) is achieved using a spline of the fifth degree of defect three. Assuming that $t_{j+4} - t_{j+3} = t_{j+3} - t_{j+2} = t_{j+2} - t_{j+1} = t_{j+1} - t_j = t_j - t_{j-1} = 1/3$ ($[t_j, t_{j+3}] = 1$), the approximate values of the first and second derivatives at the points t_j, t_{j+3} are found from (28) and (29) as:

$$\begin{cases} u_j' = \dfrac{u_j - u_{j-1}}{t_j - t_{j-1}} = 3(u_j - u_{j-1}) \\ u_{j+3}' = \dfrac{u_{j+3} - u_j}{t_{j+3} - t_j} = (u_{j+3} - u_j) \\ u_{j+4}' = \dfrac{u_{j+4} - u_{j+3}}{t_{j+4} - t_{j+3}} = 3(u_{j+4} - u_{j+3}) \\ u_j'' = \dfrac{u_{j+3}' - u_j'}{t_{j+3} - t_j} = (u_{j+3} - 4u_j + 3u_{j-1}) \\ u_{j+3}'' = \dfrac{u_{j+4}' - u_{j+3}'}{t_{j+4} - t_{j+3}} = 3(3u_{j+4} - 4u_{j+3} + u_j) \end{cases} \tag{39}$$

Substituting (39) into (38) to calculate $\alpha_i^{(j)}$ $(i = 0, 1, \dots, 5)$ and we obtain (36) as:

$$\begin{aligned} \phi_{5,3}(t) = {} & \left[-t(1-t)^3(7.5t+3)\right]u_{j-1} + \left[(1-t)^2\left(-12.5t^3 + 7t^2 + 5t + 1\right)\right]u_j + \\ & + \left[t^2\left(12.5t^3 - 30.5t^2 + 18.5t + 0.5\right]u_{j+3} + \left[t^3\left(-7.5t^2 + 18t - 10.5\right)\right]u_{j+4} \end{aligned} \tag{40}$$

Finally, substituting $t = 1/3$ and $t = 2/3$ into (38) yields formulas for calculating missing samples u_{j+1} and u_{j+2} as:

$$\begin{aligned} u_{j+1} &= -0.543u_{j-1} + 1.325u_j + 0.416u_{j+3} - 0.198u_{j+4} \\ u_{j+2} &= -0.198u_{j-1} + 0.416u_j + 1.325u_{j+3} - 0.543u_{j+4} \end{aligned} \quad (41)$$

3.3 Development of an algorithm for MDSA image recovery

In the previous subsection, the method of one-dimensional recovery of video signal samples using interpolation polynomials was investigated. For a two-dimensional function, it is possible to select the direction of interpolation (extrapolation), in which this function changes more smoothly than in other directions. Thus, during MDSA image recovery, it is possible to bypass sharp transitions in the recovered function. With additional sampling by groups of samples of adjacent lines, missing samples can be recovered in both vertical, horizontal, and diagonal directions. To recover each discrete sample, it is necessary to use all reference samples in a certain two-dimensional spatial neighborhood surrounding this sample. The choice of the recovery direction, based on the analysis of available samples in the neighborhood of the one being recovered, makes it possible to increase the accuracy of recovery since discrete samples of a smooth function are recovered most accurately.

In a digital television camera, it is usually impossible to recover missing samples in all directions using standard color-coding filters. This is due to the rigidly fixed structure of the disposition of the CFA cells and the lack of reference samples of the signal being recovered. Using the proposed structure of the CFA cell disposition (**Figure 2**) allows one to recover missing samples in the horizontal, vertical, and diagonal directions. The discrete-group method of transmitting color components of image signals makes it possible to use not only local (intra-group) changes in video information for recovering missing samples but also inter-group changes, which allows one to specify the direction of recovery or the choice of the recovered sample value, taking into account the information changes in all adjacent sample groups and the relative inter-group changes in the signal level of the recovered sample.

In the SIS camera, with the use of the proposed version of CFA (their cell disposition structures are shown in **Figures 3–5**), the current set of voltage values (corresponding to the PD elements) is three matrices corresponding to three coding colors. The matrices initially contain zero elements, which can be estimated from surrounding nonzero values and applying a micro-displacement of the light flux against the mosaic CFA itself during the frame. Therefore, in order to reduce the amount of calculations and memory during hardware implementation in real time in the form of a computer program, it is advisable to recover the missing frame samples of the signal of one coding color of the television image by dividing the samples of this frame into elementary blocks of samples, taking into account the following:

1. In each block, it is possible to recover lost samples, if possible, in horizontal, vertical, and diagonal directions. The algorithms for processing samples in all directions must be the same.

2. The number of samples in each block must be sufficient for relatively accurate recovery of lost samples using interpolation methods.

Figure 11 demonstrates the reconstruction of missing (R, G, and B) samples within each elementary block. The technique employs multi-directional interpolation (horizontal, vertical, and diagonal) to estimate central pixel values, subsequently selecting

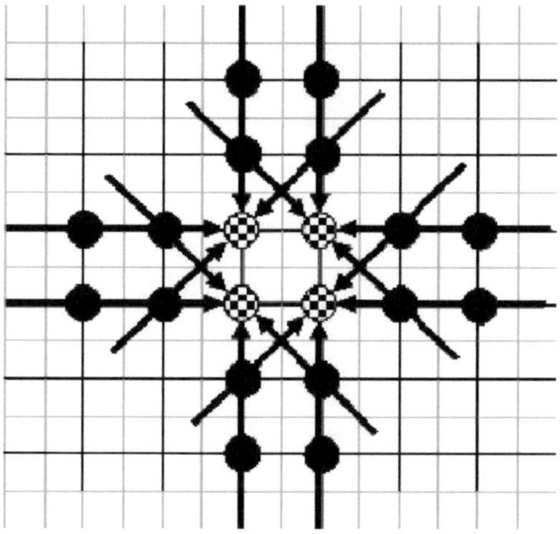

Figure 11.
Reconstruction of central pixels within elementary processing block.

the reconstruction that minimizes deviation from adjacent samples in each respective direction.

Figure 12 illustrates the developed algorithm for reconstructing missing green-channel samples in a television frame of size $M \times N$, where M = row pixels, N = row count (similarly for red and blue channels). The frame is partitioned into 6 × 6 elementary processing blocks, with a horizontal rightward shift of 4 pixels between successive blocks.

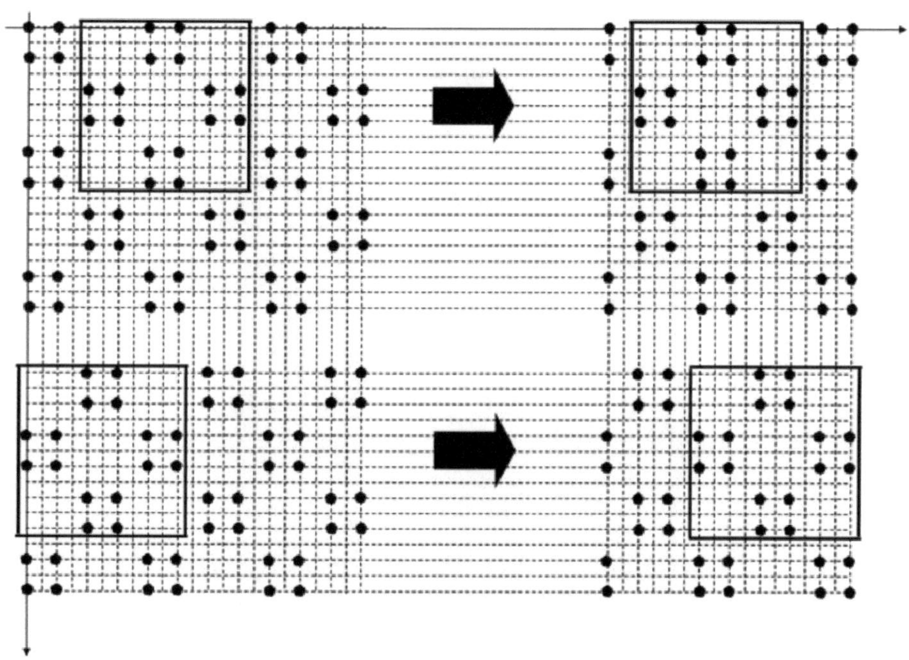

Figure 12.
Green-channel sample reconstruction algorithm for television frames.

Figure 13.
The original black-and-white image of Lena. Size: 256 × 256 (pixels), zoomed in 2 times.

To evaluate performance, the proposed MDSA method was implemented in Visual C++ and tested on standard image processing benchmarks (**Figures 13–17**). Key findings include:

1. Non-adaptive recovery (**Figure 14**): acceptable quality in low-contrast regions. Severe spiral distortions along high-contrast edges caused by mismatched recovery directions relative to actual image gradients.

2. MDSA-based recovery (**Figure 15**): high-quality reconstruction across most regions. Minor artifacts only on thin, high-contrast lines deviating from the primary recovery axes (horizontal/vertical/diagonal) (**Figure 17**).

Figure 14.
Recovered Lena image using interpolation methods in each elementary 6 × 6 block (pixels), but without the multi-dimensional spatial adaptation.

Figure 15.
Lena test image reconstructed via MDSA interpolation.

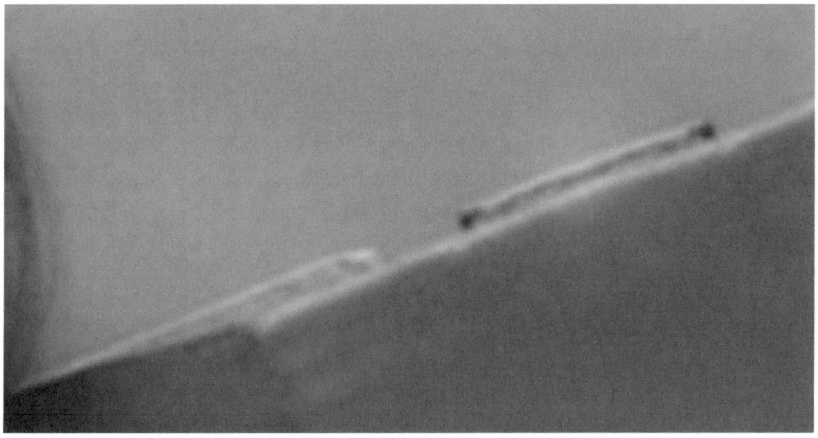

Figure 16.
Zoomed 4-times view of slender high-contrast boundaries (original size 172 × 89) against background.

4. Conclusions

An analysis of the characteristics of the spectrum of the sampling structure corresponding to the disposition of cells of the proposed CFA is carried out. A new MDSA image recovery method has been developed and investigated.

1. An increase in the real resolution of SIS cameras occurs when discretizing into groups of adjacent samples with values M = 2, N = 4, followed by recovery of the missed samples.

2. Experimental studies have proven the possibility of interpolation image recovery by using a local spline of the fifth degree of defect three in real time with high quality of the recovered image.

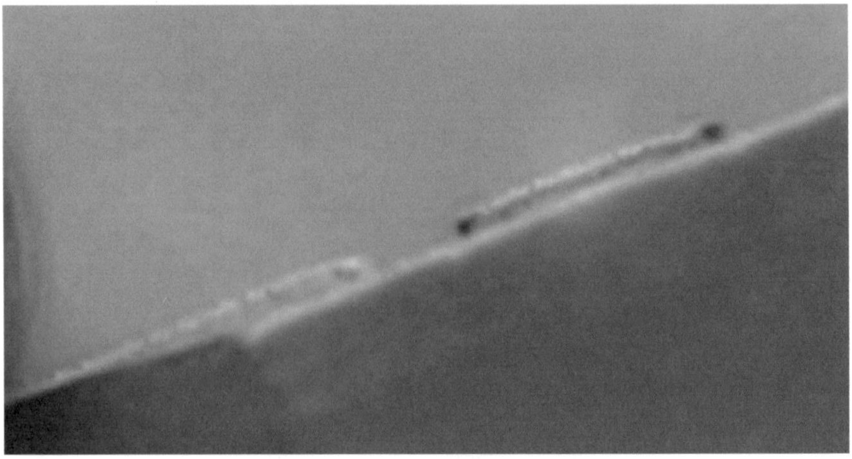

Figure 17.
Zoomed 4-times view (original size 172 × 89) demonstrating recovery inaccuracies along slender high-contrast boundaries relative to the background.

3. Computer modeling of the principles of image signal recovery developed in this chapter has shown high accuracy in calculations of the values of missing samples. Recovery errors in this case are preserved only on specifically oriented thin lines and boundaries with a high degree of brightness changes in relation to the background level when the directions of these lines do not coincide with the horizontal, vertical, and diagonal directions of recovery.

4. The proposed MDSA image recovery method can also be applied to other video compression systems.

Author details

Ha H. Cao
School of Information Technology, Thang Long University, Hanoi, Vietnam

*Address all correspondence to: caohoangha@gmail.com

IntechOpen

© 2025 The Author(s). Licensee IntechOpen. This chapter is distributed under the terms of the Creative Commons Attribution License (http://creativecommons.org/licenses/by/4.0), which permits unrestricted use, distribution, and reproduction in any medium, provided the original work is properly cited.

References

[1] Menon D, Calvagno G. Color image demosaicking: An overview. Signal Processing: Image Communication. Oct 2011;**26**(8-9):518-533

[2] Pratt WK. Digital Image Processing. New York: John W. Hanson; 1978

[3] Li X, Gunturk B, Zhang L. Image demosaicing: A systematic survey. Proceedings of SPIE. 2008;**6822**:68221J–1-68221J–15

[4] Cao HH, Nguyen HH. Novel multi-dimensional spatially-adaptive image recovery using spline interpolation. In: 2019 Signal Processing: Algorithms, Architectures, Arrangements, and Applications (SPA), Poznan, Poland. Poznan, Poland: Poznan University of Technology; 2019. pp. 319-324. DOI: 10.23919/SPA.2019.8936721

[5] Ignatyev NK. Discretization and its Application. Moscow: Svyaz; 1980. 235 p

[6] Jerri AJ. Shannon's sampling theorem, its various generalizations and applications: A review. Proceedings of the IEEE. 1977;**65**(11):53-89

[7] Ya K I, Yakovlev BP. Finite Functions in Physics and Engineering. Moscow: Nauka; 1971. 408 p

[8] Makarenko AA. Selection of interpolation methods for digital image processing. Communication Equipment Technology. TV Engineering Series. 1983;**1**:47-55

Chapter 4

Kimberley Road Degradation Detection Using Digital Image Processing

Seemeen Wookey, Christopher Mhlongo, Unarine Mukwevho, Tlotlo Fanuel Sebati and Ibidun Christiana Obagbuwa

Abstract

The city of Kimberley in the Northern Cape province of South Africa faces significant road degradation due to heavy traffic, poor road design, extreme weather, and substandard construction materials, posing safety hazards and increasing maintenance demands. Traditional monitoring methods are costly and labor-intensive; thus, this chapter explores a cost-effective solution using smartphone technology to collect data and develop a model for detecting and classifying road defects. A Kimberley-specific dataset was created with six classes of road defects, annotated using the Roboflow platform, and aligned with TRH22 guidelines for pavement management systems. The YOLOv3-CNN developed on the Kimberley dataset achieved an 83.38% accuracy. Future work will focus on improving limitations and integrating the solution into municipal road maintenance systems. This chapter provides a framework for similar applications in other regions and aligns with industry standards for civil engineering practices.

Keywords: image processing, digital image, road defects, road degradation detection, deep learning

1. Introduction

The city of Kimberley in the Northern Cape province of South Africa faces traffic congestion challenges, especially during peak hours, due to many factors, including heavy-vehicle (truck) traffic and road network limitations. Kimberley also faces extreme temperatures, which frequently fluctuate during the year, and the roads are known to be constructed from poor-quality building materials. In general, road conditions worsen over time due to traffic and weather. This can lead to potholes, cracks, and other types of road degradation, which are safety hazards for vehicles and road users. Automatic detection of these defects is important for improving road safety and comfort.

Traditionally, collecting road condition data is expensive and labor-intensive. However, researchers are exploring using smartphones as a cost-effective solution for data collection [1]. Regular and easy road surveys are important for developing maintenance plans and allocating resources effectively. Ideally, a low-cost, data-driven solution would enable this [2].

Current research focuses mainly on collecting data using smartphone technology and developing a model from the data [1, 3–5]. This chapter focuses on creating a dataset and model specific to Kimberley that aligns with specific guidelines for pavement management systems. As far as the author is aware, a Kimberley-specific dataset does not yet exist.

Due to poor road maintenance, as well as extreme weather and climate conditions, the roads of Kimberley are in deplorable condition and typically display multiple signs of degradation, which are a hazard to road users and cause further degradation down the line, which then puts more strain on the municipality for road maintenance.

2. Literature review

Asphalt pavement structures experience distress over time, primarily caused by vehicle loads and weather conditions such as dry environments and temperature decreases [1, 2]. Road deteriorations such as potholes [2], cracks [1], or loose gravel [6] pose a threat to human and automobile safety, contributing significantly to road accidents [1–7]. Potholes, in particular, can be life-threatening, and their severity can be determined by their dimensions [1], especially their depth [2]. Automatic detection of road defects is crucial in ensuring safer and more comfortable roads [1–8]. Road condition monitoring systems are typically built using GPS, audio and image data, and deep learning [1–6, 8]. Traditional methods for collecting road condition data are expensive and labor-intensive [3, 4, 8]. Researchers, therefore, employ smartphones to provide cost-effective solutions for data collection and implementation of road condition monitoring systems [2–5].

2.1 Datasets, data collection, and sensing tools

Our review of studies showed that researchers preferred collecting their data [1–8] rather than using any pre-existing datasets. This is due to the different studies considering different factors to assess road conditions when carrying out their research and needing more problem-specific data, as Roberts et al. explain about their data collection process: “It was important for the exercise to establish a model that could be used in the specific local conditions in Sicily, Italy” [4]. Roberts et al. [4] collected 7000 images for their deep learning pipeline and framework that does a hotspot analysis for pavement distress in urban road networks. Kok et al. collected image data of potholes with corresponding dimensions in Johannesburg CBD of South Africa for their pothole severity estimation pipeline [2]. Arya et al. built upon the RDD-2019 dataset and created a large-scale dataset of 26,620 road images sourced from Japan, Czech, and India, the RDD-2020 dataset, to create a detection and classification model that can work in different countries [8]. Saeed et al. [6] collected image and audio data from gravel roads in Switzerland to detect loose gravel conditions. Ramesh et al. collected image, GPS, and motion data from roads in South Carolina, USA, for their cloud-based collaborative road damage detection and monitoring system [3]. Hadj-Attou et al. only collected GPS and motion data with timestamp values for their road surface condition monitoring system [5].

Guo et al. used specialized equipment in their full-scale track test on the newly constructed highway in Gansu province, China, to collect IRI, Deflection value,

Rutting depth, and Void rate of paving to analyze hidden structural damage used to train their model for early detection of pavement structural damage [7].

Besides collecting their image and GPS data, as well as road network data from urban management centers, Boucetta et al. was the only study to use existing open-source image datasets, namely the SDNET2018, CIFAR10, and CIFAR100, MNIST datasets, to train the CNN module for their crack notification and road condition monitoring system [1]. SDNET2018 contains 56,000 images of different pavement cracks and pavements with no cracks. CIFAR10 and CIFAR100 have 60,000 images each, but CIFAR-10 has 10 classes, and CIFAR100 has 100 other classes. These two datasets contain classes relevant to the study like "Truck, Automobile", "Vehicles1, Vehicles2", but also seemingly irrelevant classes like different types of animals, insects, plants, "Household furniture", etc. The MNIST dataset contains approximately 70,000 images of handwritten digits. Boucetta et al. [1] used image datasets with the SDNET2018 dataset when training their detection and classification model to avoid overfitting their model to only pavement crack images and to allow their model to be more generalizable to the broader scene of a road and other unseen data.

To address the issue of traditional methods for collecting road condition data that are expensive and labor-intensive, as in Guo et al.'s study [7], other researchers utilized smartphone technology for cost-effective and efficient data collection [2–5, 8]. Smartphones come with a variety of sensing features besides the camera, such as location services (for GPS) and accelerometer, gyroscope, and magnetometer (for motion and orientation data) [3, 5]. In addition to their first smartphone used for data collection, Hadj-Attou et al. also used a second smartphone that connected to the first smartphone using TCP/IP sockets connected to the local network to allow the second phone to receive and sort the data gathered from the first phone [5]. Ramesh et al., Hadj-Attou et al., and Roberts et al. also utilized smartphone applications to automatically collect the data they wanted instead of relying on a manual approach [3–5]. Ramesh et al. stored their data in a cloud database using their smartphone, allowing for the collaborative cloud-based fusion that their study implemented [3]. The smartphones were typically mounted in a car either at the windscreen [3, 4, 8] or close to the car's gear lever [5]. Other than smartphones, other studies also equipped cameras onto vehicles. Boucetta et al. used a camera with an embedded GPS sensor [1], and Saeed et al. used two HERO7 GoPro cameras inside and outside a car [6]. Cars with mounted cameras and smartphones would keep a speed between 40 and 50 km/h while driving [6, 8].

2.2 Methodology, models, and limitations

The most common steps observed throughout different approaches to road condition monitoring were data collection and storage, data pre-processing, training, testing, and evaluating a detection and classification CNN, and then determining the severity of the road's condition. To evaluate the models, Intersection over Union (IoU) and mean Average Precision (mAP) were used. Arya et al. define IoU as "the division of the area overlap between predicted and ground-truth bounding boxes by the area of their union" [8]. The ioU threshold is usually set to 0.5 [3, 4, 8]. Deep learning is typically implemented using Python with Tensorflow [1, 4, 8].

Data pre-processing steps include filtering [3, 5], resampling, data transformation [6], data normalization [1, 5, 7] and augmentation [1, 3, 4], and image segmentation [2, 3, 6], sorting data into classes and also annotating with bounding boxes and class labels using either Roboflow [6] or the LabelImg annotating tool where annotations are saved in PASCAL-VOC format [2, 4]. During data transformation, Saeed et al.

converted their audio data into spectrograms [6]. With image datasets, it is also important to resize images before annotating; as Kok et al. explain, "Annotating images first and then resizing results in loss of information as the ground-truth bounding boxes no longer refer to the same image" [2]. Boucetta et al. explain the importance of data augmentation "to expose the CNN to a wide variety of image types for better learning" [1]. Data augmentation techniques include flipping, rotating, and cropping [3, 4]. Boucetta et al. mention data normalization's importance "to ensure that each input image has a similar data distribution and to avoid the influence of high- and very low-frequency noises" [1]. The data normalization techniques that Guo et al. used were to remove outliers using the "squish method" and to scale the data [7]. Guo et al. mention that some common methods for scaling data are decimal scaling, min-max normalization, and Z-Score [7]. After pre-processing, Boucetta et al. used the Hadoop framework to process and store all their data [1], and Ramesh et al. stored their data in a cloud database [3].

Boucetta et al. developed their CNN on three different public datasets to identify and categorize 10 types of road degradation features. The various classes in the data were stored as vectors [1]. Boucetta et al. used stochastic gradient descent to minimize loss Function E. Rectified Linear Unit was applied in convolutional layers, and log-sigmoid activation function was used in fully connected layers. Data was resized to 256x256 [1]. The model achieved 95% mean accuracy across all 10 classes. The severity index of the different cracks that appeared in road scans was computed. From road network data, Boucetta et al. created a graph of the road network from which they sourced their road scans [1]. They then added the severity indices to the road network graph as edge weights to create a weighted graph. From this, they made a web application that would alert drivers of road segments with high severity index and allow authorities to monitor road conditions. However, Boucetta et al. mention that human expertise is needed to supervise and update the model while it evolves with new data. This limitation could be addressed by optimizing their model and adding a feedback system where a road structure inspection expert can supervise and correct the model [1].

Kok et al. used a dataset of pothole images to train an object detector model to extract regions of interest and output bounding box coordinates [2]. The first model, object detector, also reduces the dimensionality of input for the second model, depth estimation. A dataset of potholes with corresponding depths was used to train a VGG16-based pothole depth estimation CNN. The region of interest from the first model was resized to 300x300 before passing to the second model. Kok et al. also applied zero-padding to images to avoid loss of information [2]. Kok et al. used intersection over union to evaluate the performance of the ROI extraction model (first model) and Mean Absolute Error to evaluate the depth estimator model (second model) [2]. VGG16 CNN achieved an MAE of 32.2852. Kok et al. mention that the study can be improved by combining the two proposed models and implementing a web-based application for pothole monitoring and remediation [2].

In Saeed et al.'s study, a pre-trained VGG19 was used to extract features from images and spectrograms, which were then concatenated to create a combined feature representation [6]. To reduce dimensionality, feature reduction was applied using principal component analysis, and the optimal features were selected using the elbow method. Random forest, XGBoost, and MLP were then trained on this set. Random forest achieved the best score compared to other models with an accuracy of 0.9018. This showed how feature-level fusion affects the classification decision of a model. Decision-level fusion was then investigated by training separate Densenet121-CNNs on image and audio data and applying OR and AND gates for decision fusion in the model. The decision-level approach of using the OR gate produced the best overall classification accuracy of 0.97. Saeed et al.'s study showed the effect of multimodal fusion on deep learning techniques [6]. However, the impact of different environmental conditions on classification and detection was not considered during the model development.

In Arya et al.'s study, they trained and evaluated 16 deep neural network object detection models based on data from three different countries [8]. The models included three types: models trained on data from one country and tested on a mix of data from all three countries, models trained and tested on data from only one country, and models trained and tested on a mix of data from two countries. The models had an SSD MobileNet base pre-trained on the MSCOCO dataset for transfer learning. The image data was rescaled to 300x300 before training. Arya et al. used a batch size of 24 with a Mini-batch gradient descent algorithm and a learning rate of 0.003, RMSprop optimizer, 0.9 for momentum optimizer value, and trained the models for 250,000 steps [8]. They also used the formula to calculate the number of training epochs as (batch size x training steps)/size of training data. Precision, recall, and F1-score were used to evaluate the Intersection Over Union of the models and mean Average Precision to evaluate the models' performance. Arya et al.'s study explored the effect of data and their models developed from one country on road damage detection and classification models for other countries [8]. From their results, Arya et al. offer recommended advice to future studies in this area, which is that using data from different countries increases the generalizability of a model, but using local data for a specific model improves the precision of the model and, therefore its performance as well, it is hence important to find a good balance between these two factors to create an optimum model for a specific country's road damage monitoring system [8]. Arya et al. also mention that the training data was limited to specific road conditions and regions, limiting the generalization of the results to specific road environments [8].

Ramesh et al. trained a YoloV5 model on images extracted from video frames [3]. The model was trained for 200 epochs and evaluated using mAP, IoU, and a confusion matrix. YoloV5 achieved 0.875 accuracy. A cluster of GPU nodes was used to train an LSTM model with Adam optimizer, a Batch size of 64, and a learning rate of 0.005. The LSTM performed better than the YoloV5 and achieved an accuracy of 0.94. Ramesh et al.'s cloud-based system uses survey results from various smartphones to generate a map with different road damage severity levels for drivers and authorities accessible through a web page [3]. Ramesh et al.'s study could be improved by further research and development of the cloud-based fusion algorithm regarding processing the duplicated and redundantly provided information [3]. The training dataset must also include images taken under different weather and lighting conditions.

Roberts et al.'s study uses transfer learning and several pre-trained models to avoid heavy computational resource usage [4]. Roberts et al. used the tensorboard system to monitor the progress of their model during training [4]. The Faster RCNN with InceptionV2 performed the best with Average Precision and Average Recall at 0.933 and 0.938, respectively. Roberts et al.'s hotspot analysis and pipeline works by implementing the object detection and classification model to compute the severity of road distress from the image input of road surveys and produces a road network graph with different road distress severities that are then uploaded to a database for authorities to monitor [4]. However, Roberts et al. mention that their model's accuracy was affected by weather conditions and a flexible pavement bias [4].

Hadj-Attou et al. used different kinds of sensor data from smartphone motion sensors but did not use any image data to train CNN-LSTM and CNN-GRU models [5].

Compared to another state-of-the-art CNN, the models outperformed that CNN. The CNN-GRU performed the best overall with 0.9706 accuracy. Hadj-Attou et al. combined accelerometer, gyroscope, and orientation data and found that combining the input data resulted in higher accuracy from their models [5]. They also transformed their time series data into frequency data using the Fast Fourier Transform (FFT) and Discrete Wavelet Transform (DWT). In Hadj-Attou et al.'s study, it was found that the FFT-DWT combination provided superior classification performance compared to the initial time-stamp input data [5]. Hadj-Attou et al. mention that to improve their model, they need to apply data augmentation techniques to solve the issue of unbalanced datasets [5].

Guo et al. performed state-of-the-art analysis by comparing their optimized model with a decision tree, random forest, and support vector machine models [7]. Their model outperformed the other state-of-the-art models and achieved an accuracy of 0.8333. In Guo et al.'s study, they developed their deep neural network model based on complete track test data that resulted in specialized industry-standard data. From this, their model could detect early structural damage to pavement that could not be detected by human monitoring alone. However, the specialized equipment and techniques used in Guo et al.'s study are expensive and labor-intensive [7]. Variations in track tests, road conditions, data volume, geographic regions, and pavement types also constrain the model's generalization ability.

2.3 Gaps in research

Across our broad review of the articles, we found multiple gaps in the available research. The datasets' limited scope affected the models' adaptability and generalizability [3–8]. Models need to be optimized and performance improved using different techniques like transfer learning and hyperparameter tuning [2, 7]. Implementing research of models into applications for road monitoring and automating systems [1, 2]. Developing a model that can be used by many countries globally [8]. Estimating road damage in three dimensions [3].

This chapter aims to investigate a dataset's effect on model performance and develop a road condition monitoring system specific to Kimberley. The chapter focuses on road condition issues relevant to Kimberley of the Northern Cape in South Africa, such as degradation caused by weather conditions and traffic overloading [9]. We created our dataset with six different classes of road degradation and developed a model from this dataset. We consulted a civil engineer to validate our assumptions and ensure our project aligned with the TRH22 guidelines for pavement management systems [10].

3. Methodology

The methodology consisted of two main parts: dataset development and model development. A model was trained and evaluated from the dataset, and the dataset's quality could be inferred from that model's performance. Using an optimal dataset with strong features, a well-performing model could be trained and improved in other ways apart from its dataset and features. This process is shown in **Figure 1**.

3.1 Dataset development

Three sources of data were used. Images were sampled from the Road Crack Dataset on the Roboflow website (https://universe.roboflow.com/newroadcrack/

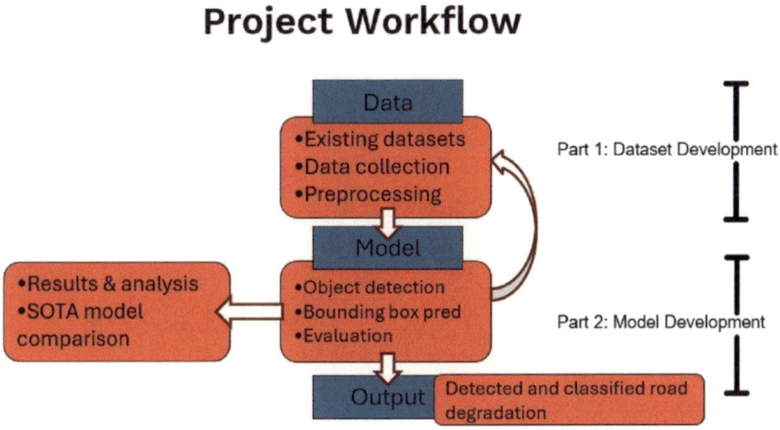

Figure 1.
Diagram showing the proposed methodology.

my-road-crack-dataset) and the Pothole Dataset from the Kaggle website (https://www.kaggle.com/datasets/sachinpatel21/pothole-image-dataset). Video data was collected from Kimberley Roads.

3.1.1 Data collection

A Samsung Galaxy A52s smartphone was mounted in a car, as shown in **Figure 2**. The smartphone recorded the road from Jacobus Smit Avenue to Gariep Mediclinic and Lawson Street to Long Street. The routes are shown in **Figures 3** and **4**.

3.1.2 Dataset creation

The Roboflow platform (https://blog.roboflow.com/getting-started-with-roboflow/) was used to create the dataset. Video recordings and collected images were uploaded to the platform, and frames were automatically sampled from the

Figure 2.
Smartphone recording setup.

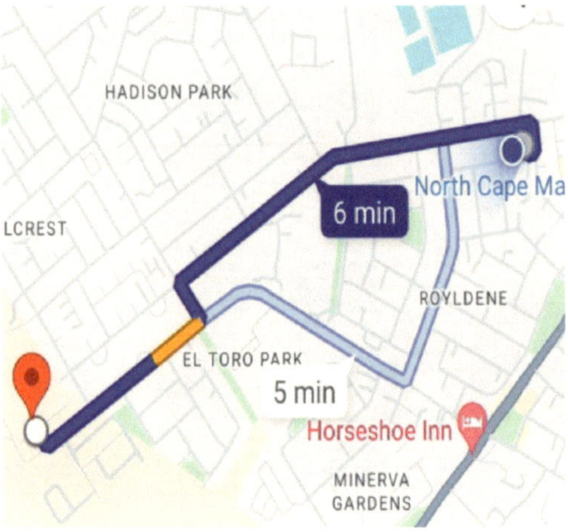

Figure 3.
Jacobus Smit to Mediclinic route.

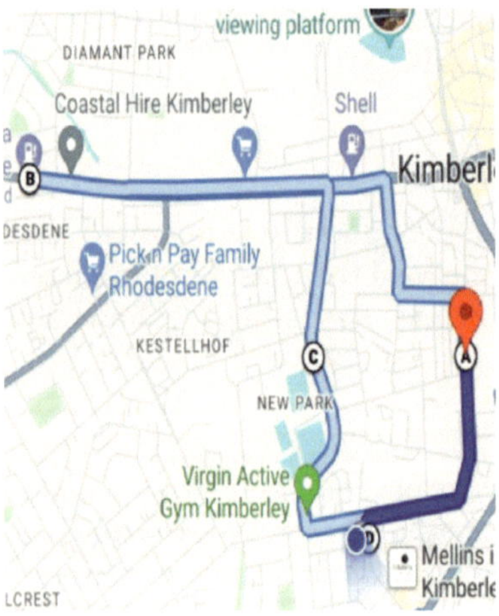

Figure 4.
Lawson to Long Str route.

video and uploaded as images. The six classes were "Crack", "Pothole", "Bump", "Sand build-up", "Water build-up", and "Loose gravel". The images were manually annotated on the Roboflow platform, as shown in **Figure 5**. Pre-processing techniques, such as auto-orient and resizing to 300x300 pixels, and data augmentation techniques, such as flipping, rotating, and cropping, were applied. After data augmentation techniques were used, the size of Dataset-1 was 2107 images.

3.1.3 Dataset evaluation and improvement

3.1.3.1 Performance evaluation metrics

The Roboflow 3.0 models trained on the different datasets were evaluated using mAP, Precision, and Recall.

Figure 5.
Roboflow annotation tool.

Precision measures how often the model's predictions are correct. It is given by:

$$Precision = \frac{\text{True Positive}}{\text{True Positive} + \text{False Positive}} \tag{1}$$

Recall measures what percentage of relevant labels were successfully identified. It is given by:

$$Recall = \frac{\text{True Positive}}{\text{True Positive} + \text{False Negative}} \tag{2}$$

mAP (mean average precision) for object detection is calculated by averaging the AP (average precision) across all classes, where AP represents the area under the precision-recall curve. This metric compares the ground-truth bounding box with the detected box, yielding a score that reflects detection accuracy. A higher mAP indicates a more accurate model characterized by higher precision and recall, meaning the model has both low false negative and false positive rates.

The results of the dataset development phase are summarized in **Tables 1** and **2**.

3.1.3.2 Dataset improvement

Dataset-1 had a big class imbalance problem despite its size, as shown in **Figure 6**. The Roboflow 3.0 Object Detection model, pre-trained on the COCO dataset, was then trained on Dataset-1 using the Roboflow platform. The results were mAP 48.5%, Precision 55.3%, and Recall 45.1%. When checking the output of this model on the Roboflow platform, a misclassification problem was identified where visually similar classes (a pothole and the water that builds up in a pothole) were incorrectly predicted as water build-up and not always as the pothole as shown in **Figure 7**.

Model	Size	No. of classes	Precision	Recall	mAP
Roboflow 3.0 Object Detection (Dataset-1.2)	2058	6	82.6%	57.9%	66.6%
YOLO-NAS Object Detection (Dataset-1.2)	2058	6	81.2%	64.5%	72.0%

Table 1.
Roboflow 3.0 and YOLO-NAS models trained on Dataset-1.2.

Model	Size	No. of classes	Precision	Recall	mAP
Roboflow 3.0 Object Detection (Dataset-1)	2107	6	55.3%	45.1%	48.5%
Roboflow 3.0 Object Detection (Dataset-2)	505	6	48.1%	26.3%	25.5%
Roboflow 3.0 Object Detection (Dataset-1.2)	2058	6	82.6%	57.9%	66.6%
Roboflow 3.0 Object Detection (Dataset-3)	815	6	70.5%	46.0%	50.5%

Table 2.
Results of Roboflow 3.0 model trained on the different datasets.

Figure 6.
Dataset-1 class distribution shown on Roboflow platform.

To improve upon Dataset-1's limitations of class imbalance and misclassification, Dataset-2 was created where the same images collected for Dataset-1 were used, except much fewer images were sampled from the Roboflow Road Crack and Kaggle Pothole Datasets to eliminate the overrepresentation of the cracks and potholes classes, and images with overlapping classes such as in **Figure 7** were removed to eliminate the misclassification issue. Dataset-2 had a size of 505 images. The Roboflow 3.0 Object Detection model was then trained on Dataset-2. The results were mAP 25.5%, Precision 48.1%, Recall 26.3%. The results show that a smaller dataset performs worse regardless of eliminating the class imbalance.

To improve upon Dataset-1, which performed better than Dataset-2, Dataset-1.2 was created, where any images or annotations causing the misclassification issue in

DOI: http://dx.doi.org/10.5772/intechopen.1010942

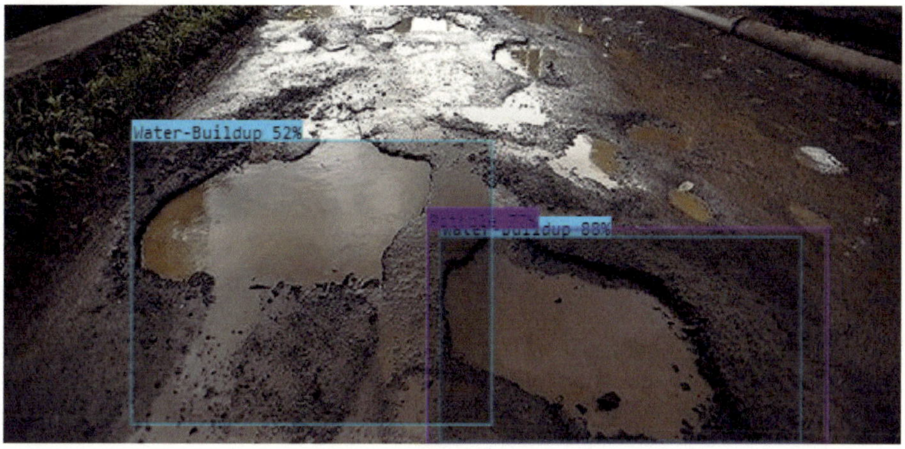

Figure 7.
Misclassification of the "Pothole" class with the "Water build-up" class.

Dataset-1 were removed, however, as shown in **Figure 8**, Dataset-1.2 still retained the class imbalance issue that was present in Dataset-1. Dataset-1.2 had 2058 images. The Roboflow 3.0 Object Detection model was then trained on Dataset-1.2. The results of the Roboflow 3.0 model were mAP 66.6%, Precision 82.6%, and Recall 57.9%. In addition to the Roboflow 3.0 Object detection model, the YOLO-NAS Object Detection model, pre-trained on the COCO dataset, was trained on Dataset-1.2 to see which would perform better. The YOLO-NAS model performed better with results mAP 72%, Precision 81.2%, and Recall 64.5%, which might imply that the YOLO series models perform well overall. These results are summarized in **Table 1**.

Dataset-3 was created to eliminate the class imbalance problem while trying to have a bigger dataset size than Dataset-2. Dataset-3 uses images web scraped from the internet to supplement the underrepresented classes and then uses the original images that were collected, excluding images causing the class imbalance, and only sampled the cracks and pothole datasets instead of using the full dataset so that the potholes and cracks classes were not overrepresented. Dataset-3's size was 815 images, as shown in **Figure 9**. The Roboflow 3.0 Object Detection model was then trained on Dataset-3. The model results were mAP 50.5%, Precision 70.5%, and Recall 46.0%.

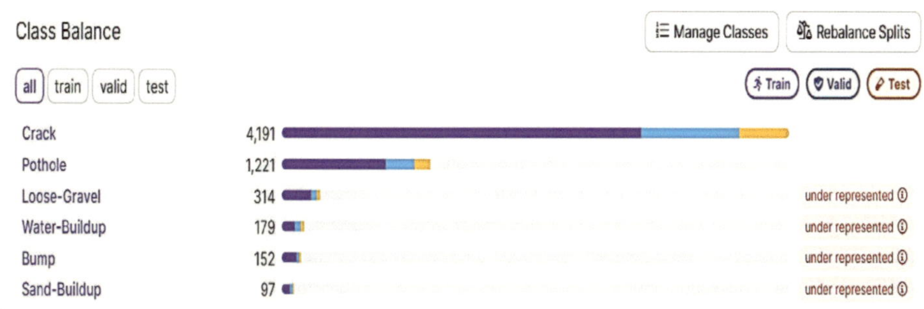

Figure 8.
Dataset-1.2's class distribution is shown on the Roboflow platform.

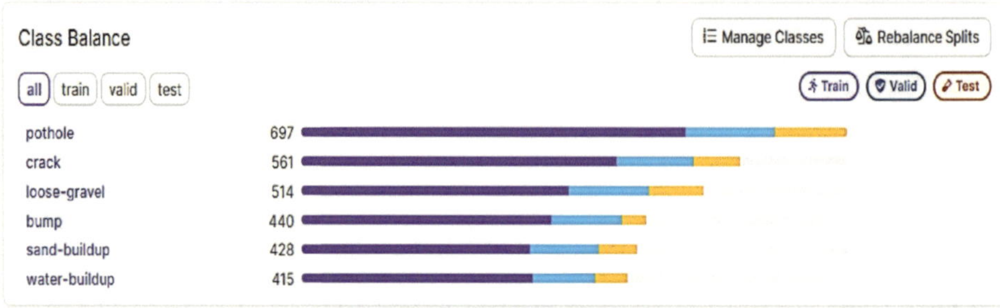

Figure 9.
Dataset-3 class distribution shown on the Roboflow platform.

The results of the Roboflow 3.0 model trained on all four datasets are summarized in **Table 2**.

4. Results

4.1 Resource links

Dataset-1.2 and Dataset-3 were made available on the Roboflow platform. Links to download Dataset-1.2 and Dataset-3 with annotation files in CSV format, as well as links to the datasets with annotation files in any format and the link to the Roboflow platform, are in **Table 3**.

4.1.1 Insights from the data

From working with and observing the collected data, a cause-and-effect relationship between the road degradation classes and their associated factors was found, as shown in **Table 4** and **Figure 10**. These insights were also confirmed by the civil engineering consultant to be valid.

Resource	Description	URL
Dataset-1.2 (for Tensorflow Object Detection)	Automatic download 2050 images + CSV format annotations	https://app.roboflow.com/ds/ca7mAnbW7o?key = xaRIbZSosA
Dataset-3 (for Tensorflow Object Detection)	Automatic download 815 images + CSV format annotations	https://app.roboflow.com/ds/SZoukZHxi5?key=xw3Ty6FQ4h
Dataset-1.2 (for any format)	Dataset labeled as "models Image Dataset" Can choose download format	https://universe.roboflow.com/sota-analysis/models-tc7jd/dataset/1
Dataset-3 (for any format)	Dataset labeled as "beta dataset road degradation Image Dataset" Can choose download format	https://app.roboflow.com/sota-analysis/beta-dataset-road-degradation/1
Roboflow Platform	Quickstart tutorial	https://blog.roboflow.com/getting-started-with-roboflow/

Table 3.
Resource links.

Cause	Issue	Effect
Soil erosion	Sand build-up	Road obstruction (Vehicle Hazard) Traps moisture + obstructs water flow
Inefficient road design Sand build-up Rain Pipe-bursts	Water build-up	Cracks Potholes Bumps Reduced pothole visibility (Vehicle Hazard)
Water build-up Excess vehicle loading	Bumps/Undulation	Vehicle Hazard Further road degradation
Extreme temperature changes Water build-up Excess vehicle loading	Cracks	Potholes Further road degradation
Cracks Water build-up Excess vehicle loading	Potholes	Vehicle Hazard Further road degradation Loose gravel
Potholes Road Degradation	Loose gravel	Vehicle Hazard

Table 4.
Cause-and-effect relationship of road degradation and associated factors.

The main insights observed were:

- The main factors that caused the road degradation issues were water build-up, excess vehicle loading, insufficient road maintenance, and roads constructed from poor building materials.
- The main causes of water build-up were weather (rain), pipe bursts, sand build-up, and poor storm drainage due to poor road design.
- The main causes of vehicle overloading were heavy-vehicle mobility on small roads and traffic congestion not being managed well because of poor road network design, as stated by Das et al. [9].

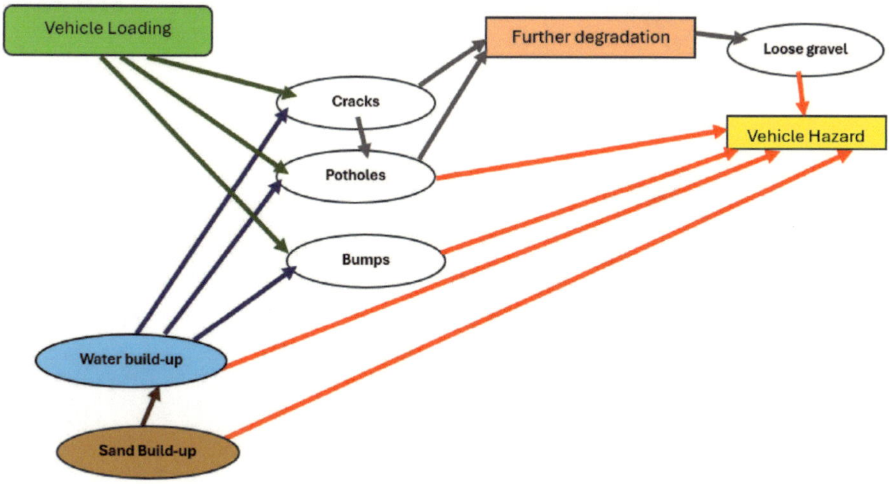

Figure 10.
Diagram showing cause-and-effect relationships of road degradation and associated factors.

- Existing road degradation is a hazard to vehicles and causes further road degradation.

- Possible solutions to combating road degradation on Kimberley roads include preventing soil erosion by paving sidewalks or implementing roadside revegetation, designing better stormwater drainage, managing traffic and road network, and implementing better road maintenance plans.

- The civil engineer mentions, "Data is fundamental in the development of maintenance plans and budgeting correctly". To improve road design and maintenance plans, the municipality would benefit from a low-cost, data-driven solution to allow better-informed decision-making and economical distribution of resources. This kind of solution would entail surveying the roads regularly and easily in a cost-effective manner, as well as monitoring the roads and tracking degradation and all the factors that cause it.

4.1.2 Images from the dataset

Different types or classes of road images from the datasets are depicted in **Figures 11–16**, which include crack, pothole, bump, water build-up, sand build-up, and loose gravel.

Figure 11.
Class: Crack.

Figure 12.
Class: Pothole.

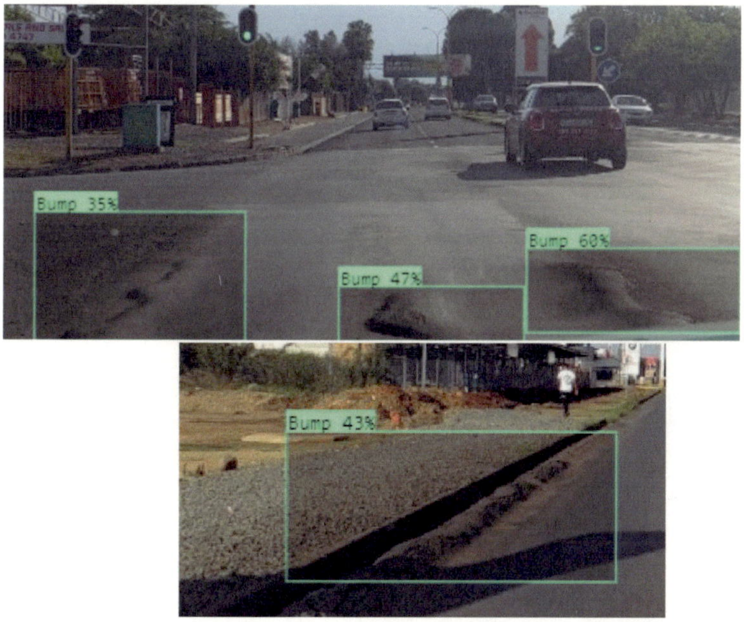

Figure 13.
Class: Bump.

Figure 14.
Class: Water build-up.

Figure 15.
Class: Sand build-up.

Figure 16.
Class: Loose gravel.

4.2 Model

4.2.1 Model architecture

The CNN was designed to classify images into six categories. The model expects input images to be 300x300 pixels with RGB color channels. It extracts features from the images using three convolutional layers with increasing filter complexity. ReLU activation is applied after each convolution to introduce non-linearity. Three max-pooling layers are inserted throughout the network to reduce data size and control overfitting. After flattening the feature maps, a fully connected layer with 64 units further processes the data. Finally, a softmax output layer with six units predicts the probabilities of each class for the image. Adam optimizer and categorical cross-entropy loss function were applied.

4.2.2 Model evaluation

The models were evaluated using the accuracy metric. Accuracy measures how often the model predicts the correct class for a given output. Its formula is given as:

$$Accuracy = \frac{\text{True Positive} + \text{True Negative}}{\text{True Positive} + \text{True Negative} + \text{False Positive} + \text{False Negative}} \tag{3}$$

5. Experiment, results, and discussion

5.1 Experiment

5.1.1 Model training and evaluation

The Google Colab environment was used for training and evaluation of the models. The YOLOv3-CNN model was trained on 10 epochs on both Dataset-1.2 and Dataset-3 in Python, using Tensorflow and Keras libraries for deep learning. Dataset-1.2 had 2058 images in total, and Dataset-3 had 815 images in total. The images were split into three folders, 70%, 20%, and 10%, for training, validation, and testing. Each folder also had a CSV file with annotations corresponding to the images in that folder. CSV file format was used for annotations as that is the format required by Tensorflow Object Detection.

The models were evaluated using an accuracy metric (Eq. (3)). The Model training log is shown in **Figure 17** for YOLOv3 trained on Dataset-1.2 and **Figure 18** for YOLOv3 trained on Dataset-3. The YOLOv3 model trained on Dataset-1.2 achieved 83.38% accuracy, and the YOLOv3 model trained on Dataset-3 achieved 64.08% accuracy. Results are summarized in **Table 5**.

```
Found 4350 validated image filenames belonging to 6 classes.
Found 1194 validated image filenames belonging to 6 classes.
Epoch 1/10
136/136 [==============================] - 636s 5s/step - loss: 0.8356 - accuracy: 0.7209 - val_loss: 0.7179 - val_accuracy: 0.7278
Epoch 2/10
136/136 [==============================] - 34s 250ms/step - loss: 0.6106 - accuracy: 0.7770 - val_loss: 0.7018 - val_accuracy: 0.7496
Epoch 3/10
136/136 [==============================] - 34s 253ms/step - loss: 0.5324 - accuracy: 0.7998 - val_loss: 0.7095 - val_accuracy: 0.7538
Epoch 4/10
136/136 [==============================] - 35s 261ms/step - loss: 0.4852 - accuracy: 0.8117 - val_loss: 0.6898 - val_accuracy: 0.7563
Epoch 5/10
136/136 [==============================] - 33s 242ms/step - loss: 0.4536 - accuracy: 0.8246 - val_loss: 0.7448 - val_accuracy: 0.7546
Epoch 6/10
136/136 [==============================] - 37s 272ms/step - loss: 0.4302 - accuracy: 0.8278 - val_loss: 0.7588 - val_accuracy: 0.7529
Epoch 7/10
136/136 [==============================] - 33s 243ms/step - loss: 0.4190 - accuracy: 0.8283 - val_loss: 0.6962 - val_accuracy: 0.7605
Epoch 8/10
136/136 [==============================] - 33s 245ms/step - loss: 0.3988 - accuracy: 0.8303 - val_loss: 0.7510 - val_accuracy: 0.7638
Epoch 9/10
136/136 [==============================] - 35s 254ms/step - loss: 0.3990 - accuracy: 0.8294 - val_loss: 0.7600 - val_accuracy: 0.7596
Epoch 10/10
136/136 [==============================] - 38s 279ms/step - loss: 0.3792 - accuracy: 0.8338 - val_loss: 0.7445 - val_accuracy: 0.7663
Found 610 validated image filenames belonging to 6 classes.
```

Figure 17.
YOLOv3 model training on Dataset-1.2.

```
Found 2681 validated image filenames belonging to 6 classes.
Found 233 validated image filenames belonging to 6 classes.
Epoch 1/10
84/84 [==============================] - 249s 3s/step - loss: 1.8363 - accuracy: 0.2227 - val_loss: 1.7642 - val_accuracy: 0.2275
Epoch 2/10
84/84 [==============================] - 24s 289ms/step - loss: 1.5959 - accuracy: 0.3655 - val_loss: 1.7257 - val_accuracy: 0.3219
Epoch 3/10
84/84 [==============================] - 25s 291ms/step - loss: 1.3480 - accuracy: 0.5080 - val_loss: 1.6661 - val_accuracy: 0.3691
Epoch 4/10
84/84 [==============================] - 25s 303ms/step - loss: 1.1904 - accuracy: 0.5632 - val_loss: 1.7718 - val_accuracy: 0.2961
Epoch 5/10
84/84 [==============================] - 24s 286ms/step - loss: 1.0761 - accuracy: 0.6050 - val_loss: 1.9522 - val_accuracy: 0.3305
Epoch 6/10
84/84 [==============================] - 24s 287ms/step - loss: 1.0010 - accuracy: 0.6270 - val_loss: 1.7626 - val_accuracy: 0.3777
Epoch 7/10
84/84 [==============================] - 24s 281ms/step - loss: 0.9414 - accuracy: 0.6248 - val_loss: 1.8165 - val_accuracy: 0.3476
Epoch 8/10
84/84 [==============================] - 24s 289ms/step - loss: 0.8987 - accuracy: 0.6315 - val_loss: 1.8572 - val_accuracy: 0.3562
Epoch 9/10
84/84 [==============================] - 25s 299ms/step - loss: 0.8952 - accuracy: 0.6382 - val_loss: 1.7353 - val_accuracy: 0.3562
Epoch 10/10
84/84 [==============================] - 24s 289ms/step - loss: 0.8866 - accuracy: 0.6307 - val_loss: 1.9233 - val_accuracy: 0.3090
Found 141 validated image filenames belonging to 6 classes.
```

Figure 18.
YOLOv3 model training on Dataset-3.

Model	Dataset Size	No. of classes	Accuracy
YOLOV3 (Dataset-1.2)	2058	6	83.38%
YOLOV3 (Dataset-3)	815	6	64.08%

Table 5.
YOLOv3-CNN trained on Dataset-1.2 and Dataset-3.

Models were able to classify classes correctly but were not correctly outputting bounding boxes, as shown in **Figures 19** and **20**.

5.2 Results and analysis

Study	Model	Dataset Size	No. of classes	Accuracy	Precision	Recall	mAP
[1]	CNN	1000	10	95%			
[2]	RESNET50 Faster-RCNN	500	1				23.3%
[6]	Densenet121	885	2	97%			
[8]	InJa_14k SSD MobileNet	15,000	4				15.7%
[3]	YOLOV5	3000	2		91%	81.2%	87.5%
[3]	LSTM	3000	2		90%		94%
[4]	Faster R-CNN with Inception v2	7000	8		93.3%	93.8%	
[4]	SSD with Inception v2	7000	8		90.9%	92.9%	
[4]	SSD with MobileNetv2	7000	8		88%	86.7%	

Table 6.
Performance of some models from the literature.

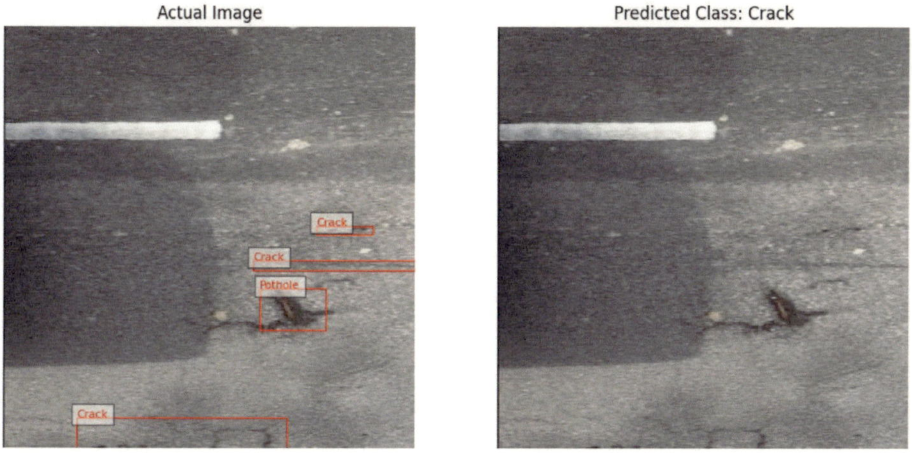

Figure 19.
YOLOv3 on Dataset-1.2 output.

Figure 20.
YOLOv3 on Dataset-3 output.

5.3 Discussion

5.3.1 Effect of dataset size

The graphs in **Figures 21–23** illustrate **Table 2**. Results of Roboflow 3.0 model trained on the different datasets.

Figures 21 and **22** show that there is a positive correlation between dataset size and the performance of the model trained on it.

The graph in **Figure 23** shows that the Roboflow 3.0 model trained on Dataset-1.2 performs best; therefore, eliminating misclassification and having a larger dataset size makes for the best dataset. **Figure 23** also shows that the Roboflow 3.0 model trained on Dataset-3 performed better than the models trained on Dataset-1, which shows that a smaller dataset with misclassification and class imbalance eliminated is still better than a larger dataset with those issues.

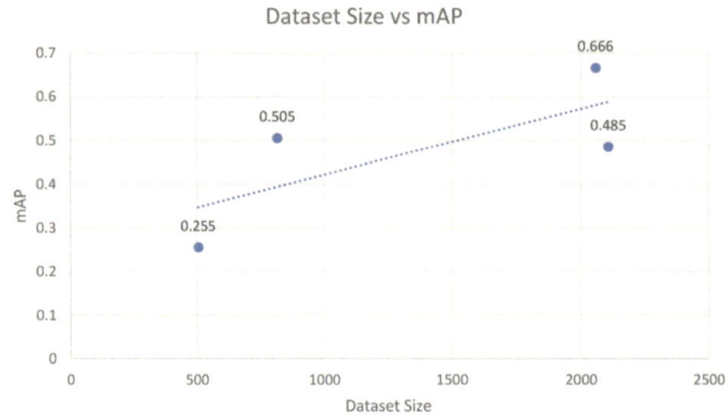

Figure 21.
Graph showing that there is a positive correlation between dataset size and performance of Roboflow 3.0 model.

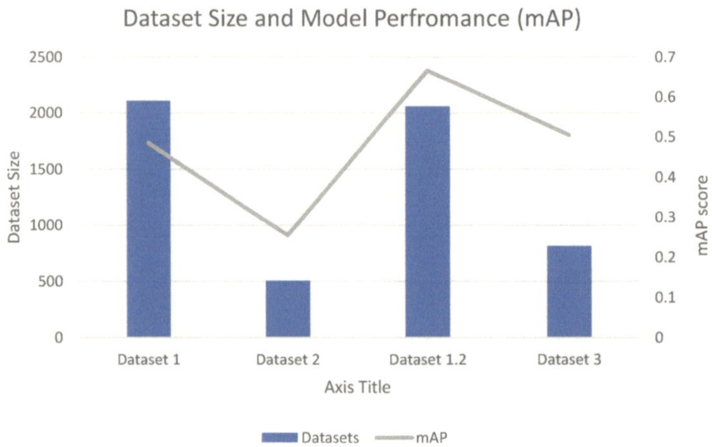

Figure 22.
Graph showing relationship between datasets of different sizes and performance of Roboflow 3.0 model trained on them.

These findings demonstrate the impact of dataset quality and size. This was also proven by the experiment in this study, where the results of training the YOLOv3 model on Dataset-1.2 and Dataset-3, as shown in **Table 5**, demonstrate that the YOLOv3 model performed better on the bigger dataset.

However, these findings do not align with the results from the literature in **Table 6**, which show that the InJa_14k SSD MobileNet model from Arya et al.'s study [8] had the lowest mAP compared to the other models [2, 3] while still having the largest dataset. This shows that other factors that affect a model's performance need to be considered.

5.3.2 Effect of different models

As shown in **Table 5**, the YOLOv3 model from this study trained and evaluated on a dataset with 2058 images achieved an accuracy of 83.38%. It performs worse than the custom-made CNN *Boucetta et al.'s* study [1], which was trained and evaluated on a dataset of 1000 images and achieved an accuracy of 95%.

Comparing the result in **Table 5** of the YOLOv3 model trained and evaluated on 815 images, which achieved an accuracy of 64.08%, to the result shown in **Table 6**

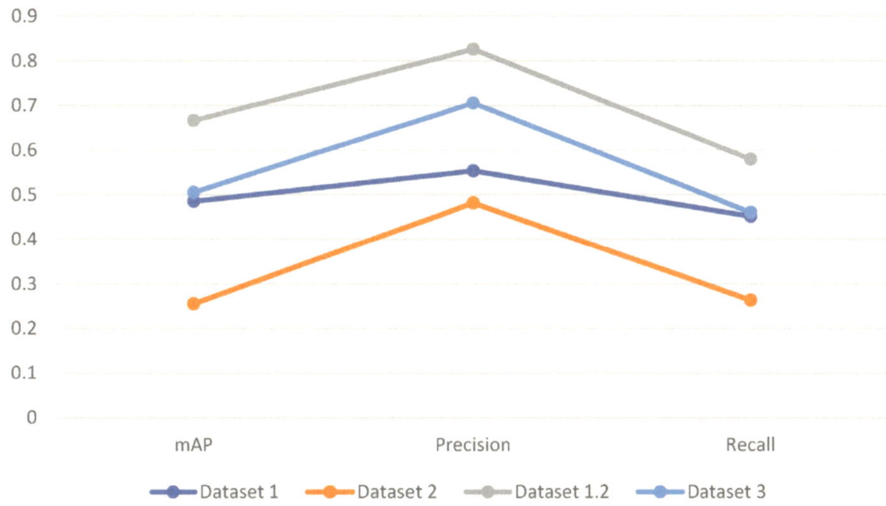

Figure 23.
Graph showing performance of Roboflow 3.0 model on different-sized datasets.

of Saeed et al.'s study [6], which had the Densenet121 model trained on 885 images achieved an accuracy of 97%, it shows that the YOLOv3 model performed worse.

The YOLOv3 model seems to perform worse than models from the literature. Still, these findings cannot ascertain that the YOLOv3 models perform poorly in general, as the datasets used in the literature and this study differed.

Comparing the results shown, which were trained on Dataset-1.2, the YOLO-NAS model achieved 72% mAP, outperforming the Roboflow 3.0 model, which achieved 66.6% mAP.

When comparing the results of Ramesh et al.'s study [3] shown in **Table 6**, the LSTM model achieved 94% mAP, outperforming the YOLOV5 model, which achieved 87.5% mAP.

These findings demonstrate that the YOLO series models perform well enough but underperform compared to other state-of-the-art models.

6. Conclusion

This chapter aimed to investigate a dataset's effect on model performance and attempted to develop a road condition monitoring system specific to Kimberley. The results highlight the significant impact of dataset quality on model performance. Models trained on Dataset-1.2, which was free of misclassifications and had a larger size, achieved considerably higher accuracy than models trained on datasets with potential issues. The YOLO series of models worked well enough for object detection. However, the authors could not develop a system further than this or create an optimal model for the Kimberley dataset.

This chapter focused on road conditions relevant to Kimberley of the Northern Cape in South Africa. A new dataset was created with six different classes of road degradation, and a model was developed from this dataset. As far as the authors were aware, a Kimberley-specific dataset did not previously exist.

The research focuses mainly on collecting data using smartphone technology and developing a model from their data. Still, most studies do not ensure that their work is suitable in real-life implementation or if it aligns with any industry standards for civil engineering. This project focused mainly on creating low-cost, data-driven solutions for assisting the Kimberley municipality with road maintenance planning, aligning with the TRH22 guidelines for pavement management systems [10].

6.1 Practical implications

The methodology of this project could be used as a framework for creating a dataset and model specific to a particular location. The authors used a smartphone to capture data and a free version of a data annotation and dataset development tool, allowing limited model training. This research could be replicated easily and with minimal to no expenses. The two main datasets, Dataset-1.2 and Dataset-3, are available for download with annotations in any format, so other researchers may train any model they prefer. **Table 3** shows download links for the datasets with CSV file annotations used in this study for Tensorflow Object Detection and links to the datasets with different annotation file formats and the dataset and model development platform. This study also aligns with TRH22 guidelines [10] and is, therefore, suitable for research or implementation of pavement management systems for South African roads.

6.2 Limitations

This chapter created a new dataset for Kimberley, but only a small dataset with no class imbalance (Dataset-3) or a bigger dataset that performed better but still had a class imbalance (Dataset-1.2). If the authors collected more data, they could have produced a much bigger dataset with no class imbalance.

The authors developed a CNN with an accuracy of 83.38% based on the Kimberley dataset using the Yolov3 pre-trained model; however, the model could not output predicted bounding boxes correctly. The YOLOv3-CNN from this study could not be directly compared to any models from the literature, but the YOLO series models do not seem to perform as well as other state-of-the-art models. The limitations of the model from this study could be improved by investigating better pre-trained models than the YOLO series and performing hyperparameter tuning.

6.3 Future work

The TRH22 manual explains that their guidelines specify four specific divisions regarding Pavement Management Systems, namely "(1) Organizational and implementation matters, (2) Facets of a basic pavement management system and the related outputs, (3) Network level enhancement of the basic system and interpretation of the outputs, (4) Updating of data and upgrading of the system" [10]. This study relates to the 4th division of "Updating data and upgrading the system" [10].

Future work would, therefore, entail improving the limitations of the dataset and model and attempting to implement them into a system for road condition monitoring that could be used by the Kimberley municipality. This might entail investigating the scalability of datasets and models.

Conflict of interest

The authors declare no conflict of interest.

Author details

Seemeen Wookey, Christopher Mhlongo, Unarine Mukwevho, Tlotlo Fanuel Sebati and Ibidun Christiana Obagbuwa*
Faculty of Natural and Applied Sciences, Department of Computer Science and Information Technology, Sol Plaatje University, Kimberly, South Africa

*Address all correspondence to: ibidun.obagbuwa@spu.ac.za

IntechOpen

© 2025 The Author(s). Licensee IntechOpen. This chapter is distributed under the terms of the Creative Commons Attribution License (http://creativecommons.org/licenses/by/4.0), which permits unrestricted use, distribution, and reproduction in any medium, provided the original work is properly cited.

References

[1] Boucetta Z, Fazziki AE, Adnani ME. A deep-learning-based road deterioration notification and road condition. International Journal of Intelligent Engineering and Systems. 2021;**14**(3):503-515

[2] Kok V, Mpofu N, Olusanya M. Severity estimation of potholes in imagery using convolutional neural networks. In: Silhavy R, editor. Artificial Intelligence in Intelligent Systems. CSOC 2021. Lecture Notes in Networks and Systems. Vol. 229. Cham: Springer; 2021. DOI: 10.1007/978-3-030-77445-5_60

[3] Ramesh A, Nikam D, Balachandran V, Guo LWR, Hu L, Comert G, et al. Cloud-based collaborative road-damage monitoring with deep learning and smartphones. Sustainability. 2022;**14**:8682

[4] Roberts R, Giancontieri G, Inzerillo L, Di Mino G. Towards low-cost pavement condition health monitoring and analysis using deep learning. Applied Sciences. 2020;**10**(1):319

[5] Hadj-Attou A, Kabir Y, Ykhlef F. Hybrid deep learning models for road surface condition monitoring. Measurement. 2023;**220**:113267

[6] Saeed N, Alam M, Nyberg RG. A multimodal deep learning approach for gravel road condition evaluation. Transportation Engineering. 2024;**16**:100228

[7] Guo X, Wang N, Li Y. Enhancing pavement maintenance: A deep learning model for accurate. Construction and Building Materials. 2023;**409**:133970

[8] Arya D, Maeda H, Ghosh SK, Toshniwal D, Mraz A, Kashiyama T, et al. Deep learning-based road damage detection and classification for multiple countries. Automation in Construction. 2021;**132**:103935

[9] Das DK, Keetse MSM. Assessment of traffic congestion in the central areas of Kimberley city. Interim: Interdisciplinary Journal. 2015;**14**(1):70-82

[10] Committee of State Road Authorities, Pretoria, South Africa. Technical Recommendations for Highways (TRH) 22. Pavement Management Systems. Committee of State Road Authorities. Pretoria, South Africa: Department of Transport; 1994

Chapter 5

GDPR Compliance in Video Surveillance Systems and Applications

Roxana Elena Mihaescu, Marian Ghenescu and Serban Carata

Abstract

With the evolution of video processing, the volume of video data has increased significantly, and access to high-risk data is becoming very easy. This chapter will classify the data regarded as high risk according to current regulations and detail both the GDPR and EDPS regulations and how they affect the processing and recording of personal data. Afterward, we will present a comprehensive review of the state-of-the-art solutions in the literature, ensuring compliance with GDPR. Throughout the chapter, we will describe the importance of ensuring compliance with the current GDPR and the challenges that a video processing system faces in this process. To exemplify the impact of GDPR on video systems, we will present our application for detecting what is considered high-risk data and how GDPR affects these applications. To adapt video surveillance systems and applications to be GDPR-compliant, we have also implemented a lightweight software solution, which can be easily integrated into any existing video processing system. This solution requires a minimal addition of computational and hardware resources, being suitable for any video application. Video surveillance systems and video analytics applications must align with GDPR and protect sensitive and personal data.

Keywords: GDPR, CCTV, video surveillance, video processing, deep learning, object detection, YOLO

1. Introduction

1.1 Evolution of video systems

The last decades have brought a considerable evolution in video surveillance [1], representing the transition from the analog era to the digital one. Subsequently, in recent years, the field has been reinvented by the introduction of artificial intelligence [2]. This last-generation algorithmic leap brought a significant evolution in video processing, adding complexity and efficiency to video processing algorithms. Along with the evolution of the field, more and more performing hardware resources appeared [3, 4]. If in the previous decade, the most used cameras were those with a resolution of 720p (1MP), nowadays, most systems use resolutions in the range of 3–6 MP, even higher. Thus, hardware resources become more efficient and more affordable.

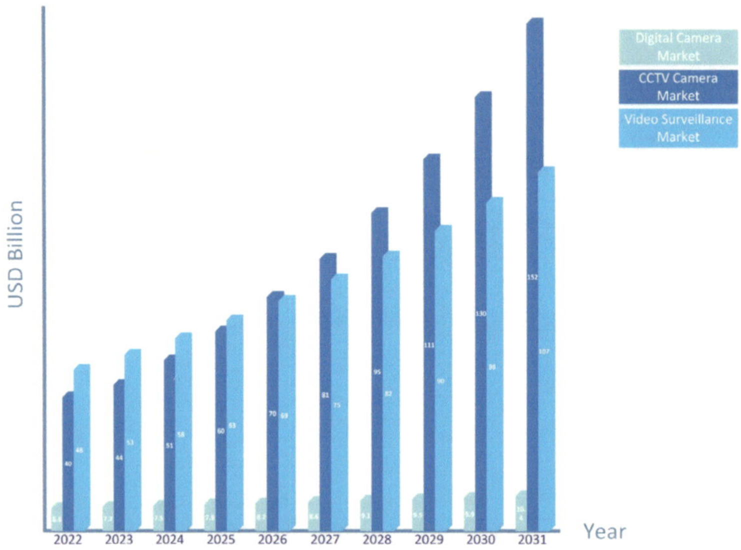

Figure 1.
Market size and trends in video surveillance systems [5–7].

As shown in **Figure 1**, specialists in the field continue to expect a considerable market size evolution for video surveillance systems and surveillance cameras. Considering the evolution of the last years and this field's exponential growth, they computed a measure called compound annual growth rate (CAGR), which represents the average growth rate between two consecutive years. A CAGR of only 4.8% [5] is expected for the digital camera market size, while the expansion for CCTV cameras and surveillance systems is much faster. Therefore, a CAGR of 16.84% for CCTV cameras was calculated according to [6], while in [7], the global video surveillance market size was estimated at an annual growth of 9.3% . The specialists made all of the analyses for the period 2024–2031.

This evolution will result in a considerable increase in video recordings for surveillance and entertainment. Using and storing them safely, without endangering people's privacy, is becoming increasingly problematic and challenging [8]. Video processing has become prone to less ethical attempts to acquire stored information [9, 10], increasing the number of incidents such as hacks and other data leaks. In the contemporary digital environment, which is full of challenges, the existing rules must provide the necessary efficiency to ensure the right to protect personal data [11]. New methods of sharing information through social networks and storing large amounts of data have become a part of life for many of Europe's 250 million Internet users.

1.2 Data protection in European Union

The General Data Protection Regulation (GDPR) is the instrument the European Union has decided to use to protect consumers' privacy and personal data [12]. The EU has assumed the role of a world leader, adopting the most complex legislative framework on privacy and data protection, starting on May 25, 2018. This GDPR law [13, 14] applies at the union level in all 28 member states. These principles were certainly known even before the introduction of the GDPR, the protection of privacy, and the right to a private life being considered fundamental human rights at the same level of importance as freedom or property rights. This critical position of the right to privacy did not appear in the GDPR legislation but has been recognized since 1948, following the adoption of the Universal Declaration of Human Rights [15].

The evolution of the law on human rights, from the first declaration in 1948 until the adoption of the GDPR (May 25, 2018), is illustrated in **Figure 2**. Over the years, the European Commission adopted a series of directives to strengthen personal data protection without restricting their free circulation. In this sense, it was adopted Directive $95/46/EC$ [16] on data protection on October 24, 1995, as well as the Directive on the processing of personal data and the safety of private life in the electronic communications sector, also known as the ePrivacy Directive [17], on June 11, 2002.

Although all these regulatory instruments aimed to introduce a harmonized approach to data protection, the lack of a common denominator at the level of the member states required the adoption of a European regulation directly applicable to all member countries without the need to transpose it into national legislation. Thus, on April 27, 2016, the regulation on the protection of humans regarding the processing of personal data and the free circulation of such data was adopted. This regulation replaces Directive 95/46/EC.

The most significant thing to note about the regulations introduced is the pivotal role they assign to companies in managing their user's data, especially in the face of hacking and other similar events. The actions companies and institutions need to take can benefit them, as the public may boycott and disregard a company that does not take the initiative to manage its data better.

1.3 Data protection in video footage

Ensuring compliance with GDPR represents a challenging task in video processing. Data captured through surveillance systems and applications are considered personally identifiable information (PII). This type of data symbolizes personal data, which companies or persons who operate the surveillance system cannot share with third parties. In video footage, PII covers an extensive category of data, such as information from documents (name, surname, addresses, identity card, bank accounts, etc.), faces or distinguishing marks (tattoos, scars), license plates numbers, locations, or location indicators. For a video system to meet the GDPR standard, all information considered

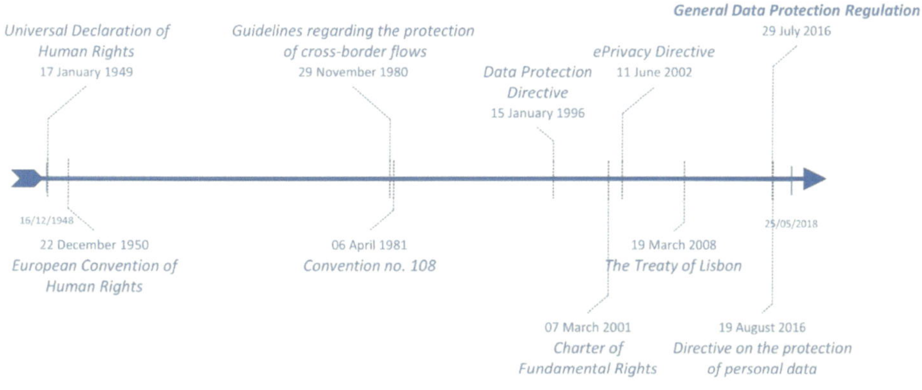

Figure 2.
Evolution of data protection in EU.

personal must be completely blurred. This ensures that no personal data is made public when the footage is shared, and the system does not violate people's privacy.

2. The general data protection regulation

The evolution of video processing systems led to the introduction of regulations aimed at defending the human right to a private life. As this field expanded and an increasingly large volume of video data was stored, a set of laws became imperative to ensure the processing of this data without affecting people's privacy. GDPR is a set of laws that establish detailed requirements relative to how personal data is collected, stored, and processed. It applies to European organizations that process EU citizens' personal data and non-EU organizations that target EU citizens. This set of laws entered into force on May 25, 2018, and applies to all 28 EU member states. The GDPR comprises 99 articles [18] and 173 recitals [19] and contains precise requirements describing how a company or organization must manage personal data.

2.1 Principles of GDPR

Today, with the proliferation of video systems, it is crucial for companies to ensure their systems comply with GDPR. With its 99 articles, this regulation forms the bedrock of laws governing personal data. The scope of personal data involved in various aspects makes GDPR compliance a significant challenge [20]. The seven essential principles of the GDPR outlined in Article 5 from [18] are critical to this compliance.

2.1.1 The principle of legality

In Article 5, the first principle described is data legality. Personal data must be collected legally, fairly, and transparently [21]. Data legality denotes the existence of a legal basis to process personal data. For companies, there are six such legal grounds:

- the consent of the person in question to process his data. Obtaining consent is the most common way to ensure GDPR compliance on video systems. The consent must be explicit, and the company must list why they use the stored data.

- the existence of a contract between the company and the data subject by which he gives his consent to the processing of his data;

- the legal obligation to process specific personal data;

- vital interest, such as medical information essential for the life of the person concerned (e.g., the medical history of a patient);

- the public interest, for instance, processing data for statistical or research purposes that benefit the public.

- the legitimate interest, which means the processing is necessary for the legitimate interests of the data controller or a third party unless these interests are overridden by the interests or fundamental rights and freedoms of the data subject.

To be GDPR compliant, a system must determine one of the legal grounds for processing personal data before starting to do so. The fairness and transparency of personal data require the companies to use personal data correctly, as the data subject has been informed. Also, the company must notify the data subject about processing its data and of the way the system will collect and store it.

2.1.2 The principle of purpose-related limitation

The second paragraph of Article 5 stipulates that companies must collect data for precise, explicit, and legitimate purposes and subsequently process it in a manner compatible with the primary purpose [22]. If the system processes data for another purpose, a new legal basis is necessary, and the concerned person will have to give new permission. According to Article 89 (from [18]), the archiving of data for subsequent processing for public, historical, or scientific purposes is considered compatible with the initial purpose.

2.1.3 The principle of data minimization

The principle of data minimization assumes that the system that collects the data processes the minimum amount of data to achieve its purpose. The requested, stored, and processed data are only appropriate, relevant, and limited to what is necessary, depending on the purposes of their processing [23].

2.1.4 The principle of accuracy

The data stored and processed must be accurate and up-to-date. If necessary, they must be deleted or updated without delay. Hallinan, D., describes this principle extensively in [24].

2.1.5 The principle of limitation related to storage

According to Article 5, paragraph 1(e), a system that stores personal data must keep it only as long as it is necessary for the intended purpose. As in the case of purpose limitation, according to paragraph 89 of the GDPR, personal data can be stored longer for archiving them for the public interest or subsequent historical or scientific research. The GDPR does not define a time limit available for data storage. This storage duration depends on the initially defined purpose and the time required to achieve that purpose. In addition, for a company not to violate the documentation laws applied by the GDPR, it will have to establish a data storage policy to inform the public how long the various categories of data are retained.

2.1.6 The principle of integrity and confidentiality

One of the most important GDPR principles is securing personal information. Any system that collects and stores data must ensure its confidentiality to not endanger the people to whom it belongs. For a system to comply with the GDPR, it should have an adequate level of cybersecurity to avoid any attack on the data and, implicitly, any leakage of personal data [25]. For this, no one should have access to personal data except for authorized employees. In addition, any system that stores data must be able to protect the data against damage and recover it in the situation in which it was damaged. According to the GDPR, system operators must conduct periodic tests to ensure the security measures work within optimal parameters.

2.1.7 The principle of responsibility

Any system that processes personal data must demonstrate at any time that it complies with the GDPR and applies these regulations in all its aspects. A data subject has the right to ensure that a system that uses his data complies with GDPR laws. Video surveillance systems and state-of-the-art applications that use artificial intelligence must notify the data owners of the purpose for which they use personal data. To ensure the principle of responsibility, the GDPR introduced the position of data protection officer (DPO) [26]. This role represents one of the novelties of the regulation compared to the former data protection directive and is described in detail in [27].

According to the GDPR standard, the role of the DPO is to ensure compliance with the protection of personal data and propose new measures for alignment. First, the DPO must facilitate and implement internal data protection policies and train employees on their responsibilities. DPO must also advise the staff and the management team on managing personal data security incidents. The DPO must permanently monitor the personal data processing procedures carried out by the system operators, analyze the requests from the concerned persons, and support in formulating the answer. Furthermore, according to GDPR, DPO must identify areas for improvement to maintain as much data protection as possible and train the staff and the management team regarding legislative news and good practices in data protection. When necessary, DPO must cooperate with the control authority.

2.2 Legal ground

GDPR comprises 99 articles and 173 recitals, in which the authorities define the rights of individuals relative to personal data and the obligations of companies to protect these rights. While the articles aim to define the legal ground and the requirements imposed on companies that collect personal data, the recitals provide more information about the laws contained in the articles. In this way, a company's obligations to comply with the GDPR standard are explained more clearly.

2.2.1 Key articles of GDPR

The GDPR insists on the most noteworthy rights: the rights of individuals, the right to be forgotten, and the right to be informed.

As it emerges from the GDPR principles described previously, this regulation is designed to protect customers' rights and secure personal information. The principle of legality requires companies to collect customer data legally and transparently. The principle of data minimization requires the collection of a minimum volume of personal data from customers from the beginning. Finally, the principle of limited storage requires that the data be deleted after a certain period. There are several articles in the GDPR introduced specifically to protect these *rights of individuals*, among which the most important are:

Article 6. This describes the situations in which collecting and processing an individual's data is legal. Among the legal circumstances are listed the direct consent of the person concerned, the protection of the vital interests of the person concerned, or particular legal circumstances that concern the individual.

Article 15. This article gives data subjects the right to obtain information about processing their data. In addition, the individual can request access to the stored data anytime.

Article 18. This article gives the individual the right to restrict the company's access to his data if he considers them inaccurate or disagrees with the purpose for which they are used. From that moment, it becomes illegal for the company to continue using the individual's data.

Data transparency is the main attribute of collected data and the basis of the GDPR's first principle. To ensure that the *right to be informed* is respected, the GDPR introduced several articles and recitals.

Article 12. This article concerns the transparency of information, communications, and ways of exercising the rights of the person concerned. According to this article, the information companies provide to collect personal data must be clear, concise, transparent, understandable, and accessible.

Recital 58. This recital was introduced to supplement Article 12, clearly describing the data transparency principle. It describes a company's obligation to provide EU citizens with details about the information to be collected. To comply with the GDPR, each system or company that collects personal data must have a privacy policy link accessible to all users. In addition, users must be notified of changes in terms and policies.

Among the rights of data subjects is the right to delete data, named by EU Regulation no. 679/2016 on the protection of personal data and the *right to be forgotten*. The right to be forgotten is more relevant, given the development of technologies that have democratized access to information and remote communications. The possibility of obtaining vast amounts of data from the World Wide Web that can be processed for purposes that are not always transparent demonstrates the need to regulate this right. To ensure this right of citizens, authorities introduced Article 17 and recitals 65 and 66 in GDPR.

Article 17. This article describes the obligation of companies to delete any personal information of an individual who withdraws his consent and the circumstances in which an individual has the right to be deleted.

2.2.2 GDPR violations and fines

With the rapid evolution of systems and technologies, the volume of data companies collect has grown exponentially. In this context, systems must comply with the GDPR rules and protect personal data. As per Article 83, failure to do so empowers supervisory authorities to levy administrative fines on companies that breach any GDPR laws. These fines are designed to be proportionate to the breach, the damages suffered, and the company's financial capacity to pay.

To determine the amount of the fine, the authorities, which are designated to monitor compliance with the GDPR, analyze the data breach using several tools. The seriousness and duration of the GDPR violation will be considered, as well as the number of affected persons and the damages they suffered. In addition, it is essential to determine the intention or negligence of the data processor and if he has taken any action to reduce the damage to the data subjects. At the same time, the history of the processor is also accessed, taking into account whether it had previous GDPR violations and whether it cooperated with the authority to resolve the breach. The total amount of the administrative fine cannot exceed the amount provided for the most severe violation.

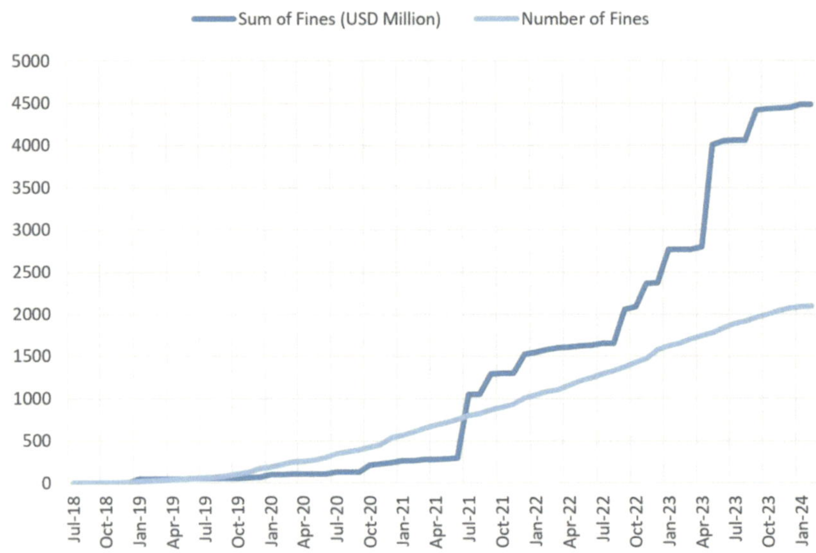

Figure 3.
GDPR fines [28].

Article 83 of the GDPR regulation categorizes violations into two types, each with its own upper limit of fines. For less severe violations, a maximum fixed fine of 10,000,000 Euros or a variable fine of up to 2% of the firm's worldwide annual revenue from the preceding financial year is imposed. However, these maximum values can double for more severe violations, underscoring the seriousness of non-compliance. **Figure 3** shows the evolution of the number of fines granted at the level of the European Union and their total value. The evolution is followed from 2018, when the GDPR entered force, until the current year. It can be observed that, with the passing of the years, the number of fines granted for non-compliance with the regulation and their value increased exponentially. The most common violations of the GDPR are non-compliance with the general principles of the GDPR, specified in Article 5, insufficient legal basis for storing and processing personal data, insufficient fulfillment of information obligation, and insufficient technical and organizational measures to ensure information security.

3. Video surveillance and GDPR

With the expansion of video systems and the technologies used, more and more people use them in their ordinary lives. Surveillance systems are increasingly used for personal purposes, to ensure the home's safety, or to supervise a business. These videos often contain images of people or other information considered personal data. Footage including a person's face or other features, medical, religious, or political information, locations such as hospitals or homes, and children under 18 years of age is considered sensitive and must be protected according to the GDPR.

In this context, closed-circuit television (CCTV) systems are one of the main subjects of complaints, reports, and notifications regarding security incidents.

Among the most common complaints, the authority received is image processing using video surveillance systems, including illegal video surveillance. Regarding security incidents, unauthorized access to closed-circuit video surveillance systems was among the most common causes. Video surveillance is a real challenge in aligning with GDPR and a real test of responsibility.

In a video surveillance system, operators must ensure compliance with GDPR throughout the process, from the cameras to the footage storage. Ensuring the system's GDPR compliance while it processes personal images presents several challenges. This chapter illustrates the challenges encountered while operating a video surveillance system, starting with installing surveillance cameras, transmitting and processing the stream safely, and storing the data. In addition, compliance with the GDPR principles described in the previous chapter must be considered even before installing the surveillance systems. Furthermore, this section describes existing solutions in the field, such as last-generation encryption techniques or state-of-the-art anonymization algorithms.

3.1 Legal bases

One of the primary challenges is the regulatory framework, from establishing the legal bases to process data to implementing privacy principles for internal regulation. Companies must understand the legislation very well before installing a video surveillance system. A video system can base data processing on one of the legal grounds: the fulfillment of a legal obligation, the legitimate interest of the operator, or the consent of the persons concerned. The company must achieve those three legal grounds in this particular order.

First, they must see if the system may fulfill a legal obligation. Then, when there is no legal obligation to video monitor a particular area, but the operator still justifies installing a surveillance system, he can invoke the legitimate interest. An example could be installing a video surveillance camera in an area with a high risk of an occupational accident. Consequently, the surveillance system may be necessary to investigate a possible incident. Obtaining the consent of the person concerned represents the last option when there is no legal obligation, and the legitimate interest cannot be proven. One of the essential characteristics of consent is that it can be withdrawn at any time, which could lead to the impossibility of processing the video recording. The erasure of any information regarding a specific person represents the right to be forgotten, according to Article 17 of GDPR.

3.2 Location of surveillance cameras

The operators should strategically place surveillance cameras so that they do not violate any person's privacy but can capture images to serve their intended purpose. In the public domain, cameras can be installed in crowded places with high traffic volume to protect people. In shops or other public spaces, they should be installed toward the entrances and exits or the cash registers so that customers have as much privacy as possible. For example, in clothing stores, the cameras should not be installed anywhere near the fitting rooms. When surveillance is conducted on a private house, the system's owner must ensure that he does not also capture the neighbors' entrances or other private places. Otherwise, the owner must obtain the neighbors' consent to install a surveillance system that is compliant with GDPR.

3.3 Security of video surveillance system

One of the most significant challenges is ensuring the security of an end-to-end video system [29], which involves securing surveillance cameras, the video stream for transmission and further processing, and the safe storage of data.

3.3.1 Choosing a password

The first and most accessible level of camera security is the password [30]. The GDPR has not defined a concrete way of setting the password, but it must be as complex as possible so that it is not easily broken following a cyberattack. First, the surveillance camera password must be long enough, preferably at least eight characters long, and contain at least one character from the five categories: uppercase and lowercase letters, numbers, special characters, and Unicode characters. In addition, security experts also advise that passwords should not contain personal information or words found in the dictionary, as they are easier to guess by outside sources. It is preferable that passwords be changed periodically and that the same password not be repeated several times.

In a study conducted in 2023, a cybersecurity center identified the most commonly used passwords globally. Among them were *123,456*, *admin*, *password*, *000000*, *Admin123*, and *user*. None of these passwords adhere to the security guidelines mentioned earlier. A surveillance system that complies with GDPR regulations should be designed to prevent users from setting weak passwords, thereby enhancing overall system security.

3.3.2 Encryption techniques

The password, as the only level of security, does not provide any degree of security to the surveillance system. It is imperative to use data stream encryption strategies in parallel [31, 32]. Encryption strategies differ in two situations: encryption of static data and encryption of data in motion. The second data category is considered more susceptible to attacks and less secure. Therefore, using encryption strategies is not just a recommendation but a necessity for a robust security system.

Encryption, the process of converting digital information into a coded format (ciphertext) to prevent unauthorized access, is a cornerstone of cybersecurity and privacy protection. In today's digital landscape, no video system can be considered secure without robust data encryption techniques.

There are two types of static data encryption: symmetric and asymmetric. [33] describes the most known and used encryption techniques. Symmetric encryption [34] uses a single encryption key and is generally used for mass data protection and local storage. Asymmetric encryption uses a public key to encrypt video streams and a private key to decrypt them and is used to secure communications on the Internet.

Symmetric encryption is also known as private key encryption. The key for encryption and decryption is a randomly generated string. The best-known algorithm with a symmetric key is the Advanced Encryption Standard (AES) technique [35, 36], considered one of the most robust encryption techniques. Currently, the AES-256 technique [37] is regarded as the most secure encryption technique, and although it is usually used for static data, it can also be applied to data in motion. Other variations of the standard, depending on the length of the key used, are AES-128 and AES-192.

Although the 128-bit key is considered safe for many systems, in the case of systems that capture sensitive images, it is preferable to use a 192-bit or even 256-bit key [38]. The AES encryption standard appeared in 2001 and replaced the Data Encryption Standard (DES) standard [39], which was widely used in the 1970s but can be easily broken nowadays.

Another known encryption method is Blowfish [40], a faster method than AES. The encryption key has a variable length from 32 to 448 bits. Blowfish was replaced in the 1990s by the Twofish algorithm [41], which, although known for its increased security, is not as widely used as AES in video systems due to its much higher complexity.

Regarding asymmetric encryption methods, the best known and widely used is the Rivest–Shamir–Adleman (RSA) algorithm [42], implemented in 1977.

3.3.3 Secure flow transmission

To safely transmit the video data stream, it is necessary to create secure channels between the surveillance cameras and the servers in the system. Video surveillance systems generally use transport layer security (TLS)/secure sockets layer (SSL), hypertext transfer protocol secure (HTTPS), or secure real-time transport protocol (SRTP) protocols to transmit data. TLS [43] is the most used protocol in video systems. It was implemented in 1999 and evolved from the SSL protocol [44]. TLS uses a combination of the two types of encryption presented previously. It ensures the best compromise between performance and security when transmitting data between surveillance cameras and the servers where they will be stored later.

HTTPS [45] implements TLS encryption over the hypertext transfer protocol (HTTP) [46] transport protocol, which is used globally. Usually, video data is transmitted using the real-time transport protocol (RTP) [47]. SRTP [48] is an extension of this protocol and can be used in 1-to-1 or multi-point transmissions. HTTPS and SRTP protocols differ because the latter can only be used for media streams. While HTTPS creates a secure channel between the camera and the servers, SRTP encrypts the RTP packets. If the clients of a surveillance system need to communicate administrative tasks to the cameras, the system will only use the HTTPS protocol. Both HTTPS and SRTP usually use AES-128 as an encryption technique.

3.3.4 Cryptographic certificates

An X.509 [49] certificate is a standardized digital credential system defined by the Internet Engineering Task Force (IETF) and represents a fundamental component of systems security. The X.509 standard defines the format and encoding of public key certificates and represents an essential part of public key infrastructure (PKI). These certificates are commonly used in secure Internet communications, such as SSL/TLS encryption. X.509 certificate is like a digital passport, providing proof of identity to a Web site or server. The certificate is issued by a trusted Certificate Authority (CA), which guarantees the entity is who it claims to be.

X.509 certificates can also be used as an authentication method instead of passwords. They are considered much more secure, improving authentication for video surveillance systems. In addition, they represent a tool that manages the identities of system users to ensure the safe sharing of personal data and not to a third party who can use the data for illegal purposes. In this way, data security and GDPR compliance of the video surveillance system are ensured.

3.3.5 Anonymization of footage

Data anonymization is an essential part of a surveillance system's security. To comply with GDPR principles, the video system must minimize users' access to the original data. Thus, access to personal data is minimized. To meet GDPR standards, a system should have a limited number of operators with access to personal data, the rest being able to access only the anonymized video streams.

Video anonymization is a powerful tool that enables the video system to adhere to GDPR rules by concealing PII. This process, which must be precise and robust, instills confidence in the system's capabilities. Regardless of changes in lighting or weather conditions that may appear in the footage, personal data must be anonymized, ensuring the confidentiality of personal data. Moreover, anonymization should be irreversible, preventing the original information from being obtained once the stream is anonymized. The anonymization of streams involves the anonymization of faces or other features by which a person can be identified, the anonymization of registration numbers, or the anonymization of certain areas of the footage. The process is complex and involves the detection of the object of interest in the first phase, followed by its anonymization.

Face detection has been one of the most researched applications in video processing in recent years. The emergence and improvement of deep learning models have considerably evolved this field. Various face detection techniques are presented in **Table 1**. The same evolution occurred in the registration plate detection (see **Table 1**).

Method name	Technologies used	Description
Face Detection	Haar Cascade Classifier [50]	A machine learning algorithm that uses a set of Haar-like features to distinguish facial features such as eyes, nose, or mouth. Haar-like features represent rectangular patterns of pixel values.
	Support Vector Machine [51]	A machine learning algorithm that searches the optimal line or hyperplane to maximize the distance between two classes. It will return a binary value, which represents the belonging to the object's class: face or non-face.
	YOLOv5 [52]	A computer vision model based on a convolutional neural network. It was developed for object detection and is very accurate in detecting small objects, such as faces.
License Plate Detection	HOG & SVM [53]	HOG generates the feature vectors, by calculating the gradient for each cell in the image and subsequently aggregating this data into a histogram. The object will thus be distinguished from the background. Then SVM decides if it is a registration plate.
	SIFT [54]	It generates the feature vectors by identifying distinct key points, invariant to changes of scale, rotation, or illumination.
	CNN [55]	Deep learning architectures that require less preprocessing than other classifiers. It learns to identify features such as geometry or texture, being able to detect plates in a new image.
Anonymization	Pixelization [56]	Reduces the resolution of an image, to make parts of it difficult to identify.
	Masking [57]	Altering sensitive data and replacing it with another set of data in real time, often using a filter over the desired areas.
	GAN [58]	GANs are used to generate synthetic data, thus replacing the original image.

Table 1.
Detection and anonymization methods.

Once the area of interest is detected, anonymization methods are applied to hide personal information. Several techniques for anonymizing video streams exist, such as pixelization, masking, techniques based on deep learning, or even real-time anonymization. **Table 1** presents some of the best-known anonymization methods.

3.3.6 Data storage

A video surveillance system offers two robust data storage methods: on-premise and on-cloud. On-premise storage involves saving data on a local network video recorder (NVR), while on-cloud storage involves storing data online, often hosted by a trusted third-party company. To fortify the stored data, surveillance systems employ advanced encryption methods and implement stringent access control techniques, ensuring the utmost security and minimizing operators' access to sensitive data. Due to the exponential growth of data in the last ten years, companies are migrating to cloud storage facilities. Virtual private network (VPN) and virtual private cloud (VPC) are two essential components for accessing resources for on-cloud storage. The storage process involves establishing an encrypted connection via VPN [59] between the camera network and the private network of the NVR in the VPC cloud [60]. VPC represents a private cloud hosted in a public cloud, which offers both the advantages of a private network and the scalability and isolation of the levels between the private network and the virtual one of the cloud.

3.4 Integrity and redundancy of stored data

According to the GDPR's accuracy principle, described in the previous section, the surveillance system operator must ensure that the stored data is accurate and up-to-date. Otherwise, they must delete and update the data with the accurate one. At the same time, according to the GDPR principle of integrity, any video surveillance system must protect its stored data to avoid alteration. However, it is challenging for such systems to keep the data intact, especially in system failure or other external circumstances. The same GDPR principle stipulates that if the data stored on the system is damaged, the system must be able to restore it. Two leading solutions to this problem are implementing a redundant system or making frequent backups.

Both data redundancy and backups play a crucial role in preventing data loss. While backups allow the system to revert to a previous state, data redundancy ensures system continuity in the event of a failure. Both practices are essential for maintaining data accuracy and integrity. To restore the data when lost or altered, they must have at least one backup copy in several locations, such as databases or storage systems. In this way, if data on the system is lost due to an event, it can restore the missing information using the copies on the external systems. The backup represents a copy of the data up to a previous point. In contrast, redundancy represents a clone of the entire system, so all copies of the data will be synchronized and updated with the original data. From this point of view, restoring the altered data is safer and more efficient in the case of a redundant system [61]. These copies also ensure high data accuracy because it is easier for a data management system to identify and evaluate any differences between the original data and their copies.

One of the most used forms of data redundancy is redundant array of independent disks (RAID) [62]. It is used against broken hard disk drives (HDDs) and involves duplicating the information in several locations, which will take over the tasks in case the first HDD breaks down [63]. There are several levels of RAID [64], but the safest and most frequently used in video surveillance systems is RAID1, which involves mirroring devices. This level offers 100% redundancy because it is unnecessary to reconstruct the data, only to copy it.

3.5 Operational procedures

Companies with video surveillance systems must regularly conduct internal audits and systematic reviews of the system to monitor its compliance with the GDPR. In addition, the operators must handle the requests of the people who appear in the videos, such as the right of access, rectification, or deletion of data. Managing a large volume of requests and maintaining a centralized system to track and respond to these requests is an additional challenge for organizations.

One solution companies resort to is forming an internal or external team of experts in personal data protection. This team's role is to monitor the system's compliance with GDPR permanently and update the internal processes constantly. It is also essential that the rest of the operators with access to personal data are periodically trained about GDPR requirements to understand their responsibility to protect personal data and the importance of GDPR compliance in the system they operate.

4. Proposed method

In this section, we propose a software solution that ensures the anonymization of video streams from a surveillance system to ensure compliance with the GDPR. The proposed solution is lightweight and simple from a computational point of view and can be easily attached to a video processing system. In addition, it requires a minimum of additional resources, making it suitable for any application and video system.

4.1 Description

Figure 4 shows the diagram of the proposed solution. The first module is the *video capture device*, which can open any video file stored in a database. The following module is the *software configuration*. The operator can select one or more intervals from the footage where the anonymization is necessary. In addition, he can select a trimming interval to save only a part of the original footage. After making the necessary configurations, the next step is the working mode selection. The surveillance system can use this solution to anonymize a wide range of PII: faces, people, cars, and license plates. Depending on the need, the operator can select one of the three working modes.

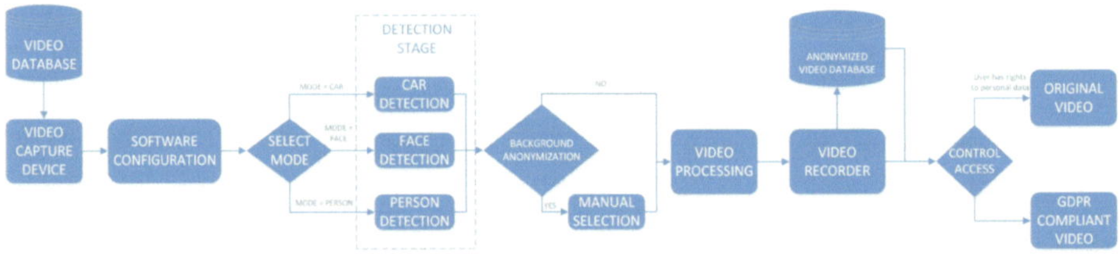

Figure 4.
Diagram of proposed method.

Regarding the *detection stage*, this solution starts from the YOLOv5 [65] detector. This model is based on a convolutional neural network (CNN) and is specially developed for object detection. We preferred this model due to its higher processing speed than other models and its increased accuracy in object detection. In addition, it is an easy model to train to fit the desired scenarios [66]. Using YOLOv5, it was possible to train and obtain a high-performance detector capable of working in real time, generating good results when detecting the classes of interest.

The software solution also ensures the blurring of certain areas or locations considered personal and prohibited by GDPR laws so that the system can be fully adapted to GDPR requirements. The *background anonymization* step involves manually selecting the desired footage areas that are considered sensitive.

Next is the *video processing* module. In this step, the video stream is anonymized according to previous configurations. For anonymization, the solution involves using the method of blurring the original stream. Thus, on each detected or manually selected area, the blurring operation is performed in two simple steps. First, the area of interest is resized to a minimal resolution of the order of 10–1 of its original size. Afterward, the area thus obtained is resized to its initial resolution. In this way, the algorithm blures sensitive information from the video stream, and the final stream complies with GDPR standards. These anonymized flows will be saved in the system database. Subsequently, only authorized operators will be able to access the original streams, while the rest of the operators will only see GDPR-compliant footage.

4.2 Key features

4.2.1 Wide applicability

One of the primary goals during the implementation of this software solution was to have a broad applicability. Therefore, the final solution supports any video format: .mp4, .avi, .mkv, and others. Additionally, depending on the scenario and scope of a video system, the solution can be set to anonymize a wide range of PII, such as faces, people, cars, license plates, or areas and locations. Thus, once attached to the surveillance system, regardless of its field, it can adapt it to comply with GDPR standards.

4.2.2 Simple and lightweight solution

We designed our solution to be simple and lightweight. It uses a straightforward blurring method with minimal computational complexity and a small detector, making it efficient and easy to use.

4.2.3 Real-time solution

One of the noteworthy features considered when implementing this software solution was the time required for processing. In order to minimize the processing time, we take several actions. First of all, the detector used is a real-time detector. Once the detections are obtained, the anonymization method is straightforward from a computational point of view, with insignificant added processing time and computing power. Another method of saving processing time is the possibility of selecting processing intervals. In this way, the whole footage is no longer processed, but only the intervals of interest, drastically reducing the processing time.

4.2.4 Simplify the camera positioning process

According to the rules in force, the installed cameras must minimize access to the public space but also not affect the privacy of other people. It is difficult to find a compromise in the positioning of the cameras so that the system captures the necessary images but ensures the privacy of the citizens. The algorithm offers as a solution the anonymization of public areas or other information that appears in the footage and must be disguised so that cameras can be positioned with a greater level of freedom.

4.2.5 Anonymization of PII

The algorithm ensures the anonymization of all categories considered personal information. **Figure 5** presents a capture of the anonymized flow generated by the algorithm. It can be seen that the algorithm blurred all the faces of the people involved, making them unidentifiable for those who see the footage. In addition, certain areas of the frame were blurred, which were wanted to be kept confidential not to affect the system's GDPR compliance.

4.2.6 Irreversibility

Along with the improvement of anonymization methods, there are also many methods of obtaining the original information from a distorted image. It is essential that the anonymization, once achieved, is an irreversible process to ensure the confidentiality of the data. In the proposed solution, once an area is resized to a very small resolution and then again to the initial resolution, most of the information of the original flow is lost. In this way, the original image cannot be recreated, and the solution ensures the irreversibility of the anonymization process.

4.2.7 Principle of data integrity and confidentiality

The presented solution ensures the principle of data integrity and confidentiality described by GDPR. The stored information will, first of all, be anonymized,

Figure 5.
Video anonymization using our proposed method.

ensuring the confidentiality of the people appearing in the video. In addition, data integrity and confidentiality are ensured by minimizing the access of unauthorized operators to the original data. In this way, only a small number of people have access to personal data, which is in line with GDPR.

5. Conclusions

Given the evolution of video processing technologies and the exponential increase in the volume of stored video data, the video surveillance systems and applications developed must comply with the GDPR standard. A surveillance system collects a considerable volume of personal data, from users' personal information, such as first and last names and IP addresses, to images containing sensitive information. For a system to be compliant with GDPR rules, it must ensure both the encryption of information and the anonymization of video streams.

GDPR was introduced to protect human rights to private life. For this, some basic principles have been described, which must be considered when implementing a system that collects and processes personal data. One of the most important is the principle of legality, which specifies that the data must be collected legally, correctly, and transparently. Any deviation from this principle brings fines up to 20 billion euros. Other important principles are purpose-related and storage limitation, but also limiting the volume of stored data. A final principle is responsibility, for which GDPR introduced the position of DPO. The DPO is entrusted with the essential task of ensuring GDPR compliance of the entire system, a responsibility that cannot be taken lightly. Finally, several GDPR articles stipulate the need for data encryption, which brings one of the most important principles of GDPR: the obligation of data processors to ensure data integrity and confidentiality.

Along with the evolution of security systems and techniques, cyberattack frequency has also increased. That is why surveillance systems must implement various security techniques to limit the access of unauthorized persons to the system. Symmetric and asymmetric key encryption techniques (AES, RSA) have been proven effective for securing static information from surveillance cameras and storage spaces. To secure the flow of information while it is transmitted over the network, systems must use secure transport protocols, such as TLS/SSL, HTTPS (for transmitting confidential data, camera configurations, and video stream), or SRTP (for transmitting the video stream). Finally, any video system must use an X.509 certificate, a digital passport that provides proof of identity to a website or server. Simultaneously, using these techniques secures personal data, ensuring the system's GDPR compliance.

In addition to system security, data anonymization is equally critical. The anonymization process involves the detection of information that is considered sensitive (faces, cars, license plates, and locations) and their anonymization using the various available methods such as pixelation, masking, or deep-learning techniques that are considered irreversible and, therefore, safer.

The method proposed in this chapter is a method of anonymizing personal data and can ensure compliance with GDPR in any situation. The developed application has several working modes, detecting and anonymizing people's faces, persons, and license plates, depending on the system's needs. In addition, the application also ensures the anonymization of other areas or places considered sensitive in the footage by manually selecting those areas. We presented a simple software solution from a computational and lightweight point of view, which ensures irreversible anonymization of the video stream and all categories of information considered personal. Once integrated into the video system, it complies with the GDPR rules and can ensure the confidentiality of stored video streams.

This chapter presented the need for the emergence of the GDPR regulation and the urgency of ensuring compliance with the rules in force. In addition, the technologies and algorithms that must be implemented in the video surveillance system in order for it to adapt to GDPR principles were presented in detail. Video surveillance systems and applications developed in video analytics have the responsibility to align with the GDPR standard and to protect people's rights and sensitive and personal data.

Acknowledgements

This research was partially supported by the Romanian Ministry of Research, Innovation and Digitalization under Romanian National Core Program LAPLAS VII - contract no. 30 N/2023 and by the Executive Agency for Higher Education, Research, Development and Innovation, UEFISCDI, contract no. 9Sol(T9)/2024 and no 5Sol(T5).

Author details

Roxana Elena Mihaescu[1], Marian Ghenescu[1,2*] and Serban Carata[1]

1 Softrust Vision Analytics, Bucharest, Roumania

2 Institute of Space Science, Magurele, Roumania

*Address all correspondence to: marian.ghenescu@softrust.ro

IntechOpen

© 2024 The Author(s). Licensee IntechOpen. This chapter is distributed under the terms of the Creative Commons Attribution License (http://creativecommons.org/licenses/by/4.0), which permits unrestricted use, distribution, and reproduction in any medium, provided the original work is properly cited.

References

[1] Tsakanikas V, Dagiuklas T. Video surveillance systems-current status and future trends. Computers & Electrical Engineering. 2018;**70**:736-753

[2] Karishma VR, Vigneswaran T. Artificial Intelligence in Video Surveillance. In: Handbook of Research on Deep Learning Techniques for Cloud-Based Industrial IoT. Pennsylvania, USA: IGI Global; 2023. pp. 1-17

[3] Haering N, Venetianer PL, Lipton A. The evolution of video surveillance: An overview. Machine Vision and Applications. 2008;**19**(5):279-290

[4] Popovic G et al. Overview, characteristics and advantages of IP camera video surveillance systems compared to systems with other kinds of camera. International Journal of Engineering Science and Innovative Technology. 2013;**2**(5):356-362

[5] Digital Camera Market Size, Share & Growth Report, 2030. Available from: https://www.grandviewresearch.com/industry-analysis/digital-camera-industry [Accessed: September 12, 2024]

[6] CCTV Camera Market Size, Share, and Trends 2024 to 2033. Available from: https://www.precedenceresearch.com/cctv-camera-market [Accessed: September 12, 2024]

[7] Global Video Surveillance Market. Available from: https://www.skyquestt.com/report/video-surveillance-market [Accessed: September 12, 2024]

[8] Vennam P et al. Attacks and preventive measures on video surveillance systems: A review. Applied Sciences. 2021;**11**(12):5571

[9] Mills JL, Harclerode K. Privacy, mass intrusion, and the modern data breach. Florida Law Review. 2017;**69**:771

[10] Cheng L, Liu F, Yao D. Enterprise data breach: Causes, challenges, prevention, and future directions. Wiley Interdisciplinary Reviews: Data Mining and Knowledge Discovery. 2017;**7**(5):e1211

[11] Blitz MJ. Video surveillance and the constitution of public space: Fitting the fourth amendment to a world that tracks image and identity. Texas Law Review. 2003;**82**:1349

[12] Asghar MN et al. Visual surveillance within the EU general data protection regulation: A technology perspective. IEEE Access. 2019;**7**:111709-111726

[13] Barnoviciu E et al. Gdpr compliance in video surveillance and video processing application. In: 2019 International Conference on Speech Technology and Human-Computer Dialogue (SpeD). Timisoara, Romania: IEEE; 2019

[14] Cliza C, Olanescu S, Olanescu A. Video surveillance: Standpoint of the eu and national legislation on data protection. In: 2018 12th International Conference Challenges of the Knowledge Society, Bucharest, Romania; 2018. pp. 465-471

[15] United Nations. General Assembly. Universal Declaration of Human Rights. Vol. 3381. United States of America: Department of State; 1949

[16] Elgesem D. The structure of rights in directive 95/46/EC on the protection of individuals with regard to the processing of personal data

and the free movement of such data. Ethics and Information Technology. 1999;**1**(4):283-293

[17] Poullet Y. About the E-Privacy Directive: Towards a Third Generation of Data Protection Legislation? Data Protection in a Profiled World. Dordrecht: Springer Netherlands; 2010. pp. 3-30

[18] Regulation (EU) 2016/679 of the European Parliament and of the Council of 27 April 2016. Available from: https://eur-lex.europa.eu/legal-content/EN/TXT/PDF/?uri=CELEX:32016R0679 [Accessed: September 2, 2024]

[19] GDPR Recitals. Available from: https://gdpr-info.eu/recitals/ [Accessed: September 2, 2024]

[20] Zaeem RN, Suzanne Barber K. The effect of the GDPR on privacy policies: Recent progress and future promise. ACM Transactions on Management Information Systems (TMIS). 2020;**12**(1):1-20

[21] Elena GG, De Hert P. Understanding the legal provisions that allow processing and profiling of personal data—An analysis of GDPR provisions and principles. In: ERA Forum. Vol. 19. No. 4. Berlin, Germany: Springer; 2019. pp. 597-621

[22] Forgó N, Hänold S, Schütze B. The principle of purpose limitation and big data. In: New Technology, Big Data and the Law. Berlin, Germany: Springer; 2017. pp. 17-42

[23] Biega AJ et al. Operationalizing the legal principle of data minimization for personalization. In: Proceedings of the 43rd International ACM SIGIR Conference on Research and Development in Information Retrieval. New York, USA: Association for Computing Machinery; 2020

[24] Hallinan D, Borgesius FZ. Opinions can be incorrect (in our opinion)! On data protection law's accuracy principle. International Data Privacy Law. 2020;**10**(1):1-10

[25] Caruccio L et al. GDPR compliant information confidentiality preservation in big data processing. IEEE Access. 2020;**8**:205034-205050

[26] Preece R. The GDPR accountability principle and the use of scenario workshops in the digital age. Journal of Data Protection & Privacy. 2018;**2**(1):34-40

[27] Lambert P. The Data Protection Officer: Profession, Rules, and Role. Florida, USA: CRC Press; 2016

[28] GDPR Enforcement Tracker Report. Available from: https://cms.law/en/int/publication/gdpr-enforcement-tracker-report/numbers-and-figures [Accessed: September 12, 2024]

[29] Kalbo N et al. The security of ip-based video surveillance systems. Sensors. 2020;**20**(17):4806

[30] Bin H et al. Research on video surveillance security system based on domestic password. In: 2023 5th International Conference on Electronic Engineering and Informatics (EEI). Wuhan, China: IEEE; 2023

[31] Abomhara M, Zakaria O, Khalifa OO. An overview of video encryption techniques. International Journal of Computer Theory and Engineering. 2010;**2**(1):1793-8201

[32] Massoudi A et al. Overview on selective encryption of image and video: Challenges and perspectives. EURASIP

Journal on Information Security. 2008;**2008**(1):179290

[33] Saleh MA et al. An analysis and comparison for popular video encryption algorithms. In: 2015 IEEE Symposium on Computer Applications & Industrial Electronics (ISCAIE). Langkawi, Kedah, Malaysia: IEEE; 2015

[34] Buhari BA et al. Performance evaluation of symmetric data encryption algorithms: AES and blowfish. Saudi Journal of Engineering and Technology. 2019;**4**(10):407-414

[35] Nechvatal J et al. Report on the development of the advanced encryption standard (AES). Journal of Research of the National Institute of Standards and Technology. 2001;**106**(3):511

[36] Abdullah AM. Advanced encryption standard (AES) algorithm to encrypt and decrypt data. Cryptography and Network Security. 2017;**16**(1):11

[37] Lanjewar R, Pande G. Implementation of AES-256 Bit: A Review. Inventi Rapid: Information Security; 2015

[38] Andriani R, Wijayanti SE, Wibowo FW. Comparsion of AES 128, 192 and 256 bit algorithm for encryption and description file. In: 3rd International Conference on Information Technology. IEEE: Information System and Electrical Engineering (ICITISEE); 2018. p. 2018

[39] Pub, F. I. P. S. Data encryption standard (des). NIPS Gaithersburg, MD, USA: FIPS PUB; 1999:46-43

[40] Mousa A. Data encryption performance based on blowfish. In: 47th International Symposium ELMAR. Zadar, Croatia: IEEE; 2005

[41] Schneier B. The Twofish encryption algorithm. Dr. Dobb's Journal: Software Tools for the Professional Programmer. 1998;**23**(12):30-34

[42] Zhou X, Tang X. Research and implementation of RSA algorithm for encryption and decryption. In: Proceedings of 2011 6th International Forum on Strategic Technology. Vol. 2. Harbin, Heilongjiang, China: IEEE; 2011

[43] Dierks Tim, Christopher Allen. The TLS protocol version 1.0. No. rfc2246. 1999

[44] Hickman Kipp, Taher Elgamal. The SSL protocol. (1995): 501

[45] Danezis George. Traffic Analysis of the HTTP Protocol over TLS. CiteSeer, Pennsylvania, USA. 2009

[46] Fielding Roy et al. Hypertext transfer protocol–HTTP/1.1. No. rfc2616. 1999

[47] Schulzrinne Henning et al. RFC3550: RTP: A transport protocol for real-time applications. 2003

[48] Baugher Mark et al. The secure real-time transport protocol (SRTP). No. rfc3711. 2004

[49] Gerck Edgardo. Overview of Certification Systems: x. 509, CA, PGP and SKIP. 1997

[50] Cuimei L et al. Human face detection algorithm via Haar cascade classifier combined with three additional classifiers. In: 2017 13th IEEE International Conference on Electronic Measurement & Instruments (ICEMI). Yangzhou, China: IEEE; 2017

[51] Lv Zhifeng. Face detection based on cascading support vector machines. In: Machine Learning

Theory and Practice. Vol. 3. London, United Kingdom: Scholar Publishing Group; 2022. pp. 36-43

[52] Qi D et al. YOLO5Face: Why reinventing a face detector. In: European Conference on Computer Vision. Cham: Springer Nature Switzerland; 2022

[53] Astawa INGA, et al. Detection of license plate using sliding window, histogram of oriented gradient, and support vector machines method. In: Journal of Physics: Conference Series. Vol. 953. Bristol, United Kingdom: IOP Publishing; 2018. pp. 012-062

[54] Wang Y et al. License plate recognition based on SIFT feature. Optik. 2015;**126**(21):2895-2901

[55] Kurpiel FD, Minetto R, Nassu BT. Convolutional neural networks for license plate detection in images. In: 2017 IEEE International Conference on Image Processing (ICIP). Beijing, China: IEEE; 2017

[56] Thomas RE, Banu SK, Tripathy BK. Image anonymization using clustering with pixelization. International Journal of Engineering &Technology. 2018;7:990-993

[57] Badgujar P. Implementing data masking techniques for privacy protection. In: Journal of Technological Innovations. Vol. 2. No. 4. Karnataka, India; 2021. Available from: https://jtipublishing.com/jti/article/view/36 [Accessed: September 16, 2024]

[58] Piacentino E, Angulo C. Anonymizing personal images using generative adversarial networks. In: International Work-Conference on Bioinformatics and Biomedical Engineering. Cham: Springer International Publishing; 2020

[59] Park S et al. Characterizing the impacts of VPN security models on streaming video. In: 2010 8th Annual Communication Networks and Services Research Conference. Montreal, Canada: IEEE; 2010

[60] Bari A, Samrin R, Khare A. VPC & public cloud optimal performance in cloud environment. Educational Administration: Theory and Practice. 2024;**30**(6):1789-1798

[61] Liu Y, Claypool M. Using redundancy to repair video damaged by network data loss. In: Multimedia Computing and Networking 2000. Vol. 3969. 1999. pp. 73-84

[62] Chen PM et al. RAID: High-performance, reliable secondary storage. ACM Computing Surveys (CSUR). 1994;**26**(2):145-185

[63] Patterson DA, Gibson G, Katz RH. A case for redundant arrays of inexpensive disks (RAID). In: Proceedings of the 1988 ACM SIGMOD International Conference on Management of Data. New York, USA: Association for Computing Machinery; 1988. pp. 109-116

[64] Shinde, Pallavi Babasaheb, Ms Santoshi Pote, and Ms Shreya Bokare. Evaluation of Performance Parameters of Commodity Storage Cluster using RAID

[65] Jocker Glenn. Ultralytics YOLOv5. Available from: https://github.com/ultralytics/yolov5 [Accessed: September 16, 2024]

[66] Solawetz Jacob. What is YOLOv5? A guide for beginners. Available from: https://blog.roboflow.com/yolov5-improvements-and-evaluation/ [Accessed: September 16, 2024]

Section 3

Deep Learning and Neural Networks

Chapter 6

Efficient DNN Algorithm Design and Hardware Acceleration for Low-Level Vision

Wendong Mao, Siyu Zhang and Zhongfeng Wang

Abstract

Deep learning has garnered widespread attention in low-level vision tasks due to its automatic feature learning capabilities. However, high computational complexity and memory requirements hinder deployment at the edge. This chapter provides a top-down solution for efficiently implementing intelligent image and video computing across algorithm, hardware, and deployment levels. Firstly, we design high-accuracy DNN algorithms for specific visual tasks, exemplified by the first text style transfer algorithm using complex image features. Secondly, we explore hardware-friendly algorithm optimizations and design efficient DNN hardware accelerators for typical visual applications such as image generation, video compression, and super-resolution. Thirdly, we introduce a precision-scalable computing method and an agile hardware mapping framework to achieve efficient deployment of algorithms. We unify convolution, deconvolution, and deformable convolution into an input-adaptive deformable convolution and design a versatile accelerator for various image enhancement tasks. Finally, we provide extensive experimental results to validate the effectiveness of the proposed hardware acceleration solutions.

Keywords: hardware design, deep learning, low-level vision tasks, image processing, video processing

1. Introduction

With the development of information technology, Artificial Intelligence (AI) has deeply permeated many aspects of human society. AI technologies have penetrated and integrated into various fields of the economy and society. The new formats, models, and products related to AI have been achieved in multiple fields such as healthcare, finance, security, transportation, logistics, industrial IoT, and more. Due to its outstanding performance, deep learning has become a significant driving force in the current development of AI, attracting attention from research institutions and industries worldwide.

In recent years, with the rise of the short video industry and 5G era, human-generated data has shown explosive growth. The abundant data provides a solid foundation for the further development of AI and increases the demand for image and video processing tasks. For example, images captured by security cameras at night have significantly lower quality compared to images taken in well-lit conditions, necessitating low-light enhancement techniques to improve image visibility. Similarly, medical images captured under endoscopes may lack clarity, requiring image super-resolution (SR) techniques to generate clear pictures. There is also an urgent need for tasks such as the transmission and storage of large-capacity videos. However, traditional visual analysis and understanding techniques are no longer sufficient to meet the demands of the modern visual imaging world, and the introduction of deep learning algorithms for image and video processing tasks such as low-light enhancement, SR, video compression, and depth estimation has become a prevailing trend. To achieve better performance, people tend to adopt deeper neural networks to carry out retrieval and processing of massive visual information. In addition, new DNNs are continuously being developed, with algorithm scales and complexities steadily increasing.

Figure 1 summarizes the typical applications of deep learning, common forms of input data, and types of DNN models. Common models include Convolutional Neural Networks (CNN), Generative Adversarial Networks (GAN), Deformable Convolutional Networks (DCN), Transformers, Graph Neural Networks (GNN), and others. A growing variety of data from different modalities can now be analyzed and processed, such as images, videos, text, language, graph structures, point cloud data, etc.

In general, due to their large number of parameters, DNNs have longer computation times on CPUs, which restricts the possibility of real-time deployment. DNN models like SRCNN, FSRCNN, and VDSR [1] have significantly higher average computation times on Central Processing Units (CPUs) compared to GPUs. Therefore, most CNN-based algorithms are currently implemented using Graphics Processing Units (GPUs). GPUs greatly enhance the speed of CNN-based algorithms compared to CPUs, but the abundant computational resources of GPUs come with significant power consumption. Therefore, for platforms with limited hardware resources and power constraints, GPUs are not the best choice. The Analyses from OpenAI indicate that the computational power required for AI training tasks has grown exponentially since 2012, doubling roughly every 3.5 months. In contrast, Moore's Law doubles

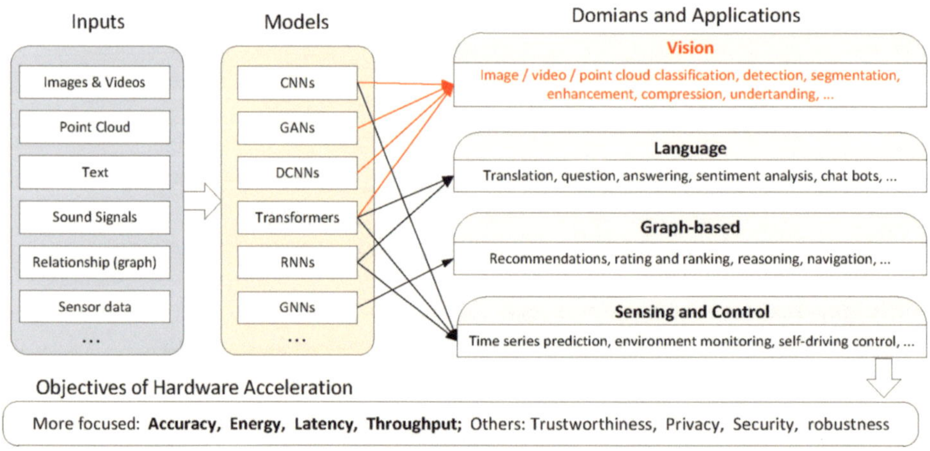

Figure 1.
Summaries of various AI application domains and their commonly used DNN models.

every 18 months. Since 2012, the demand for computational power has increased by over 300,000 times, compared to a 12-fold increase following Moore's Law. The compute and storage-intensive networks directly pose severe challenges for low-power and low-latency deployments in practical applications. In modern society, visual information systems are prevalent in various fields such as industry, daily life, and education.

With the rise of new generation AI technologies like Transformers and generative large models [2], DNNs are playing an increasingly important role in image and video processing tasks, including tasks such as style transfer, enhancement, compression of images and videos. These tasks are widely applied in visual devices in fields such as intelligent robots, digital twins, autonomous driving, virtual reality, and others. Hence, designing AI hardware accelerators for real-time embedded systems has become crucial. To address the issues from algorithm design to practical deployment of DNNs, designing high-precision visual algorithms and developing efficient hardware architectures that meet platform constraints, is one of the significant research topics in the current field of intelligence vision.

2. Recent development of low-level vision acceleration

This section briefly introduces and analyzes the differences and optimization opportunities between low-level vision tasks, such as compression, SR, and depth estimation, and high-level vision tasks, such as image classification and object detection, in terms of algorithms, hardware, and deployment. These comparisons aim to inspire the motivations behind researches into low-level vision acceleration.

In the field of SR, some advanced solutions to implement high-speed and low-power edge deployments for SR models are being gradually exploited. In Chang [3], the deconvolution (DeConv) operation, which was widely employed in SR algorithms, was converted to convolution (Conv) operations by a load balance-aware method. The designed SR system achieved promising energy efficiency for various upsampling factors. Kim *et al.* [4] developed a hardware-friendly SR method by stacking 1D Convs and depthwise separable Convs to reduce model complexity and maintain large receptive fields. They also designed effective fixed-point quantization and feature map compression strategies to save memory resource overhead. To further solve video super-resolution (VSR) task, Sun *et al.* [5] extracted temporal information by an FPGA-based recurrent CNN model to improve the temporal consistency for multiple video frames. Meanwhile, low-cost operations, normalization, and quantization were also incorporated to reduce the model complexity.

For image and video compression, due to the inherent conflict between the computational complexity of advanced neural codecs and the limited resource of mobile devices, realizing energy-efficient and high-quality image and video compression is non-trivial. To achieve efficient neural image codecs, FPX-NIC [6] extended the image compression task from software-based to FPGA-based lossy compression. The proposed system effectively accelerates the image encoding and decoding process extremely. Video compression is a more computationally intensive process than image compression. Once a video is encoded, the encoded bitstream can be transmitted to multiple mobile devices and decoded multiple times, ensuring that users can watch it anytime, anywhere. To address this issue, Rozendaal *et al.* [7] developed an efficient neural inter-frame video decoder working on a commercial mobile phone. However, relying solely on algorithmic optimizations may lead to inefficient utilization of hardware resources, resulting in a waste of performance advantages. So far, achieving high-performance video compression on embedded and mobile devices remains a hot research topic in the field of multimedia technology.

Designing dedicated stereo vision accelerators is crucial for enhancing the overall performance of robotic system. Many studies have proposed efficient solutions to improve processing speed and energy efficiency. For example, Dadu-Eye [8] constructed a cost volume and estimated optical flow by traditional methods, followed by using learnable encoders and decoders to extract depth information. However, it is limited by the reliance on handcrafted features and independent module designs, resulting in bad fault tolerance. Moreover, operations in hybrid depth estimation frameworks include not only DNN operations like Conv, pooling, and DeConv but also traditional methods' operations such as Census transform and Hamming distance. Therefore, it is necessary to allocate hardware resources separately and conduct independent designs to support these incompatible operations. Besides, most stereo vision accelerators utilize high-precision multiply-accumulate (MAC) units to perform all computations. While these precision-fixed accelerators can meet the worst-case bitwidth requirements, it faces under-utilization of computational resources. In fact, the bitwidth can be adjusted individually for each layer in the stereo-matching networks to achieve an optimal balance between bitwidth and matching score.

Compared to plain models designed for high-level tasks such as image classification and object detection, low-level vision models face numerous challenges when deployed on resource-constrained mobile devices. These challenges include: (1) Low-level vision models typically feature a topology comprising multiple independent modules and intricate connections, resulting in irregular data dependencies and extensive memory access. (2) Low-level vision models integrate a variety of heterogeneous operations, such as Convs, DeConvs, deformable convolutions (DfConvs), and attention mechanisms. The diversity of operations may lead to severe memory conflicts and computational imbalances. (3) In contrast to high-level vision models that predict semantic labels, low-level vision models reconstruct visual contents at the pixel level, making them highly sensitive to model compression techniques like light-weight structures, pruning, and quantization. (4) In practical applications, there is an increasing demand for real-time processing of high-definition (HD) and ultra-high-definition (UHD) images or videos, leading to significant data transmission pressures due to the high-resolution intermediate feature maps in low-level vision models.

In summary, the stringent requirements for resource usage, latency, energy efficiency, and visual quality highlight the importance of joint optimization across algorithms, hardware, and deployment for accelerating low-level vision models.

3. High-precision visual algorithm design

3.1 The coarse-to-fine framework for text style transfer

This section will focus on the aspect of visual algorithms and describe an example of high-precision visual algorithm design. In the field of image processing, style transfer involves transferring the style of a source image to a target image, and it is widely used in artistic design. Text style transfer is an important subtopic of style transfer, used for generating artistic fonts. Existing works only can transfer simple image features and control the scale of style to a limited extent. However, complex and intricate image features commonly used in artistic design, are challenging to transform into artistic fonts using current stylized text generation methods [9–11]. However, in the field of image processing, complex but exquisite image features have significant application demands in various areas of artistic design, while existing issues in font style transfer methods face difficulties in mapping style features, limited specialized datasets, and other key problems.

To address this issue, [12] has designed the first academic style transfer algorithm tailored to complex image features, aiming to generate refined artistic fonts with intricate textures and structures in an unsupervised manner. In addition, the method can achieve real-time control over multiple style scales. The key idea of [12] is to decompose the entire task into two steps: prototype generation and detail refinement, employing dedicated networks for each step to learn features at different levels. By cleverly combining structural characteristics of texture extrapolation and image SR reconstruction networks, the proposed framework significantly reduces the task difficulty of network learning.

The algorithm framework proposed by [12] transfers style into the targeted texts from coarse to fine granularity, as illustrated in **Figure 2**. It decomposes the style transfer task into two subtasks: (1) artistic font prototype generation and (2) image detail optimization. As shown in **Figure 2**, the generation of artistic font prototypes is modeled by a newly designed GAN model, namely pro-gen GAN (G_p), which generates a coarse stylized font from a given binary mask and clipped texture. The second subtask is executed by the Structure Network (N_s) and the Texture Network (N_t), which refine the structural and textural features meticulously. This algorithm framework extracts style features at multiple levels through these three networks, allowing each network to focus on specific levels to sequentially accomplish the overall transfer task. Due to the lack of text-effect datasets with paired data, the framework also introduces a one-shot learning method for unsupervised training. During the training steps, preprocessing of style images (Y) and binary masks (M) generates paired data, which are then used to update G_p in reverse. Subsequently, N_s is trained using a

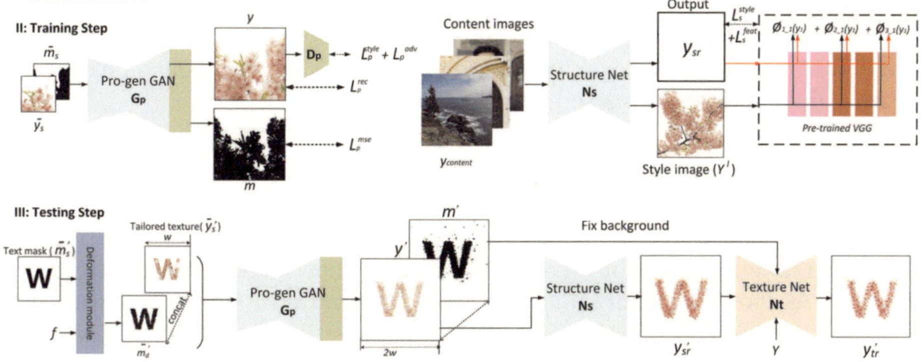

Figure 2.
Overview of the coarse-to-fine framework in [12].

general image dataset to learn the ability for structural refinement. In the testing steps, the text mask is provided to a deformable module to adjust different style scales, obtaining masked and styled images with specific style scales, which are then fed into the networks G_p, N_s, and N_t to perform forward style transfer.

In the context of style controllability, a concise style controllable module has been proposed, enabling a smooth transition of font styles from condensed to flowing without the need to retrain the network. During the detail refinement process, two networks are introduced to refine texture and structural details. Additionally, a training scheme with a hybrid attention mechanism has been proposed, allowing the network to learn more natural and comprehensive image features from different dimensions.

3.2 Visual result of the proposed framework

Figure 3 presents a qualitative comparison with five state-of-the-art methods: NST [13], T-effect [9], TET-GAN [10], Shape-Matching GAN [11], and UT-Effect [14]. Experimental results demonstrate that this method can generate artistic text with complex styles, surpassing existing research significantly in terms of texture, contours, and other visual effects.

At the same time, it can be seen that to address complex visual tasks, such as the mapping issue of complex texture structures mentioned in [11], more networks and deeper computational structures are being introduced, leading to an increase in algorithm processing time and the subsequent demand for computational acceleration. The characteristics of using various Conv operators have also sparked considerations for hardware acceleration design.

4. Algorithm and hardware co-optimization for low-level vision

4.1 Hardware acceleration for generative adversarial network

In recent years, GANs have been widely applied in the visual domain for tasks such as image and video generation, encoding and decoding, style transfer, and more, due to their superior performance. GAN models usually contain numerous DeConv operations, and involve a large amount of redundant computation, increasing computational complexity. However, the high computational complexity and parameter counts of GAN models, make it challenging to efficiently deploy them on hardware devices with limited resources and power constraints.

4.1.1 The proposed fast transformation algorithm

In [15], a widely used GAN model in visual generation tasks, a mathematical analysis and deconstruction of the abundant DeConv operators in the model were conducted. As shown in **Figure 4**, a highly universal fast transformation algorithm (FTA) was proposed for network computation acceleration, featuring concise preprocessing and postprocessing parameters that significantly reduce the corresponding hardware overhead. The two-dimensional transformation formula is shown as Eq. (1). This algorithm can reduce the complexity of the original operations

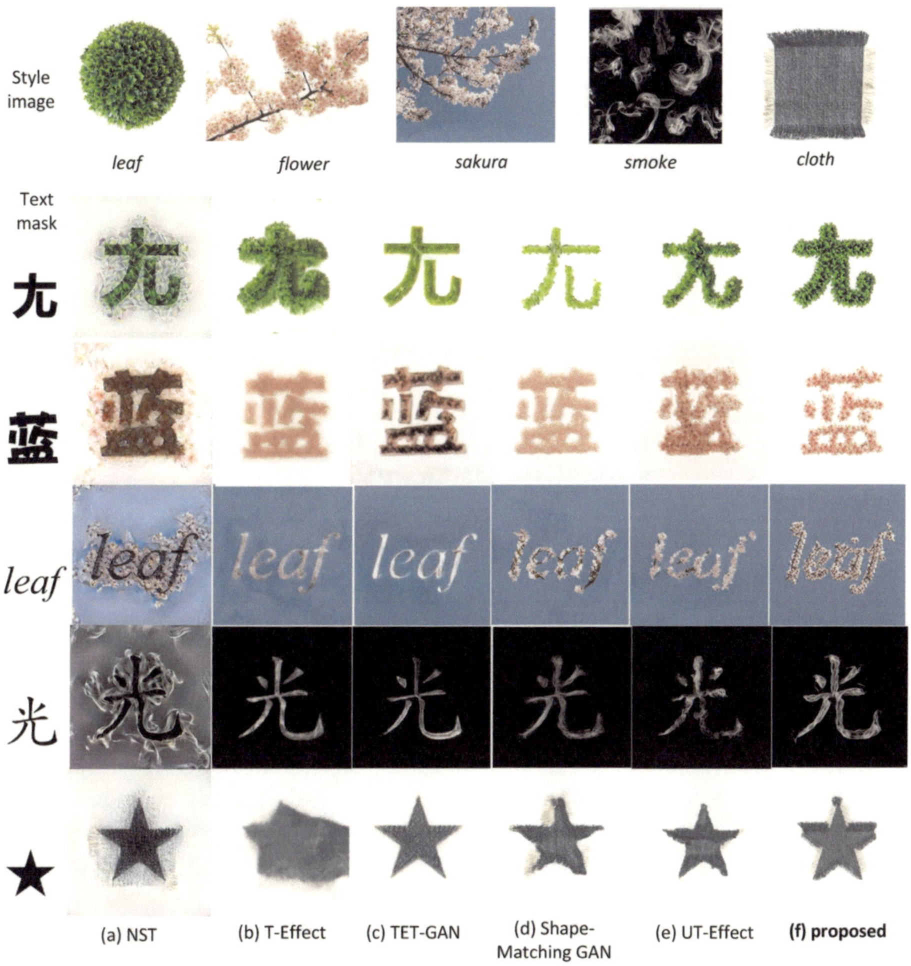

Figure 3.
Qualitative comparison with existing methods under different styles in [12]. (a) NST, (b) T-Effect, (c) TET-GAN, (d) Shape-Matching GAN, (e) UT-Effect, (f) proposed.

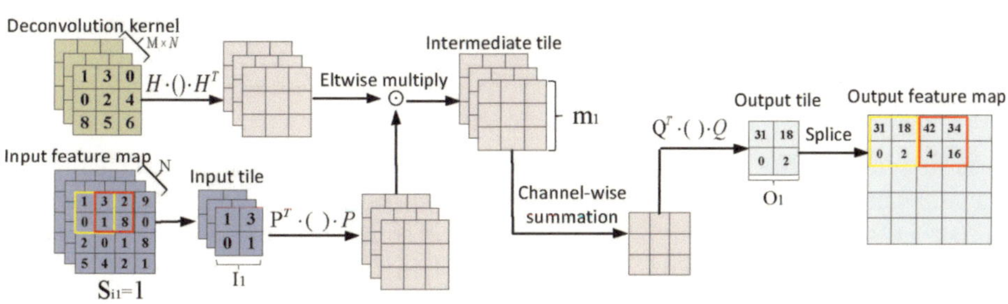

Figure 4.
Example of a fast transformation algorithm for DeConv in [15], where the DeConv kernel size is 3 and the step size is 2. The zeros inserted in the input feature map have been removed, and the blue pixels represent valid inputs.

by approximately half under the premise of algorithmic equivalence. A comparison of the computational complexity before and after applying this algorithm to DeConv operators of different sizes can be listed in **Table 1**.

	K3S2	K4S2	K5S2	K9S2	K5S3	K9S4
CPU-based	9	16	25	81	25	81
IOM [16]	2.25	4	6.25	20.25	9	5.0625
TDC [17]	4	4	9	25	9	9
Win-T [18]	1.78	1.77	4	11.11	4	4
1-FT ($ACOX_1$)	2.25	4	6.25	20.25	2.77	5.0625
2-FT ($ACOX_2$)	1.5625	2.25	3.06	7.5625	1.78	2.64

Table 1.
The comparison with computational complexity, where r-FT denotes the r-order FTA.

$$\mathbf{Y} = \mathbf{A}^{\mathrm{T}}\left[\left(\mathbf{H}\cdot\mathbf{g}\cdot\mathbf{H}^{\mathrm{T}}\right)\odot\left(\mathbf{P}^{\mathrm{T}}\cdot\mathbf{d}\cdot\mathbf{P}\right)\right]\mathbf{A}. \tag{1}$$

In addition to significantly reducing computational complexity, the algorithm also possesses multiple advantages, including:

- The algorithm does not generate overlapping parts during computation, eliminating the need for storing intermediate results, thus reducing memory requirements.

- It offers a universal block-balanced allocation scheme designed for various DeConv computations, ensuring an equal number of multiply and add calculations for each batch of data. The scheme completely resolves the issue of resource wastage due to computational imbalances present in existing methods.

- The algorithm has the simplest preprocessing parameters among published works to date, minimizing the hardware complexity of the accelerator. Based on this algorithm, an efficient hardware architecture, with a storage scheme with block-wise ping-pong storage scheme, is designed to perform different GAN models, such as EB-GAN, DCGAN, and GP-GAN.

4.1.2 Implementation result

As shown in **Table 2**, the experimental results show that work [15] can achieve 2211 GOPs under 185 MHz, surpassing previous works in various aspects notably. It is estimated that approximately 50.9% of arithmetic computing resources in regular DeConv with a 5×5 kernel can be saved by applying FTA. FTA produces up to 3× performance improvement over other works. Compared with the works using the DeConv splitting method [19], the design avoids computation imbalance and reduces computation complexity, which obtains 1.8× speedup than their designs. Compared to the state-of-the-art GAN hardware accelerators, the proposed accelerator can improve computational efficiency by 2 to 20×. This work addresses the critical issue of deploying computationally intensive GAN algorithms on chips, advancing the efficient deployment and practical applications of computer vision tasks.

	[19]	[20]	[21]	[21]	**Proposed**
Year	2020	2019	2020	2020	2020
Model	FSRCNN	DCGAN	DCGAN EBGAN ArtGAN	DCGAN WGAN EBGAN	DCGAN
Frequency	130 MHz	200 MHz	200 MHz	167 MHz	185 MHz
Precision	13bit	16-8bit	16bit	16bit	12-8bit
DSP Usage	1512	576	2520	900	1568
Multipliers	2326	576	2520	900	3136
Logic Utilization	167 k(LUTs) 158 k(FFs)	22 k(LUTs) 20 k(FFs)	265.8 k(LUTs) -(FFs)	197.7 k(LUTs) -(FFs)	69.3 k (in ALMs)
BRAM Usage	0.9Mbyte	0.8307Mbyte	0.3610Mbyte	1.36Mbyte	1.15Mbyte
performance (GOPS)	1184.84	205.95	639.2	162.5	2211.1

Table 2.
The comparison with traditional GAN accelerator.

4.2 Neural video compression

The rapid growth of video requires efficient compression to reduce transmission and memory costs. Several standards have been established, but they struggle with complex textures and fast motions, lacking versatility for diverse scenarios. Recent years have seen the rise of advanced neural video compression (NVC) models [22] that integrate DNNs into traditional methods and achieve impressive compression efficiency. However, NVC models face many challenges in real-time deployment due to irregular data dependencies from multiple modules, computational imbalances from complex operations, sensitivity to model compression methods, and transmission burdens from real-time HD video processing. Thus, it is necessary to enhance NVC performance and deployability on resource-limited devices. In this section, we propose a sparse NVC model by combining the pruning and fast algorithms and develop a dedicated hardware architecture.

4.2.1 Sparse NVC network

As shown in **Figure 5**, all stages in the NVC model execute in the latent space to achieve accurate motion estimation and compensation. In the feature extraction stage, the current frame X_t and the reference frame $\hat{X}_{t-1}$ are transformed from the pixel space to the latent space by several stacked Convs and produce frame representations F_t and F_{t-1}. To analyze the inter-frame motion relationships, the motion estimation stage learns motion vectors O_t and compresses redundant temporal information between F_t and F_{t-1}. In the motion compression and compensation stages, O_t is encoded in a lossy way by an auto-encoder style network. Then, the encoded motion information is quantized and formed as bitstreams. After that, the reconstructed motion feature $\hat{O}_t$ is compensated for F_{t-1}, and the predicted frame feature $\overline{F}_t$ is generated. Although the spatial positions of $\overline{F}_t$ and F_t have one-to-one correspondences, there is still prediction error due to intrinsic differences such as color and brightness. Thus, the residual feature R_t is encoded to ensure highly compressed video

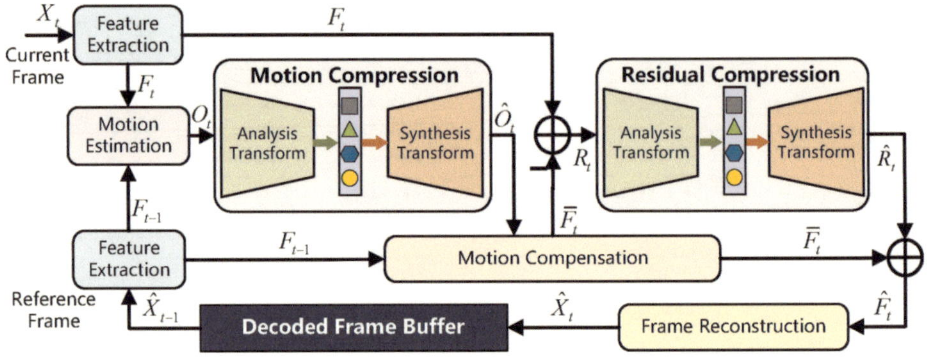

Figure 5.
Visualization of the entire process for the end-to-end NVC network.

quality in the residual compression stage. Combining the reconstructed residual feature $\hat{R}_t$ with $\overline{F}_t$, the reconstructed feature $\hat{F}_t$ is deducted and transformed from the feature space to the pixel space, and the compressed frame $\hat{X}_t$ is restored and saved in the decoded frame buffer.

Considering that substantial computational resources are needed to achieve high processing speeds for NVC, this work aims to reduce the computational complexity of NVC model through a dual approach combining weight pruning and fast algorithms. In specific, the differences between Conv and DeConv operations make concurrent acceleration challenging, a unified pruning strategy based on fast algorithms is proposed to reduce complexity. Inspired by Winograd algorithm [23] and FTA [15], the fast Conv and DeConv can be expressed by *a common formula*:

$$\mathbf{V} = \mathbf{A}^{\mathrm{T}}\left[\left(\mathbf{GWG}^{\mathrm{T}}\right)\odot\left(\mathbf{B}^{\mathrm{T}}\mathbf{XB}\right)\right]\mathbf{A}, \tag{2}$$

where **X**, **W**, and **V** denote the input, weight, and output patch, respectively. $\odot$ signifies the Hadamard product, and **A**, **B** and **G** are transform matrices. Instead of calculating each element in the output feature map separately, fast algorithms exploit structural similarities to produce output patches, significantly lowering the computational complexity for both Convs and DeConvs.

Next, a mask matrix **M** is created based on a predefined sparsity ρ to identify the redundant weights in the transform domain. Subsequently, the sparse Conv and DeConv operations can both be expressed as follows:

$$\mathbf{V} = \mathbf{A}^{\mathrm{T}}\left[\left(\mathbf{M}\odot\mathbf{GWG}^{\mathrm{T}}\right)\odot\left(\mathbf{B}^{\mathrm{T}}\mathbf{XB}\right)\right]\mathbf{A}. \tag{3}$$

4.2.2 Hardware architecture for NVC

Figure 6 illustrates the designed NVC accelerator, which comprises a Sparse Fast Transform Core (SFTC), a DfConv Core (DCC), and a Global Controller. The SFTC performs reconfigurable sparse fast Convs and DeConvs of the NVC model in a time-multiplexed manner. The Preprocessing Unit array (PreU array), Postprocessing Unit array (PostU array), and united Sparse Computation Unit array (SCU array) handle domain transforms and the Hadamard product of valid data, respectively. In terms of memory resource management, the Weight and Index Buffers store non-zero weights and their corresponding indices, while the Input Buffer is reused to store inputs and

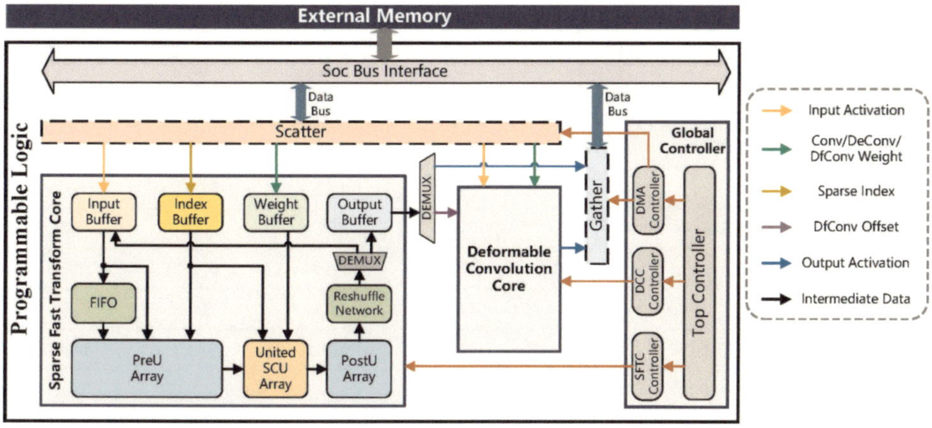

Figure 6.
Top-level block diagram of the NVC accelerator.

inter-layer features. Finally, the output of DeConvs is sent to the Output Buffer and then transferred to the external memory.

Video compression typically involves processing and transmitting large amounts of motion and residual information, leading to significant energy consumption. To address this, a novel heterogeneous layer fusion dataflow is proposed that not only supports pruning and fast algorithms but also enables on-chip fusion of Convs and DeConvs. In other words, valid data is temporarily stored in on-chip buffers to serve as input for adjacent layers, significantly reducing off-chip interactions. Invalid data that has already been processed is overwritten by new data from other layers, thereby conserving on-chip resources.

4.2.3 Implementation results

The proposed accelerator is compared with commercial GPU and CPU products, as well as several ASIC-based pixel processing accelerators [24, 25]. As shown in **Table 3**, the proposed design achieves an 11.1× increase in throughput and a 1783.9× improvement in energy efficiency compared to the CPU, and a 2.4× increase in throughput and a 799.7× improvement in energy efficiency compared to the GPU. Additionally, when compared to pixel processing accelerators [24, 25], the proposed accelerator offers an 8.7× increase in throughput and a 2.2× improvement in energy efficiency.

4.3 Video super-resolution

VSR enhances low-resolution (LR) videos into high-resolution (HR) versions. DCN can effectively achieve multi-frame alignment in the latent space to maintain temporal continuity, which is highly beneficial for enhancing the visual perception in VSR [26]. However, due to the high computational complexity introduced by offset generation and spatial deformation, as well as the dynamic and irregular memory access patterns, deploying DCNs on resource-constrained devices is challenging.

To address these challenges, a lightweight 3D-CNN and an efficient hardware architecture for deformable 3D Convs are developed to accelerate VSR tasks.

	CPU	GPU	[24]	[25]	Proposed
Technology (nm)	14	8	28	65	28
Frequency (MHz)	3500	1700	700	800	400
Precision (A-W)	FP 32-32	FP 32-32	FXP 16-16	FXP 16-16	FXP 12-16
Gate Count (M)	—	—	1.12	3.03[a]	5.01
On-Chip Memory (KB)	—	—	480	512	373
Power (W)	121.21	257.12	0.19	0.33[a]	0.76
Throughput (GOPS)	317	1493	403	833	3525
Energy Efficiency (GOPS/W)	2.6	5.8	2121.1	2524.2	4638.2

[a]*They are the scale results from 65 nm technology.*

Table 3.
Comparison with other pixel processing accelerators.

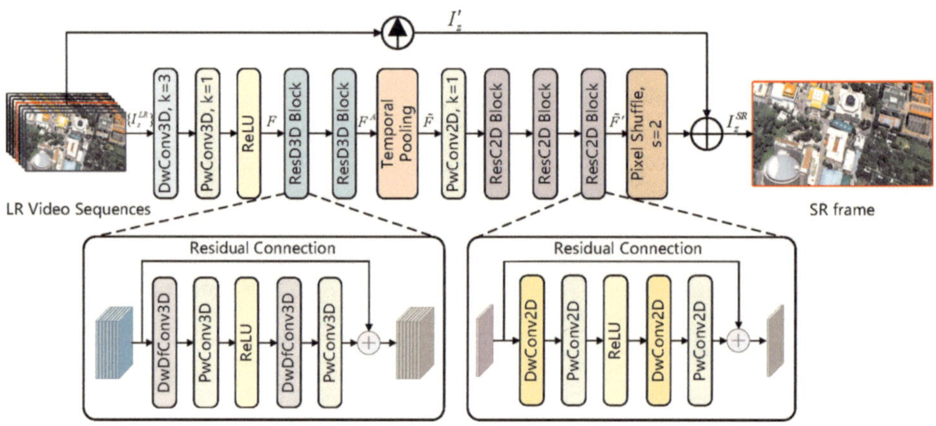

Figure 7.
Block diagrams of the proposed lightweight VSR network.

4.3.1 Lightweight VSR network

To restore an HR frame $I_z^{HR} \in \mathbb{R}^{sNix \times sNiy \times Nif}$ from an LR reference frame $I_z^{LR} \in \mathbb{R}^{Nix \times Niy \times Nif}$ and $Niz - 1$ supporting frames, a hardware-inspired deformable 3D-CNN is developed for edge devices, where $Nix \times Niy$ is the size of the LR frame, s is the upsampling factor, and Nif denotes the number of input channels.

As shown in **Figure 7**, a depthwise separable 3D Conv is first employed to extract spatio-temporal information. Then, ResD3D blocks perform spatial deformations and temporal alignments at the tile level for intermediate features $F \in \mathbb{R}^{Nix \times Niy \times Niz \times Nif}$. Each ResD3D block is stacked by two depthwise separable deformable 3D Convs. The obtained Niz frames $F^A \in \mathbb{R}^{Nox \times Noy \times Noz \times Nof}$ are further aggregated across the temporal dimension by a temporal pooling layer. ResC2D blocks, which are built by depthwise separable 2D Convs, capture deep spatial representations $\tilde{F}' \in \mathbb{R}^{Nox \times Noy \times Nof}$. Afterward, the LR reference frame I_z^{LR} and $\tilde{F}'$ are fused and upsampled to yield the final SR frame.

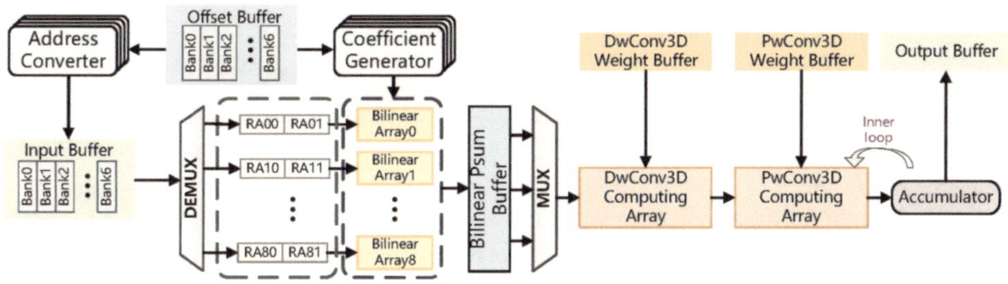

Figure 8.
Hardware architecture of deformable 3D Conv module.

4.3.2 Hardware architecture of deformable 3D Convs

As shown in **Figure 8**, the proposed design parallel computes in the temporal dimension by using an Input Buffer with several banks to store video frames, with a similar setup for the Offset Buffer. Weights are streamed into DwConv3D and PwConv3D Weight Buffer for DwConv3D and PwConv3D, and results are stored in an Output Buffer. Next, based on the scale determined by fixed-point quantization, the integer and fractional parts of the offsets are assigned to the address converter and coefficient generator, respectively, to produce the sampling indices and Bilinear coefficients. To address irregular memory access patterns and enhance input reuse in DfConvs, a block-level interleaving storage scheme is designed to cache sampling values and enable parallel execution of Bilinear operations. After the Bilinear array performs spatial deformation based on the sampled features, the aligned intermediate features are sent to the DwConv3D and PwConv3D computation arrays.

	GPU	**[4]**	**[3]**	**[27]**	**Proposed**
Platform	RTX 2080Ti	Kintex UltraScale	Kintex-7	Virtex UltraScale+	Intel Stratix 10GX 2500
Frequency (MHz)	1350	150	130	200	200
Precision (W-A)	FP 32-32	FXP 10-14	FXP 13-13	FXP 8-10	FXP 8-12
DSP Usage	—	1920	1512	1539	1305
Logic Utilization	—	151.0 k (LUTs) 121.0 k (FFs)	167.0 k (LUTs) 158.0 k (FFs)	158.0 k (LUTs) 319.5 k (FFs)	311.2 k (in ALMs)
BRAM Usage (Mbyte)	—	0.194 (7.19%)	0.945 (26.42%)	8.120 (83.54%)	6.018 (24.16%)
Power (W)	210.54	5.69	5.40	—	9.60
Throughput (GOPS)	194.04	639.57	780.00	295.29	2265.07
Energy Efficiency (GOPS/W)	0.92	112.48	144.90	—	235.94

Table 4.
Comparison with other FPGA-based SR accelerators.

4.3.3 Implementation results

The proposed accelerator is implemented on an Intel Stratix 10GX 2500 FPGA board and compared with previous FPGA-based SR accelerators [3, 4, 27] and a commercial GPU product (RTX 2080Ti). As shown in **Table 4**, the proposed design delivers 11.67× higher throughput and 256.46× better energy efficiency compared to the GPU. Additionally, our design achieves 2.75× higher throughput and 1.63× better energy efficiency than other FPGA-based designs [3, 4, 27].

5. Efficient hardware design and agile development for multiple neural networks

5.1 Variable precision accelerator for depth estimation

Scene depth serves as a crucial reference for the perception and decision-making of robots. Stereo matching determines scene depth by comparing pixel disparities between corresponding points in two or more images. However, intelligent robots often need to perform complex tasks under limited resources. Therefore, designing dedicated stereo vision accelerators is crucial for enhancing the overall performance of robotic system. In this section, a precision-scalable accelerator is designed for depth estimation tasks.

5.1.1 Novel bit-level computing strategy

Since the multiplication of two signed numbers can be flexibly implemented by fusing sub-products spatially or temporally, it can be decomposed into multiple sub-products involving signed-signed, unsigned-unsigned, and signed-unsigned pairs. **Figure 9(a)** and **(b)** illustrate the computational process of 1011×0110 using both Bit

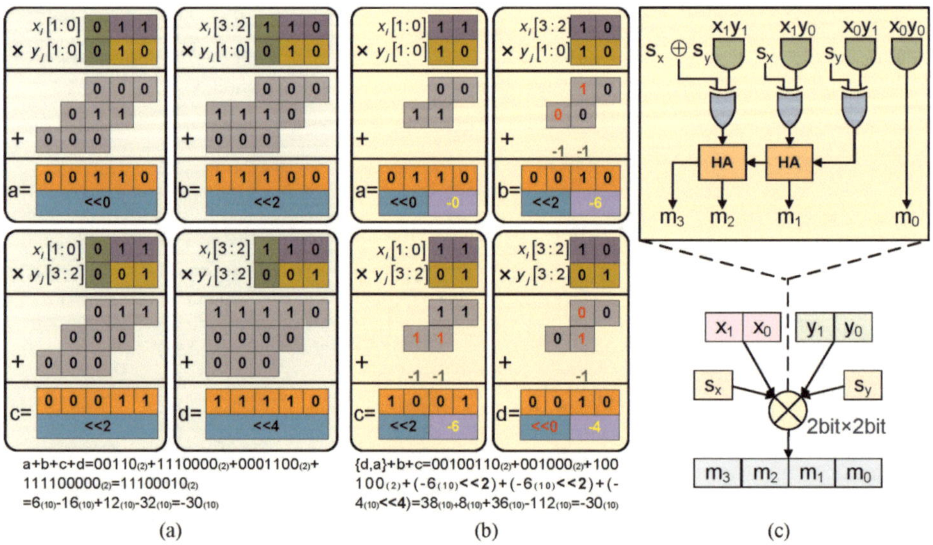

Figure 9.
Description of the computation process for 1011×0110 using (a) bit fusion and (b) proposed strategy. (c) micro-architecture of efficient BitBrick.

Fusion [28] and the proposed bit-level computing strategy. Bit Fusion performs sign extension, followed by executing 3-bit multiplications. All signed partial results undergo different shifts and accumulations to obtain the final result. In contrast, the proposed strategy does not require sign extension, and all results of 2-bit multiplications are unsigned numbers. Merging signed-signed and unsigned-unsigned 2-bit products eliminates one-shift operation.

Based on the bit-level optimization, an efficient BitBrick (EB) is developed for all kinds of decomposed 2-bit multiplications. As shown in **Figure 9(c)**, four-bit input is initially calculated through four AND operations in a 2-bit multiplication. All decomposed multiplications can be uniformly integrated using XOR operations to determine whether the outputs of the AND operations should be inverted. For the accumulation of partial products, each EB requires only two half adders, whereas a normal BitBrick needs to set up four full adders and two half adders, reflecting the significant simplification achieved by the proposed strategy.

5.1.2 Precision-scalable architecture design

Dynamic combination of EBs enables the achievement of different quantization granularity. Therefore, four EBs along with some shifting and addition (S&A) logic are initially employed to construct a bit-level processing unit (BPU), which calculates four partial sums (psums) by running the four EBs simultaneously, thereby facilitating the 4-bit×4-bit and 2-bit×2-bit working modes. The specific combination scheme is illustrated in **Figure 10(a)**. Thanks to the introduction of calibration factors [29], all outputs to the EBs are unsigned 4-bit numbers, significantly simplifying the circuit design of the BPU.

To enhance the computational resource utilization and inference speed, a large number of BPUs are arranged within a precision-scalable computing engine (PSCE), as depicted in **Figure 10(b)**. A PSCE comprises $4 \times d \times m$ BPUs. To perform Conv or DeConv operations, the input channel dimension is unrolled along the row direction, while the output channel dimension is unrolled along the column direction.

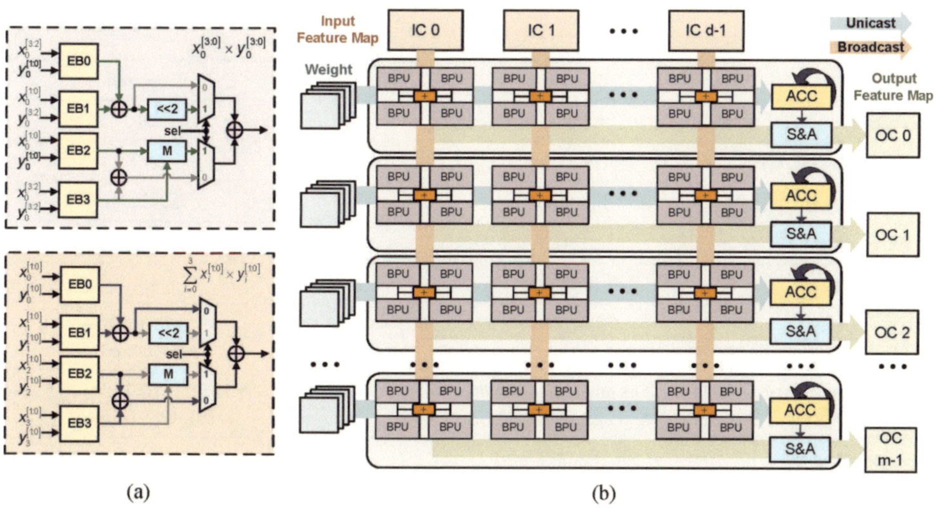

Figure 10.
(a) Description of bit-level processing unit. (b) Structure of precision-scalable computing engine.

Hence, the developed computing engine executes $m \times d$ 8-bit multiplications, or $4 \times d \times m$ 4-bit multiplications, or $16 \times d \times m$ 2-bit multiplications per cycle.

5.1.3 Implementation results

The proposed design is synthesized with the TSMC 28 nm CMOS technology. Mixed precision quantization is applied to an unsupervised monocular depth estimation network [30]. This quantization scheme has a negligible impact on the mean absolute relative error. **Table 5** presents a comparison between the proposed design and relative accelerators. The proposed design demonstrates higher energy efficiency across three precision modes, while also supporting massive operations for vision tasks.

5.2 Efficient hardware mapping method for DNNs

5.2.1 Reconfigurable hardware accelerator for Conv and DeConv

DNNs used for image processing typically require Conv and DeConv layers for feature extraction and expansion. However, using conventional Conv accelerators to handle both Conv and DeConv operations can lead to a significant waste of computational resources.

For image processing tasks, [20] introduces an efficient Conv-DeConv transforming method that converts DeConv into Conv operations, skipping redundant computations related to zero-value elements during the calculation process. This method allows flexible transformation for DeConv kernels of different sizes. Compared to other computational methods, this approach effectively avoids computational imbalance issues and greatly enhances computational efficiency.

Furthermore, a reconfigurable computing unit is proposed based on fast FIR algorithm, which can flexibly support different Conv kernel sizes, reducing computational complexity by 1.2 to 1.5 times. Leveraging the characteristics of FIR FIR algorithm, improvements have been made to the dataflow of DeConv computations, designing a

	PSEA [31]	Dadu-eye [8]	Proposed
Technology (nm)	90	40	28
Frequency (MHz)	500	500	500
Bit precision	2b, 4b,8b	8b	2b, 4b, 8b
PE number	256	4635	4096
Area (mm^2)	0.71 (@28 nm)	7.8 (@28 nm)	4.7
Throughput (TOPS)	0.274 (8b)	4.65 (peak)	4.05 (8b) 5.96 (mixed)
Energy efficiency (TOPS/W)	3.87 (8b, @28 nm), 15.3 (4b, @28 nm) 49.8 (2b, @28 nm)	4.43	4.11 (8b), 16.0 (4b) 55.5 (2b), 6.05 (mixed)
Area efficiency (TOPS/mm^2)	0.386 (8b,@28 nm)	0.596 (@28 nm)	0.862 (8b) 1.27 (mixed)

Table 5.
Comparison with other precision-scalable accelerator.

shift storage-computation data flow to ensure the synchronization of all intermediate results in the parallel computing array. This approach avoids the repeated access problem of overlapping results in traditional DeConv computation methods, thereby reducing storage requirements. Experimental results demonstrate that this design can support different types of network structures while reducing the consumption of storage resources. Compared to existing works, it exhibits significant advantages in computational efficiency and energy efficiency. The design is implemented on Xilinx Virtex-UltraScale platform and it surpasses other works by around 3 to 60 times in computation effciency. The work further enhances the computational capacity of chip design under hardware resource constraints, advancing the application of deep learning algorithms in various visual scenarios.

5.2.2 Agile development framework for DNNs

As rapidly evolving of new visual algorithms, designing specialized hardware accelerators for each specific algorithm significantly increases design time and manpower costs, restricts the hardware's application scenarios, and slows down the process of algorithm deployment and implementation. It is necessary to building a bridge between algorithm models and hardware design to imbue hardware with high flexibility across different network. Hence, agile hardware development and deployment has become another urgent research topic.

To address the aforementioned issues, [16] has focused on various visual tasks, developing a flexible and unified hardware architecture that supports multiple operations, as shown in **Figure 11**. The study explores agile hardware deployment and rapid development of computing cores. By considering the computational characteristics of classical DNNs in visual tasks, the study first proposes field-unified algorithm based on adaptive receptive fields, standardizing various types of computations into the

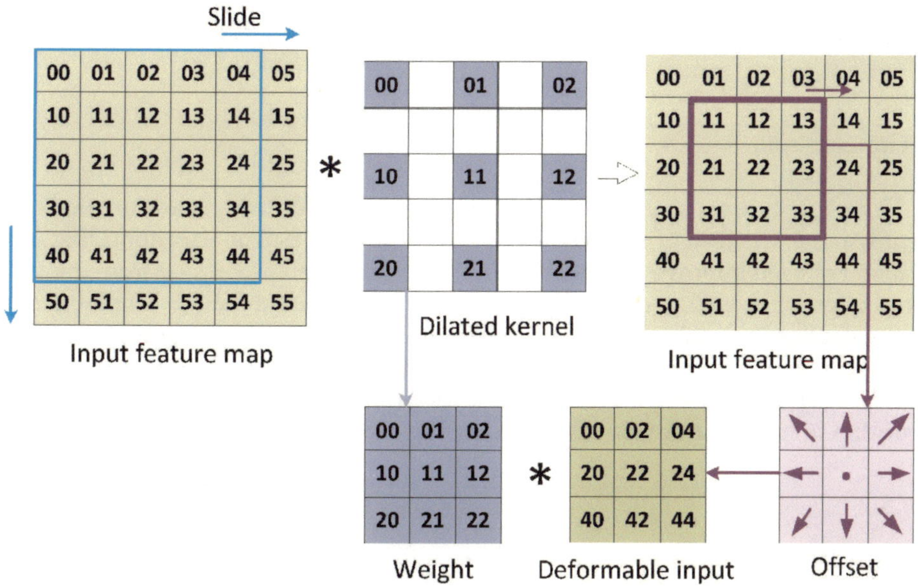

Figure 11.
The application of FUA for Dilated Conv.

FPGA device	Xinlin Zynq UltraScale+ ZCU102		
degree of parallelism (m,n,q)	8,8,8	8,8,16	12,12,16
clock frequency	230	225	220
DSP usage	513(20.36%)	1025(40.67%)	2350(91.47%)
LUT usage	15.4 k(5.6%)	19.9 k(7.23%)	21 k(8.02%)
FF usage	5 k(0.91%)	8.2 k(1.5%)	10.84 k(2%)
BRAM usage	104(11.4%)	200(21.9%)	258(28.29%)
GOPS	178	330.21	712.3

Table 6.
Resources of image processing core in different parameter settings.

same operational paradigm and resolving memory access conflicts in DfConvs. The computing process can be unified as Eq. (4).

$$y(p_0) = \sum_{p_n \in \Omega} w(p_n) \cdot u(p_0 + p_n + \Delta_{p_n}). \tag{4}$$

Furthermore, it introduces a computing flow that maintains consistency in input-output pixel arrangement, completely eliminating the additional overhead caused by data rearrangement. Lastly, to expedite the deployment process of algorithms on the edge, this work also designs a highly flexible hardware architecture and an agile development framework that can automatically generate computing cores based on specific application requirements. The proposed design is implemented on a Xilinx Zynq UltraScale+ FPGA board. Experimental results demonstrate that this framework can be flexibly configured to support multiple DNN models, achieving a computational efficiency 1.4 times higher than similar works. **Table 6** shows hardware resources of different computing cores developed by the proposed framework.

6. Conclusions

This paper focuses on enhancing visual effects and addressing hardware deployment issues in the field of intelligent vision. It explores efficient algorithms that can maintain or even improve the accuracy of image and video processing from the perspectives of algorithm model design, hardware architecture implementation, and system deployment. Additionally, it develops hardware optimization solutions to effectively reduce hardware overhead in VLSI implementation while achieving higher processing speeds. Furthermore, it introduces an agile deployment approach from algorithm to hardware, effectively reducing the hardware development cost.

Author details

Wendong Mao[1]*, Siyu Zhang[2] and Zhongfeng Wang[1]

1 School of Integrated Circuits, Sun Yat-sen University, Shenzhen, China

2 School of Electronic Science and Engineering, Nanjing University, Nanjing, China

*Address all correspondence to: maowd@mail.sysu.edu.cn

IntechOpen

© 2024 The Author(s). Licensee IntechOpen. This chapter is distributed under the terms of the Creative Commons Attribution License (http://creativecommons.org/licenses/by/4.0), which permits unrestricted use, distribution, and reproduction in any medium, provided the original work is properly cited.

References

[1] Dong C, Loy CC, Tang X. Accelerating the super-resolution convolutional neural network. In: Proceedings of the European Conference on Computer Vision (ECCV'16), 11–14 October 2016; Amsterdam. Cham: Springer; 2016. pp. 391-407

[2] She M, Mao W, Shi H, et al. S2R: Exploring a double-win transformer-based framework for ideal and blind super-resolution. In: International Conference on Artificial Neural Networks. Cham: Springer Nature Switzerland; 2023. pp. 522-537

[3] Chang J, Kang K, Kang S. An energy-efficient FPGA-based deconvolutional neural networks accelerator for single image super-resolution. IEEE Transactions on Circuits and Systems for Video Technology. 2020;**30**(1):281-295. DOI: 10.1109/TCSVT.2018.2888898

[4] Kim Y, Choi J, Kim M. A real-time convolutional neural network for super-resolution on FPGA with applications to 4K UHD 60 fps video services. IEEE Transactions on Circuits and Systems for Video Technology. 2019;**29**(8): 2521-2534. DOI: 10.1109/ TCSVT.2018.2864321

[5] Sun K, Koch M, Wang Z, et al. An FPGA-based residual recurrent neural network for real-time video super-resolution. IEEE Transactions on Circuits and Systems for Video Technology. 2022;**32**(4):1739-1750. DOI: 10.1109/ TCSVT.2021.3080241

[6] Jia C, Huang X, Wang S, et al. FPX-NIC: An FPGA-accelerated 4K ultra-high-definition neural video coding system. IEEE Transactions on Circuits and Systems for Video Technology. 2022;**32**(9):6385-6399. DOI: 10.1109/ TCSVT.2022.3164059

[7] Rozendaal T et al. MobileNVC: Real-time 1080p neural video compression on a mobile device. In: Proceedings of the IEEE/CVF Winter Conference on Applications of Computer Vision (WACV'24), 03-08 January 2024; Waikoloa. New York: IEEE; 2024. pp. 4311-4321

[8] Min F, Xu H, Wang Y, et al. Dadu-eye: A 5.3 TOPS/W, 30 fps/1080p high accuracy stereo vision accelerator. IEEE Transactions on Circuits and Systems I: Regular Papers. 2021;**68**(10):4207-4220. DOI: 10.1109/TCSI.2021.3101296

[9] Yang S, Liu J, Lian Z, et al. Awesome typography: Statistics-based text effects transfer. In: Proceedings of the IEEE Conference on Computer Vision and Pattern Recognition (CVPR'17), 21-26 July 2017; Honolulu. New York: IEEE; 2017. pp. 7464-7473

[10] Yang S, Liu J, Wang W, et al. TET-GAN: Text effects transfer via stylization and destylization. In: Proceedings of the AAAI Conference on Artificial Intelligence (AAAI'19), 27 January - 1 Feburary 2019; Honolulu. Washington: AAAI Press; 2019. pp. 1238-1245

[11] Yang S, Wang Z, Wang Z, et al. Controllable artistic text style transfer via shape-matching GAN. In: Proceedings of the IEEE/CVF International Conference on Computer Vision (ICCV'19). 27 October - 2 November 2019; Seoul. New York: IEEE; 2019. pp. 4442-4451

[12] Mao W, Yang S, Shi H, et al. Intelligent typography: Artistic text style transfer for complex texture and structure. IEEE Transactions on Multimedia. 2022;**25**:6485-6498

[13] Gatys LA, Ecker AS, Bethge M. Image style transfer using convolutional

neural networks. In: Proceedings of the IEEE Conference on Computer Vision and Pattern Recognition (CVPR'16), 27-30 June 2016; Las Vegas. New York: IEEE; 2016. pp. 2414-2423

[14] Yang S, Liu J, Yang W, et al. Context-aware text-based binary image stylization and synthesis. IEEE Transactions on Image Processing. 2018; **28**(2):952-964

[15] Mao W, Yang P, Wang Z. FTA-GAN: A computation-efficient accelerator for GANs with fast transformation algorithm. IEEE Transactions on Neural Networks and Learning Systems. 2023; **34**(6):2978-2992. DOI: 10.1109/ TNNLS.2021.3110728

[16] Mao W, Su Z, Luo J, et al. A unified acceleration solution based on deformable network for image pixel processing. IEEE Transactions on Circuits and Systems II: Express Briefs. 2023;**70**(9):3629-3633

[17] Chang JW, Kang SJ. Optimizing FPGA-based convolutional neural networks accelerator for image super-resolution. In: Proceedings of the 2018 23rd Asia and South Pacific Design Automation Conference (ASP-DAC'18), 22-25 January 2018; Jeju. New York: IEEE; 2018. pp. 343-348

[18] Yan J, Yin S, Tu F, et al. GNA: Reconfigurable and efficient architecture for generative network acceleration. IEEE Transactions on Computer-Aided Design of Integrated Circuits and Systems. 2018;**37**(11):2519-2529

[19] Chang JW, Kang KW, Kang SJ. An energy-efficient FPGA-based deconvolutional neural networks accelerator for single image super-resolution. IEEE Transactions on Circuits and Systems for Video Technology. 2018;**30**(1):281-295

[20] Mao W, Lin J, Wang Z. F-DNA: Fast convolution architecture for deconvolutional network acceleration. IEEE Transactions on Very Large Scale Integration (VLSI) Systems. 2020;**28**(8): 1867-1880

[21] Di X, Yang HG, Jia Y, et al. Exploring efficient acceleration architecture for winograd-transformed transposed convolution of GANs on FPGAs. Electronics. 2020;**9**(2):286

[22] Zhang S, Mao W, Shi H, et al. A computationally efficient neural video compression accelerator based on a sparse CNN-transformer hybrid network. In: Proceedings of the Design, Automation & Test in Europe Conference & Exhibition (DATE'24), 25–27 March 2024; Valencia. New York: IEEE; 2024. pp. 1-6

[23] Lavin A, Gray S. Fast algorithms for convolutional neural networks. In: Proceedings of the IEEE Conference on Computer Vision and Pattern Recognition (CVPR'16), 27–30 June 2016; Las Vegas. New York: IEEE; 2016. pp. 4013-4021

[24] Shao Z, Chen X, Du L, et al. Memory-efficient CNN accelerator based on interlayer feature map compression. IEEE Transactions on Circuits and Systems I: Regular Papers. 2022;**69**(2):668-681. DOI: 10.1109/ TCSI.2021.3120312

[25] Wang Y, Wang Y, Li H, et al. An efficient deep learning accelerator architecture for compressed video analysis. IEEE Transactions on Computer-Aided Design of Integrated Circuits and Systems. 2022;**41**(9): 2808-2820. DOI: 10.1109/ TCAD.2021.3120076

[26] Zhang S, Mao W, Wang Z. An efficient accelerator based on

lightweight deformable 3D-CNN for video super-resolution. IEEE Transactions on Circuits and Systems I: Regular Papers. 2023;**70**(6):2384-2397. DOI: 10.1109/TCSI.2023.3258446

[27] Zhang S, Mao W, Wang Z. An efficient accelerator of deformable 3D convolutional network for video super-resolution. In: Proceedings of the IEEE Computer Society Annual Symposium on VLSI (ISVLSI'22), 04–06 July 2022; Nicosia. New York: IEEE; 2022. pp. 110-115

[28] Sharma H, Park J, Suda N, et al. Bit fusion: Bit-level dynamically composable architecture for accelerating deep neural network. In: Proceedings of the ACM/IEEE 45th Annual International Symposium on Computer Architecture (ISCA'18), 01–06 June 2018; Los Angeles. New York: IEEE; 2018. pp. 764-775

[29] Zeng H, Mao W, Zhang S, et al. A precision-scalable vision accelerator for robotic applications. In: Proceedings of the IEEE International Symposium on Circuits and Systems (ISCAS'24), 19–22 May 2024; Singapore. New York: IEEE; 2024. pp. 1-5

[30] Ban J, Zhan H, Wang N, et al. Unsupervised scale-consistent depth learning from video. International Journal of Computer Vision. 2021;**129**: 2548-2564. DOI: 10.1007/s11263-021-01484-6

[31] Liu W, Lin J, Wang Z. A precision-scalable energy-efficient convolutional neural network accelerator. IEEE Transactions on Circuits and Systems I: Regular Papers. 2020;**67**(10):3484-3497. DOI: 10.1109/TCSI.2020.2993051

Chapter 7

Deep Learning Methods for Accelerated Cardiac MRI Reconstruction

Mertcan Özdemir and Osman Eroğul

Abstract

Cardiac magnetic resonance (CMR) imaging has emerged as the cornerstone of modern cardiovascular diagnostics, but its clinical utility has historically been limited by long acquisition times and complex reconstruction requirements. This chapter examines the transformative impact of deep learning approaches on CMR reconstruction, examining how computational methods are revolutionizing accelerated image acquisition and processing. We provide a comprehensive overview of current reconstruction methodologies, from traditional compressed sensing and low-rank modeling to state-of-the-art deep learning architectures, including generative adversarial networks and diffusion models. These methods have achieved speedup factors of 8–12x compared to fully sampled acquisitions, while maintaining diagnostic accuracy of over 95%. The integration of these techniques has enabled significant acceleration of CMR protocols in a variety of applications, reducing scan times to 15–20 minutes while maintaining diagnostic accuracy. Despite current challenges in clinical validation and computational efficiency, the ongoing development of deep learning-based reconstruction methodologies holds the potential to optimize both the clinical accessibility and diagnostic capacity of CMR and ultimately improve the quality of cardiovascular patient care.

Keywords: cardiac magnetic resonance imaging, deep learning reconstruction, generative adversarial networks, diffusion models, compressed sensing, low-rank modeling, neural networks, k-space undersampling, image reconstruction, parallel imaging

1. Introduction

Cardiac magnetic resonance (CMR) imaging is used for cardiovascular assessment, providing detailed information about the cardiac structure, function, flow dynamics, perfusion, and tissue properties [1, 2]. CMR is considered the gold standard for measuring left ventricular ejection fraction and has been effective in diagnosing various cardiac pathologies, from myocardial infarction to congenital heart defects [3]. CMR requires high spatial resolution to identify precise anatomical structures and

 IntechOpen

high temporal resolution to capture the rapid motion of the beating heart. This process makes the reconstruction process particularly challenging [4, 5].

The CMR technique differs from other modalities in its versatility in tissue characterization. Using protocols such as late gadolinium enhancement (LGE) and T1/T2 mapping, clinicians can identify conditions ranging from extensive myocardial fibrosis to fatty infiltration and necrotic areas with this technique [6–8]. This technique extends to congenital heart disease, where the flow imaging capabilities of CMR facilitate a detailed analysis of hemodynamics, including intracardiac shunts between the right and left lungs and pulmonary flow distribution [9, 10].

One of the main disadvantages of CMR is the long scanning times [11]. A comprehensive cardiac examination usually takes 45–60 minutes, during which patients must remain still and follow breath-holding instructions. However, especially in cardiac patients, the difficulties experienced during breath-holding increase motion artifacts, which lead to a decrease in image quality [12]. This process negatively affects not only cardiac patients but also a wide range of patients such as children, the elderly, or those who have difficulty holding their breath due to respiratory conditions.

Traditional reconstruction techniques based on Nyquist sampling theory and compressed sensing methods have made significant progress in speeding up CMR scans [13]. However, these approaches are usually based on complex iterative algorithms and require accurate parameter settings, resulting in long reconstruction times. These methods usually provide only a 2–3-fold speedup, which is insufficient for most cardiac applications [14]. In contrast to traditional techniques, deep learning-based methods have significantly transformed image reconstruction processes. In the literature, it is seen that deep learning algorithms support accelerated reconstruction processes, increase image quality, and enable higher subsampling rates [15–17]. Deep learning-based approaches allow the development of complex models capable of learning directly from past data. These methods effectively reduce aliasing artifacts with data-driven pattern recognition processes [18, 19].

In the context of CMR, these developments have greatly benefited especially pediatric cases and patients with respiratory problems from the reduction of the need for breath holding. These clinical successes have increased the interest in research on innovative network architectures that can learn spatiotemporal precursors [12, 20, 21]. However, there are still various challenges in image reconstruction processes. The need for large data processing, the complexity of parameterization calculations, and the difficulties in accessing clinical data stand out as important problem areas.

All these issues constitute a research area that requires comprehensive solutions that address both the theoretical basis and practical applications of deep learning-based CMR reconstruction methods. This chapter provides a comprehensive review of CMR reconstruction methodologies, starting from traditional techniques to modern deep learning approaches. Various architectures ranging from neural networks to complex generative models are discussed; how physics-based models are integrated with data-driven learning methods and how hybrid image reconstruction approaches are developed with undersampled data are examined in detail.

2. Image reconstruction theory

Traditional methods such as Parallel Imaging and Compressed Sensing have been considered as the cornerstones of this process. However, with the advent of deep learning (DL), reconstruction techniques have undergone a major transformation in terms of speed and accuracy, creating a paradigm shift in the field. In this section, the theoretical foundations of image reconstruction are examined in detail.

2.1 Inverse problem

Inverse problems arise when we aim to infer unknown causes from observed effects and are an opposite approach to forward problems where we try to predict effects from known causes. The reconstruction task in CMR represents a classical inverse problem in this context: to obtain an image from measured k-space data. This problem is inherently more difficult than the forward process of generating k-space data from an image, because multiple different images may produce similar measurements. Like most medical imaging methods, CMR reconstruction is classified as an inverse problem.

In CMR, the goal is to reconstruct an unknown image (transverse macroscopic magnetization) from sampled measurements (k-space data). However, the MRI reconstruction problem is often described as an ill-posed problem because it violates one or more of the Hadamard conditions (as shown in **Figure 1**) [22].

The three Hadamard conditions for a well-posed problem are as follows:

- *Solution existence*: The problem must have at least one solution. In CMR, if the forward model fails to capture the physics of data acquisition correctly, no solution may exist that perfectly matches the measurements.

- *Solution uniqueness*: If solutions exist, there should be exactly one solution. CMR reconstruction violates this condition when estimating a continuous

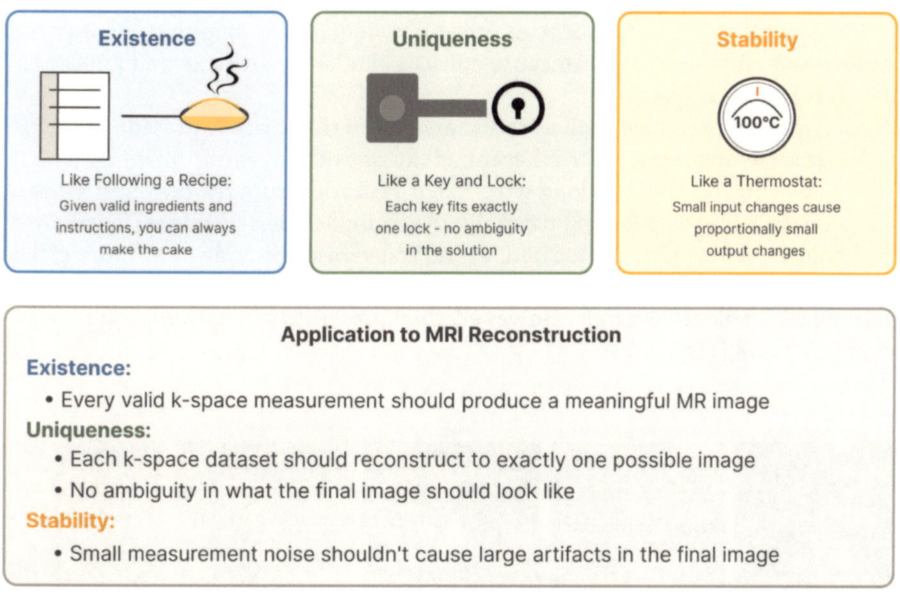

Figure 1.
Visual representation of Hadamard's three conditions for well-posed problems. Existence is analogous to a recipe where ingredients guarantee a cake can be made. Uniqueness resembles a key-and-lock system where only one solution fits. Stability is similar to a thermostat, where small input changes lead to proportional adjustments. These conditions directly apply to MRI reconstruction, where k-space measurements should produce valid, unique images with minimal artifacts from noise.

magnetization distribution from discrete k-space samples. This non-uniqueness is exacerbated by undersampling, where insufficient data is collected to determine a unique solution.

- *Solution stability*: Small changes in the input should lead to small changes in the output. The Fourier transform central to MRI is particularly sensitive to noise in high-frequency components, leading to potential instability in the reconstruction process, as described by the Riemann–Lebesgue lemma [23].

The MRI reconstruction problem can be reframed, and the difficulties arising from malpositioning can be resolved by incorporating constraints and regularization terms. The following sections will consider a general formulation of the MRI reconstruction problem, examining various methodologies for decomposing the continuous MR signal and handling its complexity.

3. Fundamental principles of k-data undersampling

K-space represents the raw data acquired during MRI scans, where data points correspond to spatial frequencies rather than direct spatial locations. In fully sampled acquisitions, k-space is populated by the Nyquist sampling criteria. However, cardiac imaging often requires acceleration that exceeds traditional sampling methods. The selection of k-space trajectories is one of the unique applications used in MRI acquisition strategies, as each pattern offers advantages and trade-offs in time-lapse imaging. Traditional Cartesian sampling is simple to implement and reconstruct, but requires long acquisition times to completely fill the linear k-space grid. Undersampling in Cartesian acquisitions can reduce scan time by systematically skipping phase encoding lines; however, this approach can cause consistent aliasing artifacts that appear as ghosts in the final image.

Non-Cartesian methods, such as radial and spiral trajectories, provide more efficient k-space coverage and offer inherent advantages for dynamic imaging. Radial sampling, which collects data along wire-like trajectories from the center of k-space, is excellent at handling motion and naturally oversamples the central region where critical contrast information is located. Spiral trajectories provide even more efficient coverage by traversing k-space in an outward spiral, allowing for fast acquisitions with reduced gradient demands. However, they present challenges related to off-resonance effects (**Figure 2**).

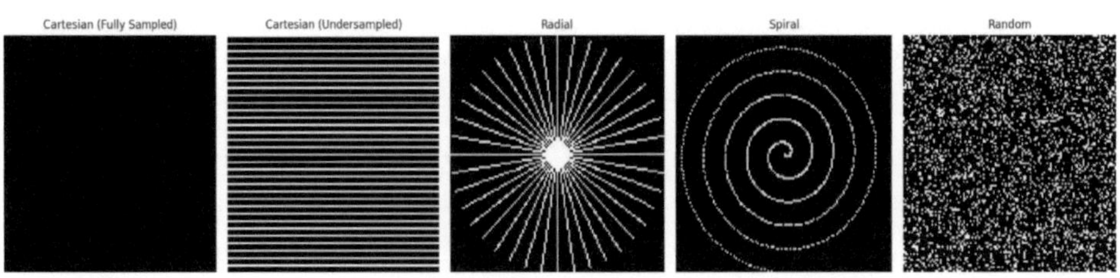

Figure 2.
Comparison of different k-space sampling patterns used in MRI acquisition: fully sampled Cartesian (left), undersampled Cartesian with regular spacing (center-left), radial sampling (center), spiral trajectory (center-right), and random sampling (right). White pixels indicate sampled locations in k-space.

Random or pseudo-random sampling patterns have gained momentum with the rise of compressed sensing, as inconsistent aliasing artifacts can be effectively mitigated through iterative reconstruction algorithms. The optimal trajectory selection depends on the specific clinical application, available reconstruction techniques, and hardware capabilities. Many novel protocols use hybrid approaches that combine multiple sampling strategies to take advantage of their advantages [24, 25].

3.1 Reconstruction of undersampled CMRI

The challenge of recovering CMR images often presents itself as ill-posed problems. Leading methods, such as SENSE, tackle this issue through an optimization framework, mathematically expressed as $\mathbf{x} = \arg\min_{\mathbf{x}} \mathscr{L}(\mathbf{x})$, where the objective function takes the following form [14]:

$$\mathscr{L}(\mathbf{x}) = \underbrace{\|\mathbf{Ax} - \mathbf{y}\|_2^2}_{\text{data consistency}} + \underbrace{\lambda\mathscr{R}(\mathbf{x})}_{\text{regularization}} \tag{1}$$

This formulation combines two key components: a data consistency measure and a regularization term, denoted as the prior $\mathscr{R} : \mathbb{C}^n \to \mathbb{R}_+$ for acceptable solutions. Notably, this prior exhibits a unique characteristic: It assigns lower values to images aligning with expected properties, while assigning higher values to those deviating from them. In the context of compressed sensing, wavelet domain sparsity emerges as a prominent prior for recovering images, characterized by a small number of nonzero wavelet coefficients or a specific subset thereof.

Algorithm 1 outlines the pseudocode for a basic iterative reconstruction algorithm tailored for MRI. This algorithm reconstructs images from undersampled k-space data through the following steps: (1) initializing the image estimate, (2) iteratively updating it by enforcing consistency with sampled k-space values and applying the Fourier transform, and (3) terminating the process once the change in the estimate becomes sufficiently small.

From a Bayesian perspective, this approach can be reframed as a posterior estimation problem. The objective is to identify an image $\mathbf{x}$ that maximizes the posterior distribution:

$$p(\mathbf{x}|\mathbf{y}) = \frac{p(\mathbf{y}|\mathbf{x}) \cdot p(\mathbf{x})}{p(\mathbf{y})}. \tag{2}$$

Equivalently, this estimation can be obtained by minimizing the negative log posterior:

$$-\log p(\mathbf{x}|\mathbf{y}) = -\log p(\mathbf{y}|\mathbf{x}) - \log p(\mathbf{x}). \tag{3}$$

This reformulation provides valuable insights: The data consistency term emerges as the mean-squared error when the likelihood $p(\mathbf{y}|\mathbf{x})$ is modeled as a Gaussian distribution.

Algorithm 1. Reconstruction of Undersampled MR Image.

Require: *k_space_data* (Undersampled k-space data)
Require: *sampling_mask* (Binary mask indicating sampled locations)

```
Ensure: Reconstructed image x
Initialize x ← 0 (array of zeros with the same shape as k_space_data)
max_iter ← 100
tolerance ← 10^-6
for i ← 0 to max_iter − 1 do
    x_k ← FourierTransform(x)
    for all sampled locations in sampling_mask do
        x_k[location] ← k_space_data[location]
    end for
    x_new ← InverseFourierTransform(x_k)
    x_new ← ApplyRegularization (x_new)
    if Norm(x_new − x) < tolerance then
        break
    end if
    x ← x_new
end for
return x
```

3.2 Compressed sensing

Compressed sensing enables accelerated CMR by employing pseudo-random undersampling strategies to reduce the amount of k-space data required. This approach introduces incoherent aliasing artifacts, which necessitate robust reconstruction algorithms to recover high-quality images [26].

The image reconstruction problem can be formulated as an inverse optimization problem:

$$x^* = \arg\min_x \frac{1}{2} \|Ax - y\|_2^2 + \lambda R(x), \tag{4}$$

where x represents the reconstructed image or a time series of images, y is the acquired k-space data, and A denotes the MRI forward operator that incorporates the Fourier transform and coil sensitivity maps. The term $R(x)$ acts as a regularization function imposing prior constraints such as sparsity or low-rank structures, while λ is a tunable parameter balancing data fidelity and prior enforcement. The optimization balances consistency with acquired data and adherence to prior knowledge.

3.3 Parallel imaging

Multiple receiver coils and their spatial sensitivity patterns can be used to perform MRI scanning. Since its introduction in the late 1990s, parallel imaging has become a widely used technique in clinical MRI. This technique reduces scan times by requiring fewer k-space measurements, while eliminating image quality degradation [27]. Since its introduction in the late 1990s, parallel imaging has become a widely used technique in clinical MRI.

3.3.1 Image domain methods (SENSE)

SENSitivity Encoding (SENSE) operates directly in the image domain by utilizing known coil sensitivity profiles to unwrap aliased images. The reconstruction can be formulated as:

$$\rho = \left(S^H \Psi^{-1} S\right)^{-1} S^H \Psi^{-1} y \tag{5}$$

where:

$$S = \begin{bmatrix} S_{1,1} & S_{1,2} & \cdots & S_{1,R} \\ S_{2,1} & S_{2,2} & \cdots & S_{2,R} \\ \vdots & \vdots & \ddots & \vdots \\ S_{N,1} & S_{N,2} & \cdots & S_{N,R} \end{bmatrix} \tag{6}$$

Here:
ρ = unfolded/reconstructed image
S = sensitivity matrix containing coil sensitivities
S^H = conjugate transpose of S
Ψ = noise correlation matrix
y = vector of aliased images from each coil
N = number of coils
R = acceleration/reduction factor
$S_{i,j}$ = sensitivity of coil i at aliased position j

In cardiac applications, SENSE reconstruction takes into account the complex motion of the beating heart [4]. Acceleration factors are usually varied between 2 and 3 to preserve diagnostic image quality [28]. The accuracy of coil sensitivity estimation can be achieved with various calibration techniques [29]. Recent deep learning approaches are leading the way by providing more robust sensitivity estimation methods [30].

3.3.2 K-space methods (GRAPPA)

GRAPPA operates by synthesizing missing k-space lines using spatial correlation patterns learned from acquired data. The reconstruction process can be expressed as [31]:

$$S_j\left(k_x, k_y + m\Delta k_y\right) = \sum_{l=1}^{L} \sum_{b \in \mathcal{B}} n(j, l, b, m) \cdot S_l\left(k_x + b_x \Delta k_x, k_y + b_y \Delta k_y\right) \tag{7}$$

where:

- $S_j\left(k_x, k_y + m\Delta k_y\right)$ represents the target k-space point to be synthesized for coil j
- $S_l\left(k_x + b_x \Delta k_x, k_y + b_y \Delta k_y\right)$ are the acquired source points from coil l
- $n(j, l, b, m)$ are the GRAPPA weights learned from auto-calibration data
- L is the total number of coils
- $\mathcal{B}$ represents the set of spatial offsets in the kernel
- m is the distance between the target point and acquired points
- $\left(b_x, b_y\right)$ are the kernel offset coordinates.

A key advantage of GRAPPA is its robustness to phase errors and motion artifacts, making it particularly suitable for cardiac imaging. The method requires an auto-calibration signal (ACS) region in k-space, which provides training data for determining the reconstruction weights.

3.4 Low-rank and sparse modeling

At the intersection of compressed sensing and low-rank image modeling lies a powerful mathematical synergy. While these approaches may appear distinct—one utilizing fixed sparsifying bases, the other employing adaptive bases—they share a remarkable compatibility in their data acquisition requirements, often achieved through randomized sampling techniques.

The optimization framework can be expressed through three fundamental equations [32]:

$$\left\{\hat{\mathbf{A}}, \hat{\phi}\right\} = \arg\min_{\mathbf{A}, \phi} \|\mathbf{E}(\mathbf{A}\phi) - \mathbf{y}\|_2^2 + \lambda\|\Psi, (\mathbf{A}\phi)\|_1 \tag{8}$$

$$\hat{\mathbf{X}} = \arg\min_{\mathbf{X}} \|\mathbf{E}(\mathbf{X}) - \mathbf{y}\|_2^2 + \lambda\|\Psi, (\mathbf{X})\|_1 \tag{9}$$

$$\hat{\mathbf{X}} = \arg\min_{\mathbf{X}} \|\mathbf{E}(\mathbf{X}) - \mathbf{y}\|_2^2 + \lambda_1\sum_{i\geq 1} R_{\text{rank}}(\mathbf{P}_i\mathbf{X}) + \lambda_2\|\Psi, (\mathbf{X})\|_1 \tag{10}$$

The transform function Ψ can take multiple forms:

- Fixed transform as in [33, 34]

- Direct sparse transform on X

Adaptive transform with $\phi' : \Psi(\mathrm{X}) = \Psi\mathrm{X}\phi' = \Psi\mathrm{A}$.

3.5 Low-rank plus sparse decomposition

Low-rank plus sparse (L + S) decomposition has emerged as a powerful framework for dynamic CMR reconstruction [35, 36]. The approach separates temporal variations into low-rank background components and sparse dynamic components:

$$\min_{x_L, x_S} \frac{1}{2}\|A(x_L + x_S) - y\|_2^2 + \lambda_L\|M(x_L)\|_* + \lambda_S\|Sx_S\|_1 \tag{11}$$

where $\|\cdot\|_*$ denotes the nuclear norm (sum of singular values), x_L and x_S represent the low-rank and sparse components, respectively, and $M(\cdot)$ reshapes the data into a Casorati matrix. This decomposition is particularly effective for cardiac cine imaging, where the beating heart motion can be captured in the sparse component, while background structures remain in the low-rank component.

3.6 Low-rank Hankel-structured matrix

The Hankel matrix approach leverages the relationship between spatial domain sparsity and spectral domain rank used. It is proposed as a general framework for a sparsity-driven k-space interpolation method that unifies parallel imaging and compressed sensing MRI [37]. For sparsely sampled measurements on $\Omega \subseteq \{0, 1, \ldots, n-1\}$, the reconstruction problem becomes:

$$\arg\min_{\mathbf{m} \in \mathbb{C}^n} \|H(n,d)(\mathbf{m})\|_* \quad \text{s.t.} \quad P_\Omega(\mathbf{m}) = P_\Omega(\hat{\mathbf{x}}) \tag{12}$$

with the Hankel matrix structure:

$$H(n,d)(\mathbf{m}) = \begin{pmatrix} m(0) & m(1) & \cdots & m(d-1) \\ \vdots & \vdots & \ddots & \vdots \\ m(n-d) & m(n-d+1) & \cdots & m(n-1) \end{pmatrix}$$

This approach has shown particular promise in accelerated cardiac imaging when combined with parallel imaging techniques [35].

4. Relevance to deep learning

Although traditional methods provide reliable solutions, due to their computational complexity and limited adaptability to undersampled data, it has been necessary to develop DL-based approaches. These methods combine traditional frameworks with data-driven priors learned from historical datasets. By replacing the priors with learned priors, DL-based techniques generate higher-quality images, enable higher undersampling rates, and accelerate CMRI.

4.1 Regularization techniques

Modern DL-based regularization approaches have significantly improved traditional sparsity constraints by incorporating sophisticated learning mechanisms that can capture complex image features and anatomical patterns. These techniques can be broadly categorized into several complementary approaches:

4.1.1 Transform domain regularization

The learned transform space regularization offers significant advantages over traditional fixed transforms like wavelets or Fourier basis by enabling the network to adapt its representation basis specifically to CMRI data characteristics. The network can develop learned wavelet-like transforms that automatically discover optimal multi-scale decompositions for cardiac structures, while adaptive sparsifying operators evolve during training to capture both spatial and temporal patterns specific to cardiac motion. Through multi-scale decomposition networks, the system can simultaneously process features at different spatial resolutions, enabling better preservation of both fine details and global structure. This data-driven approach allows for automatic identification of relevant anatomical and physiological patterns, making the overall system more flexible and effective at handling the unique aspects of cardiac imaging data.

4.1.2 Temporal regularization

Cardiac imaging faces distinct challenges due to its dynamic nature, but modern temporal regularization techniques have developed effective solutions to address these complexities. Motion-aware constraints work by explicitly modeling both cardiac and respiratory motion patterns, while cardiac phase-specific priors take into account the varying appearance and motion characteristics that occur throughout the cardiac cycle. The approach incorporates dynamic feature learning mechanisms that can adapt to different temporal resolution requirements as needed, allowing for flexible processing of time-varying data. Additionally, coherence constraints play a crucial role in ensuring temporal consistency across frames while simultaneously preserving the natural motion patterns essential for accurate cardiac imaging.

4.1.3 Anatomical priors

Deep learning enables the incorporation of sophisticated anatomical knowledge into the reconstruction process through multiple key mechanisms. The use of cardiac structure preservation techniques helps maintain anatomical fidelity even when dealing with high acceleration factors, while motion pattern consistency constraints work to ensure physiologically plausible deformation throughout the reconstruction. The approach also leverages physiological constraints that are derived from large-scale analysis of both normal and pathological cardiac motions, providing a robust foundation for accurate reconstruction. Additionally, shape and texture priors learned from population-level studies further enhance the reconstruction quality by incorporating broader statistical patterns observed across many cases.

4.2 Optimization methods

The optimization problem can be solved using various iterative approaches. Proximal gradient methods are commonly used when the regularization function has a closed-form proximal operator. These methods alternate between data consistency and proximal regularization steps. For instance, the Fast Iterative Shrinkage-Thresholding Algorithm (FISTA) uses the following updates [38]:

$$z^{k+1} = x^k - \alpha A^H\left(Ax^k - y\right), \tag{13}$$

$$x^{k+1} = \mathrm{prox}_{\alpha\lambda R}\left(z^{k+1}\right), \tag{14}$$

where α is the step size. For more complex regularization terms, methods like Half-Quadratic Splitting introduce an auxiliary variable z to provide greater flexibility. The updates in this case are:

$$x^{k+1} = \arg\min_x \frac{1}{2}\|Ax - y\|_2^2 + \frac{\rho}{2}\|Tx - z^k\|_2^2, \tag{15}$$

$$z^{k+1} = \arg\min_z \lambda Q(z) + \frac{\rho}{2}\|z - Tx^{k+1}\|_2^2, \tag{16}$$

where T is a sparsifying transform. These approaches are foundational for traditional reconstruction methods.

The Alternating Direction Method of Multipliers (ADMM) [39] has proven to be an effective optimization algorithm for accelerating cardiac MRI reconstruction, particularly in cases involving undersampled k-space data. Its ability to decompose optimization problems into separable components makes it a suitable approach for reconstruction problems where both data consistency and regularization play critical roles.

In the context of cardiac MRI reconstruction, the problem can be formulated as:

$$\min_{x,z} f(x) + g(z) \quad \text{subject to} \quad Ax + Bz = c, \tag{17}$$

where:

- x represents the reconstructed MRI image,
- z corresponds to auxiliary variables enforcing constraints or regularization terms,
- $f(x)$ encodes the data fidelity term to ensure consistency with the acquired k-space data,
- $g(z)$ incorporates regularization terms, such as sparsity or smoothness (e.g., Total Variation or wavelet-based regularization),
- A and B are system model and transformation matrices,
- c is the acquired undersampled k-space data.

4.3 Deep learning-based reconstruction

Supervised deep learning methods address this ill-posed problem by leveraging prior knowledge obtained during offline training. The reconstruction process can be formulated as:

$$I = \arg\min_{I} \frac{1}{2} \|y - F_p C I\|_2^2 + \lambda R(I), \tag{18}$$

where: I is the reconstructed MR image, $R(I)$ is the regularization term guided by prior knowledge, such as sparsity or learned features, λ is the regularization weight, balancing data fidelity, and prior knowledge.

In supervised reconstruction frameworks, the regularization term $R(I)$ encapsulates the mapping between undersampled and fully sampled acquisitions learned during the training phase. Neural networks, particularly convolutional neural networks (CNNs), are trained on large datasets of paired undersampled and fully sampled images, enabling them to predict high-quality reconstructions directly from undersampled data.

In recent years, deep learning methods have shown great promise for accelerating CMR acquisition while maintaining high-quality image. This chapter provides an overview of the main categories of deep learning methods for accelerated CMR reconstruction, as depicted in **Figure 3**.

4.3.1 Plug-n-Play (PnP) methods

PnP methods modularly combine conventional reconstruction algorithms with deep learning models. For cardiac MRI specifically, PnP approaches like Deep ADMM-Net [40] integrate learned CNN denoisers into traditional optimization frameworks while preserving their mathematical properties. They have proven to be particularly effective for challenging cardiac applications like free-breathing imaging [41] and dynamic cine

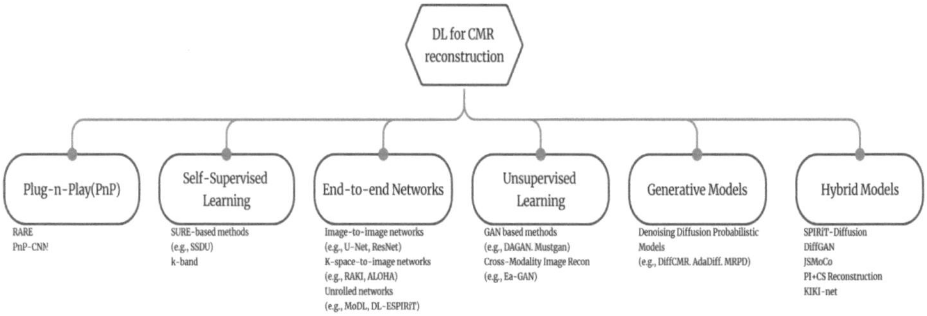

Figure 3.
Overview of deep learning (DL) approaches for cardiac MRI (CMR) reconstruction, categorizing methods into six main branches: Plug-n-Play, Self-Supervised Learning, End-to-end Networks, Unsupervised Learning, Generative Models, and Hybrid Models.

MRI [42]. Key advantages include flexibility in adapting to different cardiac protocols, preservation of data consistency, better interpretability compared to pure deep learning methods, and ability to handle complex cardiac motion. Recent work has demonstrated their effectiveness for real-time cardiac MRI reconstruction [30], enabling high acceleration factors while maintaining diagnostic quality.

4.3.2 Self-supervised learning

Self-supervised learning approaches aim to learn representations from the data itself without requiring fully sampled ground truth images for training. SURE-based methods [43, 44] train networks to minimize Stein's Unbiased Risk Estimator, which provides a surrogate for the reconstruction error that can be computed from undersampled data alone. Another example is k-band [43], which learns to interpolate missing k-space samples by exploiting correlations within and across nearby k-space bands. Self-supervised learning enables training on large datasets of undersampled acquisitions, which can improve robustness and generalization compared to supervised methods that require fully sampled data.

4.3.3 End-to-end networks

End-to-end networks learn a direct mapping from undersampled k-space data or aliased images to high-quality reconstructions. U-Net [45] and ResNet [46] architectures have been popular choices for this category, demonstrating strong performance on various CMR reconstruction tasks. Unrolled networks, such as MoDL [42] and RAKI [47], incorporate domain knowledge by unrolling iterative optimization algorithms and learning the algorithm parameters end-to-end. VN-Net [48] is another unrolled network that combines a variational network with a gradient descent scheme for improved reconstruction. End-to-end networks offer a streamlined approach to CMR reconstruction, but may require larger training datasets and careful design to avoid overfitting.

4.3.4 Unsupervised learning and generative models

Unsupervised learning approaches aim to learn image representations or generative models without paired training data. Generative adversarial networks (GANs) have been widely used for this purpose, with examples including DAGAN [49] for dynamic CMR reconstruction and MustGAN [50] for multi-contrast synthesis. These methods train a generator network to synthesize realistic images, while a discriminator network learns to distinguish real from synthesized images. Cycle-consistent adversarial architectures like DiamondGAN [51] enable unsupervised learning from unpaired data by enforcing forward and backward consistency.

GANs consists of two components that compete during training: a generator $G(\cdot)$ and a discriminator $D(\cdot)$. The generator aims to produce realistic data, while the discriminator attempts to distinguish between real data and the data generated by $G(\cdot)$ [52]. The input to a GAN is typically represented as $z \sim p_z(z)$, where z is a noise variable sampled from a probability distribution $p_z(z)$. The generator maps this noise z to the data domain, generating outputs $G(z)$. These outputs are expected to resemble the real data distribution $p_{\text{data}}(x)$. The discriminator, in contrast, outputs a scalar value indicating the likelihood that its input is real data rather than generated by $G(\cdot)$ (**Figure 4**).

This framework leads to the following optimization problem, based on cross-entropy:

$$\min_G \max_D \mathbb{E}_{x \sim p_{\text{data}}(x)}[\log D(x)] + \mathbb{E}_{z \sim p_z(z)}[\log(1 - D(G(z)))], \tag{19}$$

where D is optimized to maximize the probability of correctly classifying real and generated data, that is, maximizing $D(x)$ and minimizing $1 - D(G(z))$ (both in logarithmic form). Meanwhile, the generator G is trained to minimize $\log(1 - D(G(z)))$, effectively improving its ability to produce realistic data. Both optimizations are performed in expectation over their respective distributions. Over time, several improvements to GANs have been proposed, focusing on better loss functions and

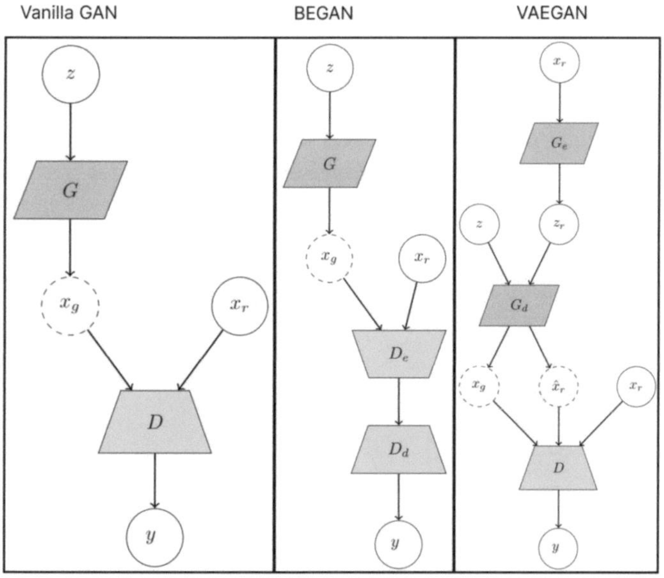

Figure 4.
Architectural variants of Generative Adversarial Networks (GANs). Left: Standard GAN with generator G and discriminator D. Center: Enhanced GAN with separate encoder-decoder discriminator (De, Dd). Right: Advanced GAN architecture featuring both encoder (Ge) and decoder (Gd) components in the generator, where z represents latent noise, xg the generated samples, xr the real samples, and y the output classification.

network architectures. Notable examples include WGAN [53], which replaces the cross-entropy loss with the Wasserstein distance-based loss; LSGAN [54], which uses a least-squares loss; the VGG19-based GAN [55]; and the consistency-enforced CycleGAN [56].

Generative models learn the distribution of high-quality CMR images, allowing for realistic image synthesis and reconstruction from undersampled data. Denoising diffusion probabilistic models (DDPMs) [57] have recently emerged as a powerful class of generative models, demonstrating impressive performance on various inverse problems. In CMR reconstruction, DDPM-based methods such as Score-based Diffusion Models [58] and Adaptive Diffusion Priors [59] have shown promising results, enabling high-quality reconstruction from highly undersampled data (**Figure 5**). Other generative approaches include the Deep Decoder [60], which learns a low-dimensional manifold of CMR images, and Noise2Noise [61], which trains a denoising network using only noisy image pairs.

4.3.5 Hybrid models

Hybrid models combine aspects of different deep learning approaches to leverage their complementary strengths. For example, SPIRiT-Diffusion [62] integrates the SPIRiT parallel imaging model with a diffusion prior, enabling high-quality reconstruction from multi-coil data. DiffSPIRIT [63] combines a pre-trained diffusion model with a self-supervised k-space interpolation network, demonstrating strong generalization to different acquisition settings. JS-MoCo [64] jointly estimates coil sensitivity maps and motion parameters using a score-based diffusion model, enabling motion-robust reconstruction. Hybrid models offer a promising direction for future research, potentially combining the benefits of physics-driven and data-driven approaches.

4.3.6 Novel architectures and advanced techniques

Recent developments have seen the emergence of more sophisticated architectures. The variational network approach, introduced by Hammernik et al. [48], reinterprets the traditional optimization-based reconstruction as a deep learning problem, leading to improved reconstruction quality. Similarly, the model-based deep learning (MoDL) framework [42] combines data consistency with learned regularization in an end-to-end trainable network.

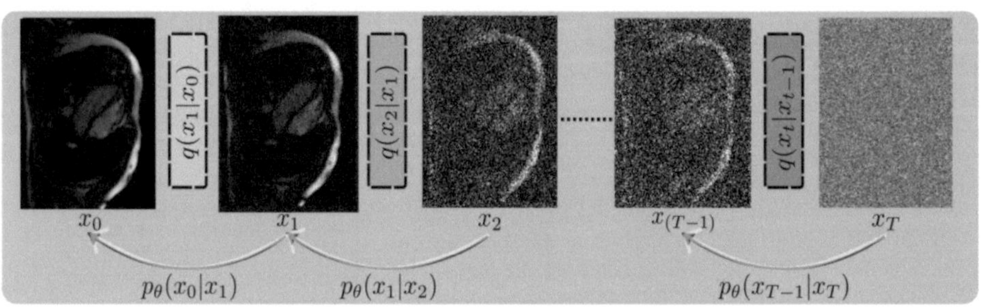

Figure 5.
The figure illustrates the forward diffusion process in a diffusion model for MRI reconstruction, showing the progressive degradation of an initial cardiac MR image (x_0) through multiple timesteps ($x_1, x_2, \ldots, x_t$) by gradually adding Gaussian noise. Each transition $p_\theta(x_{t-1}|x_t)$ represents a step in the diffusion process, with $q(x_t|x_{t-1})$ denoting the conditional distribution at each timestep, ultimately resulting in pure noise (x_t) at the final timestep.

A particularly promising direction has been the development of diffusion models for CMR reconstruction [65]. These models have shown remarkable ability to generate high-quality images from highly undersampled data, while providing uncertainty estimates in their reconstructions. The integration of transformer architectures has also begun to show promise, particularly in capturing long-range dependencies in the image data [66].

4.4 Cardiac cine imaging

Cardiac cine imaging represents one of the most important applications of deep learning-based reconstruction in CMR. The need to capture both spatial and temporal dynamics of cardiac motion while maintaining high-quality image makes this a particularly challenging problem [67]. Recent advances have shown remarkable success in accelerating cine imaging while preserving diagnostic quality.

DL-ESPIRiT, proposed by Sandino et al. [5], demonstrated that deep learning reconstruction could achieve up to threefold reduction in scan time while maintaining image quality comparable to standard protocols. This method combines traditional parallel imaging principles with learned priors, showing particular robustness in handling reduced field-of-view acquisitions common in cardiac imaging. The clinical validation of this approach showed only minimal differences in diagnostic quality compared to conventional acquisitions, with scan times reduced from approximately 3 minutes to under 1 minute [20].

For 3D cardiac cine imaging, CINENet [21] introduced a novel approach using 4D spatio-temporal convolutions, enabling the acquisition of whole-heart coverage in a single breath-hold of less than 10 seconds. This represents a significant advancement over traditional multi-slice 2D acquisitions that require multiple breath-holds and several minutes of scan time.

4.5 Flow imaging and quantification

Four-dimensional flow MRI (4D Flow) has emerged as a powerful tool for comprehensive assessment of cardiovascular hemodynamics [68]. However, the need to encode velocity in three directions while maintaining temporal resolution traditionally results in long acquisition times. Deep learning reconstruction has shown particular promise in this domain.

Vishnevskiy et al. [69] demonstrated that deep variational networks could enable acceleration factors of up to 12.4× while maintaining accuracy in flow measurements. Their approach showed comparable measurements of peak velocity and flow rates compared to conventional parallel imaging methods, while significantly reducing scan time.

A particularly innovative approach was demonstrated by Kim et al. [70], who developed a method to produce three-directional velocities from only three flow encodings, eliminating the need for a separate reference scan. This approach not only reduces scan time but also shows robustness to background phase errors, a common challenge in flow imaging.

4.6 Late gadolinium enhancement and tissue characterization

Late gadolinium enhancement (LGE) imaging is crucial for myocardial viability assessment and scar characterization. Deep learning reconstruction has enabled significant improvements in both acquisition speed and image quality. El-Rewaidy et al.

[71] developed a complex-valued network for reconstructing 3D LGE volumes, achieving high acceleration factors while preserving the ability to accurately quantify scar extent.

For parametric mapping, novel deep learning approaches have emerged that combine reconstruction with direct parameter estimation. Recent work by Jeelani et al. [72] demonstrated the feasibility of simultaneous T1 mapping and image reconstruction using recurrent neural networks, potentially streamlining the quantitative imaging workflow.

5. Conclusions

The field of CMR imaging has witnessed transformative advancements, particularly in the realm of image reconstruction. Traditional methods such as parallel imaging and compressed sensing have laid the foundation for faster acquisition and high-quality image reconstruction. However, these approaches often face limitations in computational complexity and adaptability to highly undersampled data.

DL has emerged as a revolutionary solution, offering unprecedented capabilities in tackling the inherent challenges of CMR reconstruction. From convolutional neural networks (CNNs) to GANs and DDPMs, DL methods have demonstrated remarkable potential in reducing scan times, enhancing image quality, and improving diagnostic accuracy. These approaches leverage data-driven priors, enabling higher undersampling factors and integrating seamlessly into clinical workflows.

Despite these advancements, challenges remain. The need for robust, generalizable models, access to diverse and high-quality training datasets, and efficient computational resources are critical areas for continued exploration. Innovations such as hybrid models, self-supervised learning, and the integration of novel architectures like transformers and diffusion models are promising directions that hold the potential to address these gaps.

The ongoing evolution of DL-based techniques in CMR reconstruction underscores their significance in improving patient outcomes and expanding the scope of clinical applications. Future research should focus on refining these methodologies, optimizing their integration into clinical settings, and addressing the practical challenges to realize their full potential. Through collaborative efforts across disciplines, the advancements in DL-based CMR reconstruction will continue to shape the future of cardiovascular imaging, ultimately enabling faster, more accurate, and patient-centered diagnostics.

Abbreviations

ADMM	alternating direction method of multipliers
ACS	auto-calibration signal
CMR	cardiac magnetic resonance
CNN	convolutional neural network
DAGAN	deep attention generative adversarial network
DDPM	denoising diffusion probabilistic model
DL	deep learning
DL-ESPIRiT	deep learning extended SPIRiT
FISTA	fast iterative shrinkage-thresholding algorithm

GAN	generative adversarial network
GRAPPA	generalized autocalibrating partially parallel acquisitions
JS-MoCo	joint score-based motion compensation
L + S	low-rank plus sparse
LGE	late gadolinium enhancement
LSGAN	least squares GAN
MoDL	model-based deep learning
MRI	magnetic resonance imaging
NRMSE	normalized root mean square error
PnP	Plug-n-Play
PS	partial separability
PSNR	peak signal-to-noise ratio
RAKI	robust artificial-neural-networks for K-space interpolation
SENSE	sensitivity encoding
SPIRiT	self-consistent parallel imaging reconstruction
SSIM	structural similarity index measure
SURE	stein's unbiased risk estimator
VN-Net	variational network
WGAN	Wasserstein GAN
4D Flow	four-dimensional flow MRI

Author details

Mertcan Özdemir* and Osman Eroğul†
TOBB University of Economics and Technology, Ankara, Türkiye

*Address all correspondence to: mertcanozdemir@etu.edu.tr

† These authors contributed equally.

IntechOpen

© 2025 The Author(s). Licensee IntechOpen. This chapter is distributed under the terms of the Creative Commons Attribution License (http://creativecommons.org/licenses/by/4.0), which permits unrestricted use, distribution, and reproduction in any medium, provided the original work is properly cited.

References

[1] Bustin A, Fuin N, Botnar RM, Prieto C. From compressed-sensing to artificial intelligence-based cardiac MRI reconstruction. Frontiers in Cardiovascular Medicine (Switzerland). 2020

[2] Ismail TF, Strugnell W, Coletti C, Božić-Iven M, Weingärtner S, Hammernik K, et al. Cardiac MR: From theory to practice. Frontiers in Cardiovascular Medicine (Switzerland). 2022;**9**

[3] Humbert M, Kovacs G, Hoeper MM, Badagliacca R, Berger RMF, Brida M, et al. 2022 ESC/ERS guidelines for the diagnosis and treatment of pulmonary hypertension: Developed by the task force for the diagnosis and treatment of pulmonary hypertension of the European Society of Cardiology (ESC) and the European Respiratory Society (ERS). Endorsed by the International Society for Heart and Lung Transplantation (ISHLT) and the European reference network on rare respiratory diseases (ERN-lung). European Heart Journal. 2022;**43**: 3618-3731

[4] Cheng JY, Hanneman K, Zhang T, Alley MT, Lai P, Tamir JI, et al. Comprehensive motion-compensated highly accelerated 4d flow MRI with ferumoxytol enhancement for pediatric congenital heart disease. Journal of Magnetic Resonance Imaging. 2016;**43** (6):1355-1368

[5] Sandino CM, Lai P, Vasanawala SS, Cheng JY. Accelerating cardiac cine MRI using a deep learning-based ESPIRiT reconstruction. Magnetic Resonance in Medicine. 2021;**85**:152-167

[6] Amano Y, Takayama M, Kumita S. Contrast-enhanced myocardial T1-weighted scout (look–locker) imaging for the detection of myocardial damages in hypertrophic cardiomyopathy. Journal of Magnetic Resonance Imaging: An Official Journal of the International Society for Magnetic Resonance in Medicine. 2009;**30**(4):778-784

[7] Demirel OB, Ghanbari F, Hoeger CW, Tsao CW, Carty A, Ngo LH, et al. Late gadolinium enhancement cardiovascular magnetic resonance with generative artificial intelligence. Journal of Cardiovascular Magnetic Resonance. 2025;**27**:101127

[8] Kellman P, Arai AE, McVeigh ER, Aletras AH. Phase-sensitive inversion recovery for detecting myocardial infarction using gadolinium-delayed hyperenhancement. Magnetic Resonance in Medicine: An Official Journal of the International Society for Magnetic Resonance in Medicine. 2002;**47**(2): 372-383

[9] Shin T, Lustig M, Nishimura DG, Hu BS. Rapid single-breath-hold 3D late gadolinium enhancement cardiac MRI using a stack-of-spirals acquisition. Journal of Magnetic Resonance Imaging. 2014;**40**:1496-1502

[10] Ntsinjana HN, Hughes ML, Taylor AM. The role of cardiovascular magnetic resonance in pediatric congenital heart disease. Journal of Cardiovascular Magnetic Resonance. 2011;**13**(1):51

[11] Burrage MK, Ferreira VM. The use of cardiovascular magnetic resonance as an early non-invasive biomarker for cardiotoxicity in cardio-oncology. Cardiovascular Diagnosis and Therapy. 2020;**10**(3):610

[12] Oscanoa JA, Middione MJ, Syed AB, Sandino CM, Vasanawala SS, Ennis DB.

Accelerated two-dimensional phase-contrast for cardiovascular MRI using deep learning-based reconstruction with complex difference estimation. Magnetic Resonance in Medicine. 2023;**89**:356-369

[13] Lustig M, Donoho D, Pauly JM. Sparse MRI: The application of compressed sensing for rapid MR imaging. Magnetic Resonance in Medicine. 2007;**58**:1182-1195

[14] Pruessmann KP, Weiger M, Scheidegger MB, Boesiger P. Sense: Sensitivity encoding for fast MRI. Magnetic Resonance in Medicine. 1999; **42**:952-962

[15] Knoll F, Hammernik K, Kobler E, Pock T, Recht MP, Sodickson DK. Assessment of the generalization of learned image reconstruction and the potential for transfer learning. Magnetic Resonance in Medicine. 2019;**81**:116-128

[16] Muckley MJ, Riemenschneider B, Radmanesh A, Kim S, Jeong G, Ko J, et al. Results of the 2020 fastMRI challenge for machine learning MR image reconstruction. IEEE Transactions on Medical Imaging (New York). 2021;**40** (9):2306-2317

[17] Hammernik K, Schlemper J, Qin C, Duan J, Summers RM, Rueckert D. Systematic evaluation of iterative deep neural networks for fast parallel MRI reconstruction with sensitivity-weighted coil combination. Magnetic Resonance in Medicine. 2021;**86**(4):1859-1872

[18] Bai W, Sinclair M, Tarroni G, Oktay O, Rajchl M, Vaillant G, et al. Automated cardiovascular magnetic resonance image analysis with fully convolutional networks. Journal of Cardiovascular Magnetic Resonance. 2018;**20**:65

[19] Wang K, Tamir JI, Goyeneche AD, Wollner U, Brada R, Yu SX, et al. High fidelity deep learning-based MRI reconstruction with instance-wise discriminative feature matching loss. Magnetic Resonance in Medicine. 2022; **88**:476-491

[20] Zucker EJ, Sandino CM, Kino A, Lai P, Vasanawala SS. Free-breathing accelerated cardiac MRI using deep learning: Validation in children and young adults. Radiology. 2021;**300**:539-548

[21] Küstner T, Fuin N, Hammernik K, Bustin A, Qi H, Hajhosseiny R, et al. Cinenet: Deep learning-based 3D cardiac cine MRI reconstruction with multi-coil complex-valued 4D spatio-temporal convolutions. Scientific Reports. 2020; **10**:1-13

[22] Hadamard J. Leçons sur la propagation des ondes et les équations de l'hydrodynamique. Paris: A. Hermann; 1903

[23] Serov V. The Riemann–Lebesgue lemma. In: Fourier Series, Fourier Transform and their Applications to Mathematical Physics. Switzerland: Springer; 2017. pp. 33-35

[24] Al-Haidri W, Matveev I, Al-antari MA, Zubkov M. A deep learning framework for cardiac MR under-sampled image reconstruction with a hybrid spatial and k-space loss function. Diagnostics. 2023;**13**:1120

[25] Arshad M, Najeeb F, Khawaja R, Ammar A, Amjad K, Omer H. Cardiac MR image reconstruction using cascaded hybrid dual domain deep learning framework. PLoS One. 2025;**20**(1): e0313226

[26] Lustig M, Donoho DL, Santos JM, Pauly JM. Compressed Sensing MRI: A Look at How CS Can Improve on Current Imaging Techniques. IEEE Signal Processing Magazine; 2008

[27] Larkman DJ, Nunes RG. Parallel Magnetic Resonance Imaging. Bristol, England: IOP Publishing; 2007

[28] Hollingsworth KG. Reducing acquisition time in clinical MRI by data undersampling and compressed sensing reconstruction. Physics in Medicine & Biology. 2015;**60**(21):R297

[29] Uecker M, Lai P, Murphy MJ, Virtue P, Elad M, Pauly JM, et al. Espirit - An eigenvalue approach to autocalibrating parallel MRI: Where sense meets grappa. Magnetic Resonance in Medicine. 2014; **71**:990-1001

[30] Sandino CM, Cheng JY, Chen F, Mardani M, Pauly JM, Vasanawala SS. Compressed sensing: From research to clinical practice with deep neural networks: Shortening scan times for magnetic resonance imaging. IEEE Signal Processing Magazine. 2020;**37**: 117-127

[31] Griswold MA, Jakob PM, Heidemann RM, Nittka M, Jellus V, Wang J, et al. Generalized autocalibrating partially parallel acquisitions (GRAPPA). Magnetic Resonance in Medicine. 2002; **47**:1202-1210

[32] Christodoulou AG. Low-rank matrix and tensor–based reconstruction. In: Advances in Magnetic Resonance Technology and Applications. Vol. 7. Amsterdam, Netherlands: Elsevier; 2022. pp. 223-247

[33] Lingala SG, Hu Y, DiBella E, Jacob M. Accelerated dynamic MRI exploiting sparsity and low-rank structure: k-t SLR. IEEE Transactions on Medical Imaging. 2011;**30**(5):1042-1054

[34] Zhao B, Haldar JP, Christodoulou AG, Liang Z-P. Image reconstruction from highly undersampled (k, t)-space data with joint partial separability and sparsity constraints. IEEE Transactions on Medical Imaging. 2012;**31**(9):1809-1820

[35] Zhang W, Xiao Z, Tao H, Zhang M, Xu X, Liu Q. Low-rank tensor assisted k-space generative model for parallel imaging reconstruction. Magnetic Resonance Imaging. 2023;**103**:198-207

[36] Ye JC, Kim JM, Jin KH, Lee K. Compressive sampling using annihilating filter-based low-rank interpolation. IEEE Transactions on Information Theory. 2017;**63**:777-801

[37] Cheng JY et al. DeepSPIRiT: Generalized parallel imaging using deep convolutional neural networks. In: Annual Meeting of the International Society of Magnetic Resonance in Medicine. 2018

[38] Beck A, Teboulle M. A fast iterative shrinkage-thresholding algorithm for linear inverse problems. SIAM Journal on Imaging Sciences. 2009;**2**(1):183-202

[39] Boyd S, Parikh N, Chu E, Peleato B, Eckstein J, et al. Distributed optimization and statistical learning via the alternating direction method of multipliers. Foundations and Trends® in Machine Learning. 2011;**3**(1):1-122

[40] Yang Y, Sun J, Li H, Xu Z. Deep ADMM-net for compressive sensing MRI. In: Advances in Neural Information Processing Systems. arXiv preprint. 2016. arXiv:1705.06869

[41] Demirel OB, Yaman B, Dowdle L, Moeller S, Vizioli L, Yacoub E, et al. 20-fold accelerated 7T fMRI using referenceless self-supervised deep learning reconstruction. In: 2021 43rd Annual International Conference of the IEEE Engineering in Medicine & Biology Society (EMBC). IEEE; Nov 2021. pp. 3765-3769

[42] Aggarwal HK, Mani MP, Jacob M. MoDL: Model-based deep learning architecture for inverse problems. IEEE Transactions on Medical Imaging. 2019; **38**:394-405

[43] Dar SU, Yurt M, Shahdloo M, Ildiz ME, Tinaz B, Cukur T. Prior-guided image reconstruction for accelerated multi-contrast MRI via generative adversarial networks. IEEE Journal on Selected Topics in Signal Processing. 2020;**14**:1072-1087

[44] Chen F, Taviani V, Malkiel I, Cheng JY, Tamir JI, Shaikh J, et al. Variable-density single-shot fast spin-echo MRI with deep learning reconstruction by using variational networks. Radiology. 2018;**289**:366-373

[45] Hyun CM, Kim HP, Lee SM, Lee S, Seo JK. Deep learning for undersampled MRI reconstruction. Physics in Medicine and Biology. 2018;**63**:135007

[46] Zhu B, Liu JZ, Cauley SF, Rosen BR, Rosen MS. Image reconstruction by domain-transform manifold learning. Nature. 2018;**555**:487-492

[47] Akçakaya M, Moeller S, Weingärtner S, Uğurbil K. Scan-specific robust artificial-neural-networks for k-space interpolation (RAKI) reconstruction: Database-free deep learning for fast imaging. Magnetic Resonance in Medicine. 2019;**81**(1):439-453

[48] Hammernik K, Klatzer T, Kobler E, Recht MP, Sodickson DK, Pock T, et al. Learning a variational network for reconstruction of accelerated MRI data. Magnetic Resonance in Medicine. 2018; **79**:3055-3071

[49] Yang G, Yu S, Dong H, Slabaugh G, Dragotti PL, Ye X, et al. Dagan: Deep de-aliasing generative adversarial networks for fast compressed sensing MRI reconstruction. IEEE Transactions on Medical Imaging. 2018;**37**:1310-1321

[50] Yurt M, Dar SU, Erdem A, Erdem E, Oguz KK, Çukur T. Mustgan: Multi-stream generative adversarial networks for MR image synthesis. Medical Image Analysis. 2021;**70**:5

[51] Medical image computing and computer assisted intervention–MICCAI 2019. In: 22nd International Conference, Shenzhen, China, October 13–17, 2019, Proceedings, Part IV 22. Springer International Publishing; 2019

[52] Goodfellow I, Pouget-Abadie J, Mirza M, Xu B, Warde-Farley D, Ozair S, et al. Generative adversarial networks. Communications of the ACM. 2020;**63**: 139-144

[53] Arjovsky M, Chintala S, Bottou L. Wasserstein generative adversarial networks. In: International Conference on Machine Learning. MIT, USA: PMLR; 2017. pp. 214-223

[54] Mao X, Li Q, Xie H, Lau RY, Wang Z, Paul Smolley S. Least squares generative adversarial networks. In: Proceedings of the IEEE International Conference on Computer Vision. 2017. pp. 2794-2802

[55] Ledig C, Theis L, Huszár F, Caballero J, Cunningham A, Acosta A, et al. Photo-realistic single image super-resolution using a generative adversarial network. In: Proceedings of the IEEE Conference on Computer Vision and Pattern Recognition. 2017. pp. 4681-4690

[56] Zhu J-Y, Park T, Isola P, Efros AA. Unpaired image-to-image translation using cycle-consistent adversarial networks. In: Proceedings of the IEEE International Conference on Computer Vision. 2017. pp. 2223-2232

[57] Ho J, Jain A, Abbeel P. Denoising diffusion probabilistic models. In: Advances in Neural Information Processing Systems. Vol. 33. 2020. pp. 6840-6851

[58] Liu Y, Cui Z-X, Qin S, Liu C, Zheng H, Wang H, et al. Score-based diffusion models with self-supervised learning for accelerated 3D multi-contrast cardiac magnetic resonance imaging. arXiv preprint. 2023. arXiv:2310.04669

[59] Güngör A, Dar SU, Şaban Öztürk Y, Korkmaz HA, Bedel G, Elmas MO, et al. Adaptive diffusion priors for accelerated MRI reconstruction. Medical Image Analysis. 2023;**88**:102872

[60] Heckel R, Hand P. Deep decoder: Concise image representations from untrained non-convolutional networks. arXiv preprint. 2019. arXiv:1810.03982

[61] Lehtinen J et al. Noise2Noise: Learning image restoration without clean data. ArXiv abs/1803.04189. 2018

[62] Cui Z-X, Cao C, Wang Y, Jia S, Cheng J, Liu X, et al. Spirit-diffusion: Self-consistency driven diffusion model for accelerated MRI. IEEE Transactions on Medical Imaging. 2024;**44**(2):1-1

[63] Gao Z, Zhou SK. MRPD: Undersampled MRI reconstruction by prompting a large latent diffusion model. arXiv preprint. 2024. arXiv:2402.10609

[64] Chen L, Tian X, Wu J, Feng R, Lao G, Zhang Y, et al. JSMoCo: Joint coil sensitivity and motion correction in parallel MRI with a self-calibrating score-based diffusion model. arXiv preprint. 2023. arXiv:2310.09625

[65] Yoo J, Jin KH, Gupta H, Yerly J, Stuber M, Unser M. Time-dependent deep image prior for dynamic MRI. IEEE Transactions on Medical Imaging. 2021; **40**:3337-3348

[66] Korkmaz Y, Dar SU, Yurt M, Ozbey M, Cukur T. Unsupervised MRI reconstruction via zero-shot learned adversarial transformers. IEEE Transactions on Medical Imaging. 2022; **41**:1747-1763

[67] Kramer CM, Barkhausen J, Bucciarelli-Ducci C, Flamm SD, Kim RJ, Nagel E. Standardized cardiovascular magnetic resonance imaging (CMR) protocols: 2020 update. Journal of Cardiovascular Magnetic Resonance. 2020;**22**:2

[68] Dyverfeldt P, Bissell M, Barker AJ, Bolger AF, Carlhäll CJ, Ebbers T, et al. 4D flow cardiovascular magnetic resonance consensus statement. Journal of Cardiovascular Magnetic Resonance. 2015;**17**:1-19

[69] Vishnevskiy V, Walheim J, Kozerke S. Deep variational network for rapid 4D flow MRI reconstruction. Nature Machine Intelligence. 2020;**2**:228-235

[70] Kim D, Jen ML, Eisenmenger LB, Johnson KM. Accelerated 4D-flow MRI with 3-point encoding enabled by machine learning. Magnetic Resonance in Medicine. 2023;**89**:800-811

[71] El-Rewaidy H, Neisius U, Mancio J, Kucukseymen S, Rodriguez J, Paskavitz A, et al. Deep complex convolutional network for fast reconstruction of 3D late gadolinium enhancement cardiac MRI. NMR in Biomedicine. 2020;**33**(7): e4312

[72] Jeelani H, Yang Y, Zhou R, Kramer CM, Salerno M, Weller DS. A myocardial T1-mapping framework with recurrent and U-net convolutional neural networks. In: 2020 IEEE 17th International Symposium on Biomedical Imaging (ISBI). IEEE; 2020. pp. 1941-1944

Chapter 8

Enhancing Speech Emotion Recognition through Bone-Conducted Speech

Md. Sarwar Hosain and Tetsuya Shimamura

Abstract

In this chapter, we analyze the EmoBone dataset, a new and large multinational audio dataset of emotional bone-conducted (BC) speech using advanced deep learning techniques, specifically focusing on bidirectional long short-term memory (BiLSTM) networks combined with attention mechanisms. Although BC speech provides notable benefits in noisy environment and improves user privacy, deep learning models sometimes encounter difficulties like as deterioration and information loss as network depth escalates. To tackle these issues, our proposed model effectively employs attention mechanisms, allowing the network to focus on the most pertinent characteristics and temporal patterns in the BC speech data. This concentrated emphasis substantially reduces the negative impacts of deterioration, resulting in a notable enhancement in emotion recognition accuracy. Our findings indicate that the BiLSTM model incorporating attention mechanisms attains an accuracy of 91.45%, in contrast to 85.17% without attention. This improvement not only illustrates the model's resilience across all emotional categories but also highlights the capacity of attention-based deep learning methods to transform emotion detection systems in BC speech applications, enhancing their reliability and applicability in practical contexts.

Keywords: speech emotion recognition, BiLSTM, bone-conducted speech, air-conducted speech, EmoBone dataset

1. Introduction

In recent years, the development of human-computer interaction (HCI) systems has increasingly focused on making interactions more natural and responsive. A key aspect of achieving this goal is the ability to accurately recognize human emotions from speech. By identifying human emotions from voice signals, speech emotion recognition (SER) finds applications in diverse areas such as robotics, mobile services, contact centers, gaming, and psychological assessments [1]. A lot of research has been done on air-conducted (AC) speech in the SER system, but bone-conducted (BC) speech has its benefits, especially in noisy locations and when privacy is important. BC speech propagates auditory signals directly to the cochlea using bone conduction

 IntechOpen

of the skull [2]. Despite its potential, research on emotion recognition from BC speech remains largely unexplored [3].

The process of creating efficient SER systems comprises several stages, starting with the construction of a strong dataset specifically designed for the desired language and mode of communication. Emotional databases can be created in different formats, such as acted, simulated, or evoked, and may contain audio-only, audio-visual, or face expression data. Choosing suitable features for emotion categorization is a crucial component of constructing a SER system. Acoustic characteristics, such as prosodic elements, spectral properties, voice quality, and energy operators, are frequently employed and can be classified as either temporal or spectral qualities. Due to the lack of a real dataset of BC speech, we created an EmoBone dataset, the first of its kind specifically created for BC speech emotion recognition [3].

With the growing complexity of SER tasks, deep learning models have gained popularity because of their capacity to autonomously acquire complex patterns in data. The temporal dynamics of speech have been captured with encouraging results by recurrent neural networks (RNNs), especially BiLSTM networks. To improve the accuracy of emotion categorization, attention mechanisms are added to these models. This tells the network to concentrate on the numerous important sections of the input, which in turn improves their performance. The combination of BiLSTM with attention mechanisms has proven to be effective in various SER tasks [4]. We desire to solve problems that come up a lot in SER tasks, like the degradation problem and information loss in the higher layers of deep neural networks. These problems can make emotion detection systems less accurate and less reliable. Utilizing BiLSTM and attention mechanisms in this context presents a new strategy for enhancing the precision and robustness of SER systems, especially in situations where conventional AC methods may struggle.

For these problems, we suggest using a Bi-LSTM network that has an attention algorithm added to it (**Figure 1**). The attention method lets the model focus on the most important parts of the input data. This lowers the bad effects of degradation and raises the system's total performance [5]. The results of our experiments clearly show that this strategy is effective. The BiLSTM model achieved an overall accuracy of 85.17% without the use of the attention mechanism. However, when the attention mechanism is incorporated, the model's accuracy significantly improves, reaching 91.45%.

The confusion matrices, classification accuracy, training and testing loss and accuracy data, and receiver operating characteristic (ROC) curves show that the attention mechanism improves not only the overall recognition accuracy but also classification performance for certain emotional categories. The present research signifies a notable advancement in the domain of speech emotion identification by bone conduction, offering a promising new approach that could be applied in various real-world scenarios where traditional air-conducted methods may not suffice.

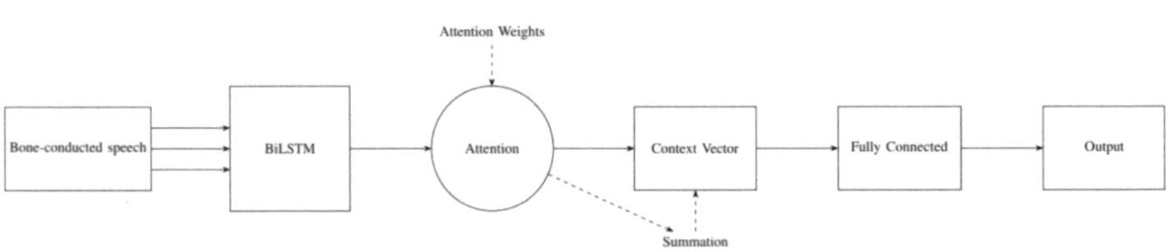

Figure 1.
BiLSTM with attention mechanism for BC speech emotion recognition.

These outcomes, which constitute the main contributions of the chapter, are as follows:

- This research develops a deep learning-based model incorporating an attention mechanism, achieving a high perception accuracy of more than 91% using the largest emotional speech corpus, EmoBone, specifically designed for this purpose.

- A relative analysis is provided, demonstrating that the suggested architecture significantly improves emotion detection capabilities compared to other comparable models.

- This achieves state-of-the-art performance on the EmoBone dataset, establishing a new benchmark for emotion recognition in BC speech.

The remainder of this chapter is classified as follows: Section 2 introduces a thorough review of current literature on BC speech, deep learning (DL), BiLSTM, and attention techniques. Section 3 outlines the detailed protocol and evaluation methodology employed in this investigation. In Section 4, we deliver the comparative experimental results and engage in a thorough discussion of the findings. This section also addresses related topics and constraints. Finally, Section 5 finalizes the chapter, outlining the key discoveries and implications of our research.

2. Literature review

The use of speech in emotion recognition, particularly focusing on pitch or fundamental frequency, has been extensively studied. Pitch, as a speech characteristic, has a significant role in defining emotional nuances. Several researchers have discussed and validated the prominence of various pitch statistics in conveying emotions [6, 7]. On the other hand, a recent report has highlighted the advantages of BC speech over AC speech in pitch detection, especially in noiseless environments [8, 9]. This distinction is crucial because BC speech captures the body's vibration, resulting in more accurate pitch detection, which can be critical for SER.

The noise-robust feature of BC speech, which captures the body's vibrations and makes it less susceptible to outside noise, is what drives its application in SER. This property of BC speech not only enhances the low-frequency components but also improves the accuracy of speech analysis [10]. In Ref. [10], although SER takes AC speech as input, there have been promising results in converting AC speech to equivalent BC speech using an infinite impulse response (IIR) filter. The expectation is that BC speech provides more valuable information for SER due to its enhanced low-frequency components, which are essential for recognizing emotions. They got 72.50% accuracy for recognizing BC speech emotion using convolutional neural networks (CNNs) with synthetic data. The authors of Ref. [11] have also emphasized the improved accuracy rates for speaker recognition when AC and BC speech are used together under noiseless conditions. Their findings indicate that the error rates for BC and AC speech are comparable, which suggest that BC speech can serve as a compensatory feature, potentially leading to better accuracy in SER models.

DL techniques have become a cornerstone in advancing SER, particularly using CNNs and LSTM networks. According to Ref. [12], three convolutional layers and three fully connected (FC) layers made up their CNN architecture. They trained it on the Berlin database of emotional speech (Emo-DB) to tell the difference between seven emotions using spectrograms and got an average prediction accuracy of 56%. In the same way, the researchers in Ref. [13] used a CNN-LSTM architecture for SER and computed log-spectrograms as feature vectors. For the interactive emotional dyadic motion capture (IEMOCAP) dataset, they got prediction rates of 66% for convolution-only and 68% for convolution-LSTM deep neural networks. In Ref. [14], they explored a CNN-LSTM framework for classifying emotions using spectrogram information. The researchers conducted many experiments, testing different combinations such as a shallow CNN with a deep BiLSTM, a deep CNN with a shallow BiLSTM, and a deep CNN with a deep BiLSTM. They found that the most successful configuration consisted of four convolutional layers and one BLSTM layer. They got a weighted accuracy (WA) of 64.5% using IEMOCAP. The researchers in Ref. [15] employed 3-D attention-based convolutional recurrent neural networks (ACRNN) to classify emotions. They trained the model using the Emo-DB corpus and supplemented it with data from the IEMOCAP corpus. The resulting recognition accuracies were 82.82 and 64.74% for the two datasets, respectively. A different research conducted a deep learning model for end-to-end speech emotion recognition, which combined a CNN with an LSTM [16]. The WA of this model, which was trained and evaluated using spectrograms from the IEMOCAP dataset, reached 68%. The architecture utilized attention-based BiLSTM layers to extract sequential features and fully convolutional network (FCN) layers to learn the spectro-temporal characteristics of the spectrograms.

Various speech emotion datasets have been used in SER studies, including the IEMOCAP, Ryerson audio-visual database of emotional speech and song (RAVDESS), Emo-DB, crowd-sourced emotional multimodal actors dataset (CREMA-D) and others. The IEMOCAP and RAVDESS datasets are widely used benchmarks, offering a rich collection of emotionally charged dialogs. Several studies have demonstrated the effectiveness of deep learning models on this dataset. For instance, researchers [17] employed a connections temporal classification (CTC) approach combined with an attention-based BLSTM for SER, achieving a 69% accuracy on the IEMOCAP dataset in 2019. Their method involved extracting log mel-spectrograms from each audio file for classification. The researchers in Ref. [18] introduced a deep stride convolutional neural network (DSCNN) model that attained mean accuracies of 81.75 and 79.5% for the IEMOCAP and RAVDESS datasets, respectively. In contrast, the newly developed EmoBone dataset, designed specifically for BC speech, has shown state-of-the-art performance in recent studies. The dataset's unique features, such as enhanced low-frequency components and noise-robust characteristics, make it particularly suitable for SER using deep learning techniques. The attention mechanism, applied successfully in image processing and later adopted in natural language processing, has been integrated into LSTM networks for SER, optimizing the network's output and improving accuracy [19, 20]. Arjun et al. [21] utilized a CNN with an attention framework and an LSTM model with a channel-attention autoencoder. They conducted experiments on three databases: the Database for emotion analysis using physiological signals (DEAP), the SJTU emotion EEG dataset (SEED), and the children's hospital Boston-Massachusetts institute of technology scalp EEG database (CHB-MIT). Using the DEAP dataset, their method achieved an average accuracy of 65.9 and 69.5% for valence and arousal classification, the positive-negative classification accuracy in the SEED dataset is 76.7%. In the CHB-MIT dataset, the accuracy for Pre-Ictal Vs Ictal classification is 69.1%, for Inter-Ictal Vs Ictal classification is 67.6%, and for Pre-Ictal Vs Inter-Ictal classification is 72.3%. BiLSTM networks have been extensively used in

SER tasks, with or without attention mechanisms. Wöllmer [22] was among the first to apply LSTM to continuous emotion recognition, extracting numerous features for each utterance as input for the LSTM. The authors in Ref. [23] introduced a pooling operation of CNNs to the output of LSTM for emotion classification tasks. Another research in Ref. [24] suggested an attention mechanism that utilizes an attention parameter vector to calculate weights for frames, hence optimizing the output of the LSTM. This approach considers the memory capacity of LSTM and assigns higher weights to the most relevant outputs, often taken as the final output of the LSTM. Applying the attention mechanism to the feature dimension of the output of LSTM improves its ability to be distinguished.

The application of BC speech in SER using deep learning techniques has shown significant promise, especially when compared to traditional AC speech. The integration of attention mechanisms with LSTM networks has further improved the accuracy and efficiency of SER models. The development of new datasets like EmoBone has also contributed to advancing the field, providing more robust and accurate models for speech emotion recognition.

3. Methodology and structure

This research explores the use of BiLSTM networks in the field of speech emotion recognition. To test this idea, we examine how well the model works with and without an attention mechanism. We think that attention can help the model focus on important parts of the speech data. The methodology is well organized to cover all stages of the study, which include data collection, preprocessing, model architecture design, training processes, and evaluation measures. This thorough approach ensures the validity and reliability of our results.

3.1 EmoBone dataset

The dataset comprises a collection of 28 speakers from 10 separate countries. It is composed of 15,680 files, representing 7 emotions (anger, calm, fear, happy, sad, surprise, and neutral), 10 sentences, and 8 repetitions for each sentence. The sentences were recorded in a dedicated audio recording studio. Sufficient time was allocated for speakers to thoroughly prepare themselves to effectively deliver the appropriate emotions. During the recording sessions, the principal investigator visually monitored the recordings on a laptop and provided immediate feedback to the speakers using specified gestures. Headphones connected to a control device linked to the microphone in the recording room were utilized to listen to the recordings. The prominent audio editor "Ocenaudio" was employed for recording and editing the speech files. Audio clips that did not meet the specified criteria were eliminated, and the remaining recordings were stored on the computer for future processing, pending expert validation. All sentences representing the intended emotional categories were recorded separately for each speaker, necessitating the scheduling of multiple sessions. The recordings were post-processed to prepare the data for prosodic analysis and automatic feature extraction. Each speaker delivered approximately 700–800 recordings, requiring a recording time of 3 to 4 hours. From those takes, eight were selected as the most effective, resulting in each speaker having 560 final tracks. The audio recordings were edited to have an average duration of 4.5 seconds, ensuring that no words were cut off and that any periods of quiet were removed during the editing process.

Each speaker was assigned an individual serial number according to their gender, and the statements were recorded in a preset sequential manner. Serial numbers were allocated based on the speakers' intended recording schedules. After the editing procedure, each audio file was given a unique and distinctive file name. For example, the file name "BC_F_14_SH_Angry_S6(7).wav" provides information on the speech type (BC), speaker gender (M), identification number (14), speaker name (SH), emotional state (angry), sentence number (6), take number (7), and file extension (.wav).

The reliability of the audio recordings was assessed by evaluating how accurately unskilled raters could identify the emotions conveyed in the recordings. Higher identification accuracy is indicative of superior recording quality. For this assessment, a total of 80 university students from Bangladesh were selected as evaluators. The group comprised 40 males and 40 females, all within the age range of 18 to 25. Only individuals, who were native speakers of Bengali, had normal auditory abilities, and had no history of speech or language impairments were included. To eliminate potential bias, the raters were not present during the recording sessions and did not receive any specific training. To assess speech emotion, 40 random audio sets, each containing an equal number of stimuli representing each emotion, were utilized, with each set comprising 392 stimuli. Each audio set was assigned to pairs of raters to ensure that each clip was evaluated twice, once by a male and once by a female rater. The raters assessed the speech samples and determined the emotion conveyed by the speaker. Their evaluations were subsequently compared against the speaker's intended emotion. Both correct and incorrect responses were counted, and percentage scores were computed for each emotion. To mitigate potential biases arising from raters' tendencies to select certain emotion categories, the unbiased hit rate was calculated using Wagner's approach [25]. Wagner's unbiased hit rate, Hu, is determined by squaring the number of correct predictions for a certain emotion, such as sadness, and dividing it by the total number of recordings of sad emotions and the total number of guesses made for sad emotions.

3.2 Data collection and preprocessing

The EmoBone dataset utilized in this research comprises 15,680 audio files, systematically organized within a directory structure that categorizes files by actor and emotion class. Each audio file represents a unique utterance expressing one of seven emotions: neutral, calm, happy, sad, angry, fear, and surprise. This dataset was accessed through a publicly available repository, providing a diverse set of vocal samples to train and evaluate the models. The files were processed using Python's torchaudio library, which facilitated the reading and transformation of raw audio data into a form suitable for model consumption. To maintain consistency across all audio samples, we resampled the audio files to a uniform sample rate of 16,000 Hz. This standardization ensures that the temporal resolution of the audio signals is consistent, thereby eliminating potential discrepancies arising from variable sampling rates.

Once resampled, the audio files were transformed into a feature representation using mel-frequency cepstral coefficients (MFCCs). MFCCs are commonly used in speech processing because they effectively capture the timbral texture of sound, which is crucial for distinguishing between different emotional states. The transformation involved computing a MelSpectrogram for each audio file, followed by a discrete cosine transform to derive the MFCC features. This process resulted in a feature vector of 23 coefficients for each audio frame. The parameters for the MFCC computation were carefully selected to optimize the feature representation: the number of Mel bins was set to 40, the fast Fourier transform (FFT) window size was fixed at a constant value of 400, and the hop length was established as 160. These parameters were picked based on established practices in speech processing to ensure the features accurately capture the nuances of the audio signals. After computing the MFCCs, the features were standardized using StandardScaler from the sklearn library, ensuring that each feature had a mean of zero and unit variance. This normalization step is critical as it enhances the model's ability to learn by preventing any single feature from disproportionately influencing the training process.

3.3 Model architecture: BiLSTM without attention

The LSTM is a variant of the RNN that consists of memory blocks connected and capable of maintaining temporal states through self-connections. It has three gate units: input, output, and forget gates. LSTM solves long-term dependence issues in RNNs and implements refined internal processing units for better storage and updating context information. It also overcomes gradient vanishing or explosion problems in standard RNNs. The BiLSTM model utilizes contextual information in both the forward and backward directions, enhancing its robustness by detecting hidden emotions through directional analysis [26].

The initial model architecture developed in this study was a BiLSTM network without an attention mechanism. This model was built to take advantage of the sequential structure of voice data by capturing both forward and backward temporal dependencies. The architecture consists of several layers that hierarchically process the input data. The input layer receives the MFCC feature vectors, which serves as the model's raw data input. This layer is followed by a stack of two bidirectional LSTM layers, each with 128 hidden units. These LSTM layers are responsible for processing the input sequences and generating a sequence of hidden states that capture the temporal dependencies within the data. The LSTM layers in the model can include both past and future context when processing each time step due to their bidirectional nature, enhancing its ability to capture relevant features for emotion classification.

The final output of the LSTM layer is sent into a fully linked layer, which transforms the LSTM's output into the seven emotion classes. This mapping is achieved through a linear transformation, followed by a Softmax activation function. The Softmax function converts the raw scores into probabilities, providing a measure of the model's confidence in each emotion class. The choice of a Softmax activation function is motivated by its ability to normalize the output probabilities, ensuring that they sum to one. This property is essential for multi-class classification tasks, as it allows the model to express uncertainty in its predictions. The model was implemented using the PyTorch framework, which offers a versatile and effective framework for constructing and instructing deep learning models. To optimize the parameters of the model, we employed the Adam optimizer, a modified version of stochastic gradient descent that adjusts the learning rate for each parameter using estimates of its first and second moments. The learning rate was set to 0.001, a commonly used value that balances the need for quick convergence with the risk of overshooting the optimal solution. The model performed 100 epochs of training, utilizing a batch size of 8, to achieve sufficient exposure to the training data while also retaining computational efficiency.

3.4 Model architecture: BiLSTM with attention

To enhance the performance of the BiLSTM model, we incorporated an attention mechanism. The attention mechanism enables the model to pick and focus on those segments of the input process that are more essential for classification, hence potentially enhancing the model's capacity to distinguish between comparable emotions. The architecture of the BiLSTM with attention is similar to the vanilla BiLSTM model, with the addition of an attention layer after the second LSTM layer. The attention layer computes a context vector by assigning weights to the hidden states of the LSTM layer. These weights, or attention scores, are learned during training and indicate the relative importance of each hidden state for the final prediction. By adding up all of the hidden states with weights derived from attention scores, we can get the context vector. This context vector is then fed into a fully connected layer, which maps it to the seven emotion classes.

The attention mechanism was implemented using a linear layer with a dimensionality of 1, allowing the model to assign a single weight to each hidden state. A tanh activation function was applied to the attention layer's output before the Softmax function was used. The tanh activation function introduces nonlinearity into the attention scores, enhancing the model's ability to differentiate between important and unimportant hidden states. Highlighting the most important portions of the input sequence, the attention mechanism helps the model make more accurate predictions, particularly for challenging cases where the differences between emotions are subtle.

3.5 Training and evaluation

Both the BiLSTM model and the BiLSTM model with attention were trained using the same training dataset and procedure to ensure a fair comparison. In order to train the model, we minimized the cross-entropy loss, which is the difference between the actual emotion labels and the predicted probabilities. To avoid overfitting, we checked the accuracy of the model on a validation set while it was being trained. We used an early stopping mechanism to cease training after three consecutive epochs if the validation loss failed to improve. This method is useful for preventing the model from becoming "overfit" to its training data, thereby improving its generalization performance. If the validation loss did not improve, a learning rate scheduler was employed to lower the learning rate, so assisting the model in achieving a more optimal minimum.

The performance of both models was evaluated using classification accuracy on a held-out test set. The vanilla BiLSTM model achieved an accuracy of 85%, indicating its ability to capture temporal dependencies in the speech data. However, the BiLSTM model with attention significantly outperformed the vanilla model, achieving an accuracy of 91.45%. The ability of the model to distinguish between various emotions is improved because the attention mechanism may zero in on the most important bits of the input sequence. To further analyze the models' performance, we computed confusion matrices and classification reports for both models. The confusion matrix for the BiLSTM with attention model showed a significant reduction in misclassifications compared to the vanilla model, particularly for similar emotion classes like calm and happy. The classification report highlighted the improvement in precision, recall, and F1-score for most of the emotion classes, indicating a more balanced and robust performance.

The experimental results demonstrate the effectiveness of the attention mechanism in improving the performance of BiLSTM models for speech emotion recognition. The attention-based BiLSTM model not only achieved higher accuracy but also provided more interpretable results by highlighting the most relevant features for classification. This study underscores the importance of incorporating attention mechanisms in sequential models, particularly for tasks that require fine-grained analysis of temporal data.

4. Experimental results

The EmoBone dataset was utilized to train and evaluate the BiLSTM models. The dataset's distribution across the seven emotion classes (neutral, calm, happy, sad, angry, fear, and surprise) is visualized in **Figure 2**. The figure illustrates a relatively balanced distribution, with each emotion class represented by a substantial number of samples. This balance is crucial for preventing the model from being biased toward any particular emotion class during training.

The performance of the BiLSTM model without the attention mechanism is depicted in **Figure 3**. The figure presents the training and validation loss and accuracy curves over 100 epochs. The loss curves demonstrate a steady decrease in both training and validation loss, indicating that the model is learning to fit the training data effectively. The accuracy curves show a corresponding increase in both training and validation accuracy, further confirming the model's learning progress. The intersection of the training and validation curves implies that the model is not overfitting, which is a positive sign for its generalization capabilities. The confusion matrix for the BiLSTM model without attention is presented in **Figure 4**. The matrix provides a thorough analysis of the approach estimates, highlighting its advantages and disadvantages in categorizing various emotions. The diagonal elements of the

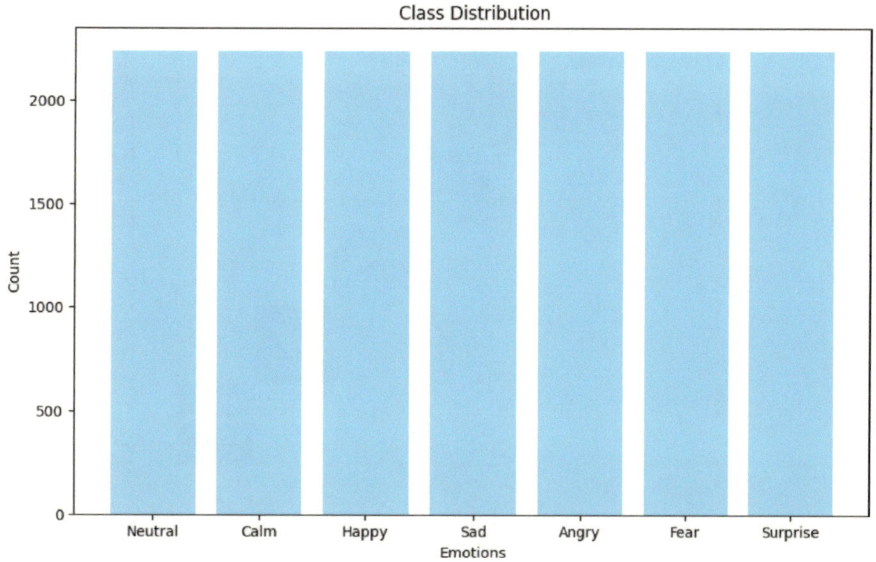

Figure 2.
Emotion class distribution.

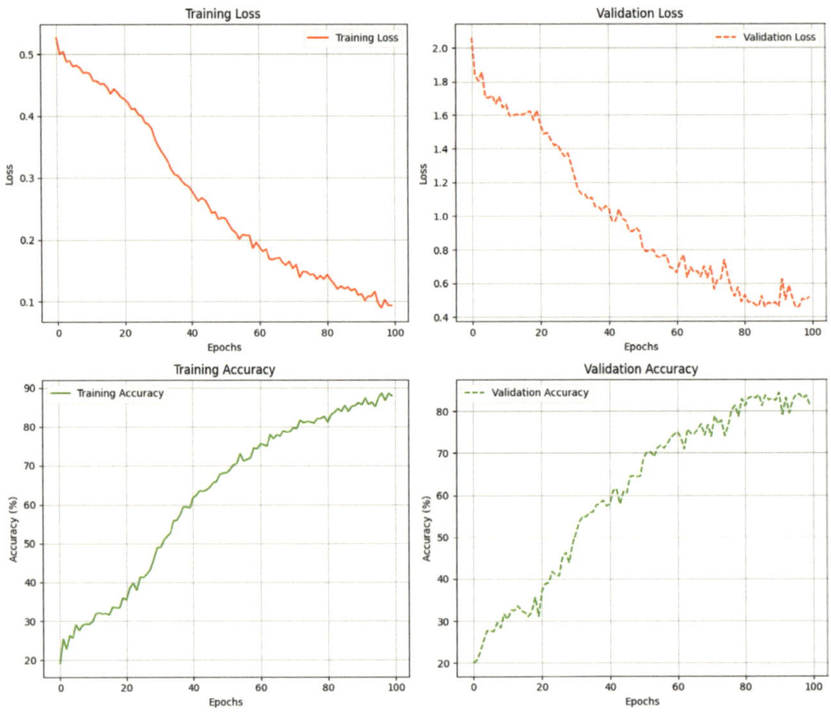

Figure 3.
Loss and accuracy without attention.

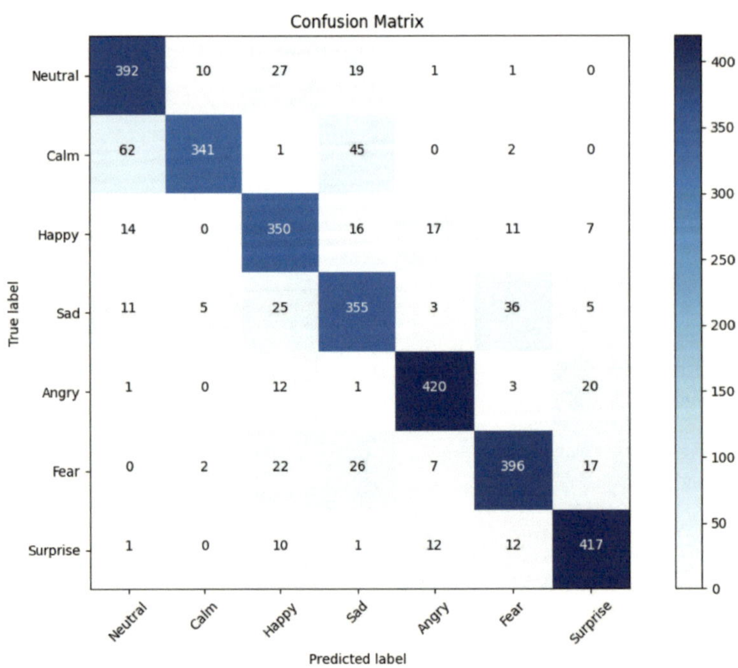

Figure 4.
Confusion matrix without attention.

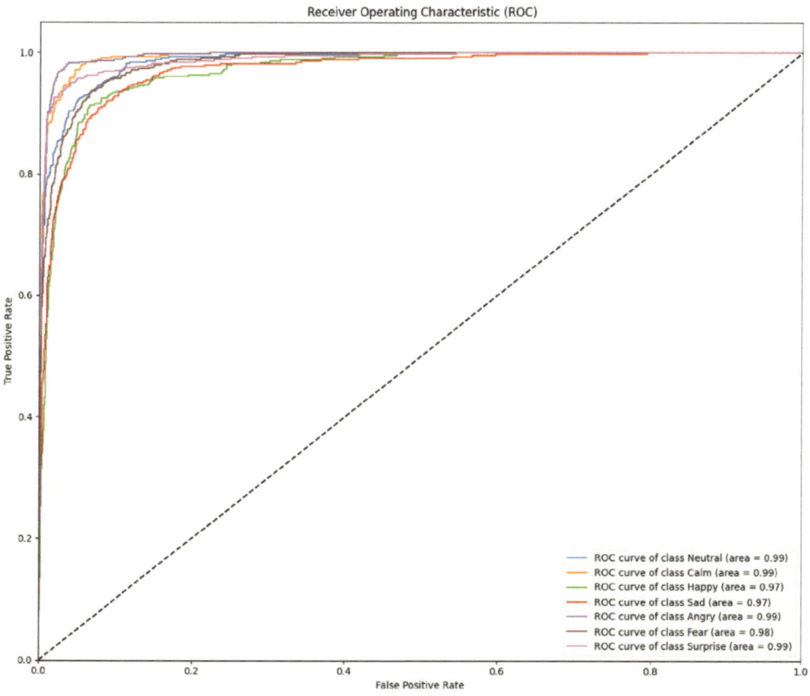

Figure 5.
ROC curve of emotions.

matrix represent the number of correct predictions for each emotion class, while the off-diagonal elements indicate misclassifications. The matrix shows that the model performs well for most emotion classes, with high accuracy for emotions like angry and surprise. However, there is some confusion between similar emotions like calm and neutral, suggesting room for improvement.

Figure 5 presents the ROC curves for the BiLSTM model. ROC curves graphically represent the relationship between the true-positive rate and the false-positive rate across various classification levels. The curves illustrate the ability of the model to differentiate across several emotion categories. The area under the curve (AUC) for each emotion class is also provided, serving as a quantitative measure of the model's performance. The AUC values are generally high, indicating good discriminative power for most emotions.

The overall classification accuracy for the BiLSTM model without attention is presented in **Figure 6**. The figure shows that the model achieves an accuracy of 85.17%, which is a respectable performance considering the complexity of the task. This result serves as a baseline for comparison with the Bi-LSTM model with attention.

The performance of the BiLSTM model with the attention mechanism is illustrated in **Figure 7**. The figure presents the training and validation loss and accuracy curves, similar to **Figure 3**. The curves show a similar trend of decreasing loss and increasing accuracy, indicating that the model with attention is also learning effectively. However, the validation accuracy for the model with attention is consistently higher than that of the vanilla model, suggesting that the attention mechanism is contributing to improved performance.

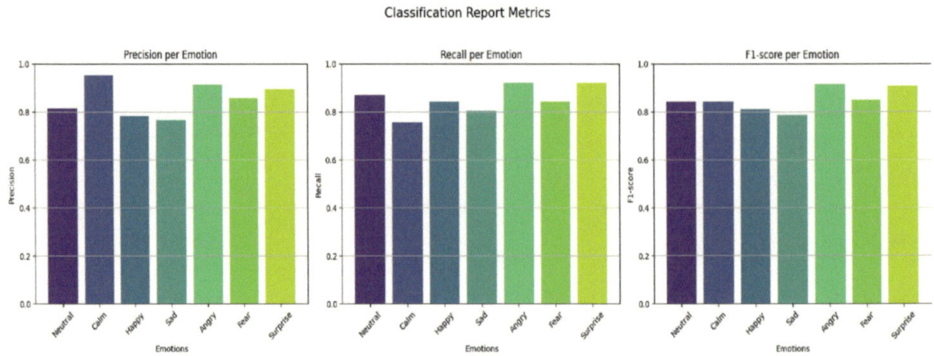

Figure 6.
Classification accuracy without attention.

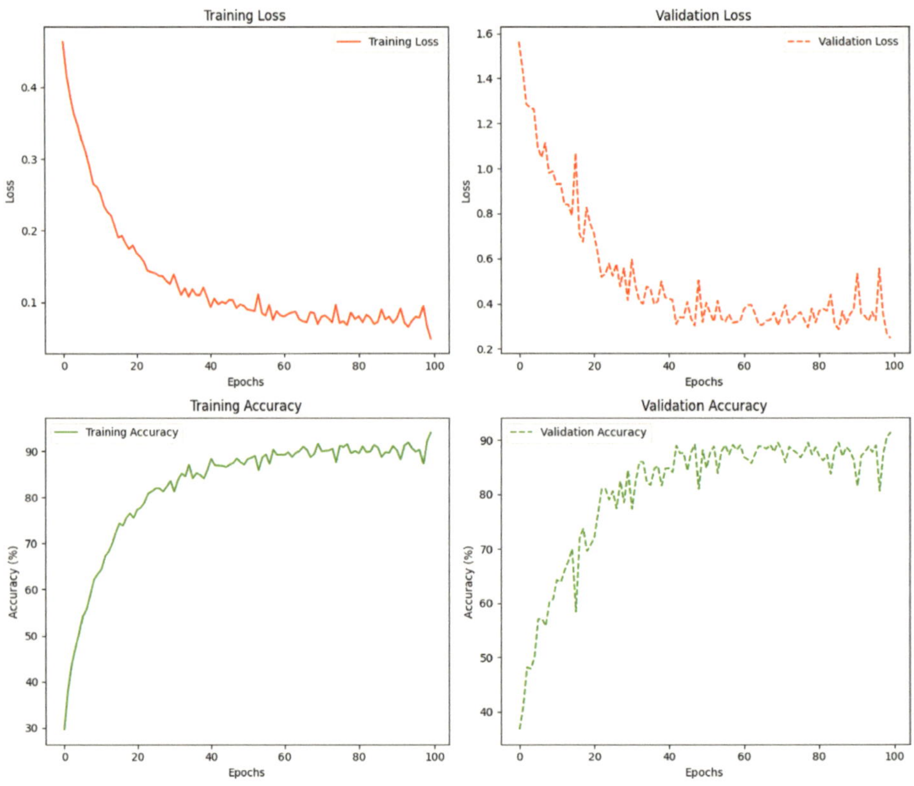

Figure 7.
Loss and accuracy with attention.

The confusion matrix for the BiLSTM model with attention is shown in **Figure 8**. The matrix reveals a significant reduction in misclassifications compared to the vanilla model. The diagonal elements are more prominent, indicating higher accuracy for each emotion class. The presence of the attention mechanism in the model appears to be diminishing the ambiguity between calm and neutral, indicating that it aids in directing its focus toward the most significant characteristics for discerning between these emotions.

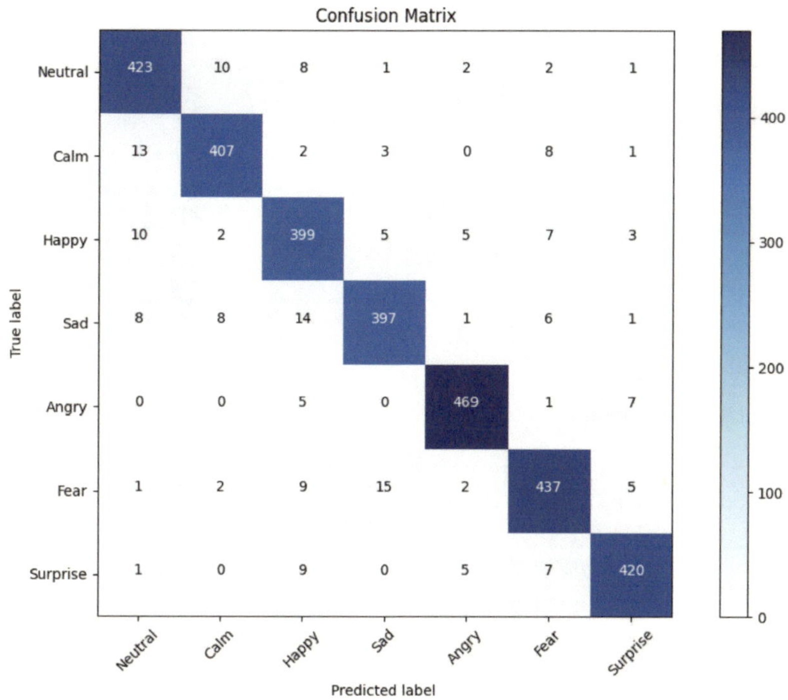

Figure 8.
Confusion matrix with attention.

The accuracy for each emotion class for the Bi-LSTM model with attention is presented in **Figure 9**. The figure shows a consistent improvement in accuracy for all emotion classes compared to the vanilla model. The accuracy for calm is notably higher, confirming the positive impact of the attention mechanism.

The overall classification accuracy for the Bi-LSTM model with attention is shown in **Figure 10**. The figure reveals a significant improvement in accuracy, reaching 91.45%. The detail values are presented in **Table 1**. This outcome emphasizes how well

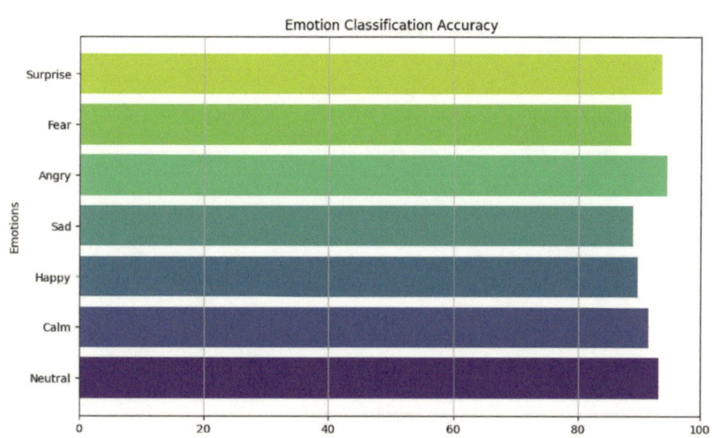

Figure 9.
Emotion accuracy with attention.

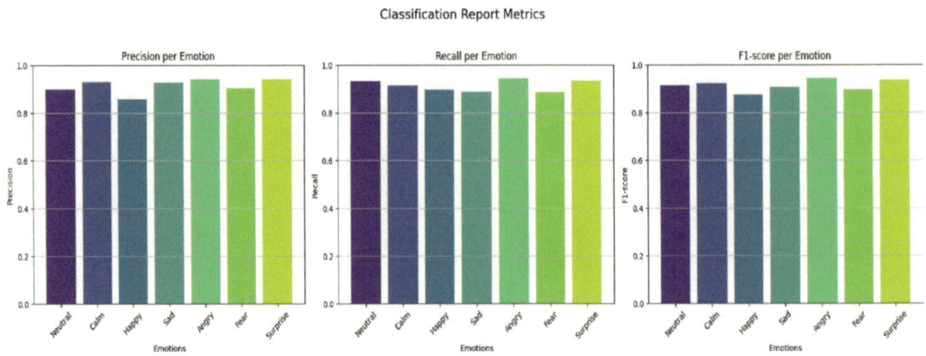

Figure 10.
Classification accuracy with attention.

Emotion	Precision	Recall	F1-Score	Support
Neutral	0.900844	0.932314	0.916309	458.000
Calm	0.929825	0.915767	0.922742	463.000
Happy	0.856823	0.896956	0.876430	427.000
Sad	0.926887	0.889140	0.907621	442.000
Angry	0.942350	0.944444	0.943396	450.000
Fear	0.906040	0.886214	0.896018	457.000
Surprise	0.940367	0.936073	0.938215	438.000
Accuracy	0.914514	0.914514	0.914514	0.91451
Macro avg	0.914734	0.914416	0.914390	3135.00
Weighted avg	0.915037	0.914514	0.914593	3135.00

Table 1.
Classification accuracy with attention.

Work	Dataset	Accuracy
Proposed model (BiLSTM + Attention)	EmoBone	91.45%
Zhao et al. (2019) [19]	IEMOCAP	69%
Mustaqeem and Kwon (2020) [27]	IEMOCAP	81.75%
Mustaqeem and Kwon (2020) [27]	RAVDESS	79.5%
Chen et al. [15]	Emo-DB	82.82%
Chen et al. [15]	IEMOCAP	64.74%
Etienne et al. [14]	IEMOCAP	64.5%
Zhao et al. [16]	IEMOCAP	68%
Satt et al. [13]	IEMOCAP	66%
Badshah et al. [12]	Emo-DB	56%
Hosain et al. [10]	Synthetic BC speech data	72.50%

Table 2.
Comparison of accuracy across different studies.

the attention mechanism improves the accuracy of the emotional classification of the model. A comparative analysis is presented in **Table 2**.

5. Conclusions

This chapter examined the use of BiLSTM networks, with and without an attention mechanism, for speech emotion recognition employing the EmoBone dataset. The findings indicate that the BiLSTM model with attention outperforms the standard Bi-LSTM model, with an accuracy of 91.45 versus 85.17%. The attention mechanism's capacity to concentrate on pertinent characteristics in the speech data was essential for enhancing classification accuracy, especially in differentiating between identical emotions. The research demonstrates that attention-based BiLSTM models can markedly enhance speech emotion identification systems, facilitating more precise and dependable emotion detection in practical applications. Future study may investigate the incorporation of more advanced methodologies, such as transfer learning and multi-modal fusion, to further improve the efficacy and resilience of speech emotion identification systems.

Conflict of interest

The authors declare no conflict of interest.

Abbreviations

BiLSTM	bi-directional long short-term memory
HCI	human-computer interaction
SER	speech emotion recognition
AC	air-conducted
BC	bone-conducted
RNNs	recurrent neural networks
ROC	receiver operating characteristic
CNNs	convolutional neural networks
IEMOCAP	interactive emotional dyadic motion capture
ACRNN	attention-based convolutional recurrent neural networks
FCN	fully convolutional network
RAVDESS	Ryerson audio-visual database of emotional speech and song

Author details

Md. Sarwar Hosain[1,2*†] and Tetsuya Shimamura[2†]

1 Pabna University of Science and Technology, Pabna, Bangladesh

2 Saitama University, Saitama, Japan

*Address all correspondence to: sarwar.ice@pust.ac.bd

†These authors contributed equally.

IntechOpen

© 2025 The Author(s). Licensee IntechOpen. This chapter is distributed under the terms of the Creative Commons Attribution License (http://creativecommons.org/licenses/by/4.0), which permits unrestricted use, distribution, and reproduction in any medium, provided the original work is properly cited.

References

[1] Khare SK, Blanes-Vidal V, Nadimi ES, Acharya UR. Emotion recognition and artificial intelligence: A systematic review (2014-2023) and research recommendations. Information Fusion. 2024;**102**:102019. DOI: 10.1016/j.inffus.2023.102019 [Accessed: July 14, 2024]

[2] Zhou Y, Chen Y, Ma Y, Liu H. A real-time dual-microphone speech enhancement algorithm assisted by bone conduction sensor. MDPI Sensors. 2020;**20**(18):5050. Available from: https://www.mdpi.com/1424-8220/20/18/5050 [Accessed: July 14, 2024]

[3] Hosain MS, Sugiura Y, Rahman MS, Shimamura T. EmoBone: A multinational audio dataset of emotional bone conducted speech. IEEJ Transactions on Electrical and Electronic Engineering. 2024;**19**(9):1492-1506. DOI: 10.1002/tee.24110 [Accessed: May 29, 2024]

[4] Xie Y, Liang R, Liang Z, Huang C, Zou C, Schuller B. Speech emotion classification using attention-based LSTM. IEEE/ACM Transactions on Audio Speech and Language Processing. 2019;**27**(11):1675-1685. DOI: 10.1109/taslp.2019.2925934 [Accessed: July 14, 2024]

[5] Chen S, Zhang M, Yang X, Zhao Z, Zou T, Sun X. The impact of attention mechanisms on speech emotion recognition. Sensors. 2021;**21**(22):7530. DOI: 10.3390/s21227530 [Accessed: July 14, 2024]

[6] Busso C, Lee S, Narayanan S. Analysis of emotionally salient aspects of fundamental frequency for emotion detection. IEEE Transactions on Audio, Speech and Language Processing. 2009;**17**(4):582-596 [Accessed: July 14, 2024]

[7] Sudhkar RS, Anil MC. Analysis of speech features for emotion detection: A review. In: Proceedings of the International Conference on Computing Communication Control and Automation. Uttar Pradesh, India: IEEE Uttar Pradesh Section; 2015. pp. 661-664. Available from: https://api.semanticscholar.org/CorpusID:15403862 [Accessed: July 17, 2024]

[8] Rahman MS, Shimamura T. Pitch determination from bone conducted speech. IEICE Transactions on Information and Systems. 2015;**E99.D**(1):283-287. DOI: 10.1587/transinf.2015edl8134 [Accessed: July 17, 2024]

[9] Rahman MS, Shimamura T. Pitch characteristics of bone conducted speech. In: European Signal Processing Conference. Aalborg, Denmark: European Association for Signal Processing (EURASIP); 2010. pp. 795-799. Available from: https://dblp.uni-trier.de/db/conf/eusipco/eusipco2010.html#RahmanS10 [Accessed: July 19, 2024]

[10] Hosain MS, Sugiura Y, Yasui N, Shimamura T. Deep-learning-based speech emotion recognition using synthetic bone-conducted speech. Journal of Signal Processing. 2023;**27**(6):151-163. DOI: 10.2299/jsp.27.151 [Accessed: July 19, 2024]

[11] Tsuge S, Koizumi ND, Fukumi M, Kuroiwa S. Speaker verification method using bone-conduction and air-conduction speech. In: Proceedings of the International Symposium on Intelligent

Signal Processing and Communication Systems (ISPACS) [Internet]. Kanazawa, Japan: IEEE; 2009. DOI: 10.1109/ispacs.2009.5383806 [Accessed: July 24, 2024]

[12] Badshah AM, Ahmad J, Rahim N, Baik SW. Speech emotion recognition from spectrograms with deep convolutional neural network [Internet]. In: Proceedings of the International Conference on Platform Technology and Service (PlatCon); 13-15 February 2017; Busan, Korea (South). Busan, South Korea: IEEE; 2017. DOI: 10.1109/platcon.2017.7883728 [Accessed: August 6, 2024]

[13] Satt A, Rozenberg S, Hoory R. Efficient emotion recognition from speech using deep learning on spectrograms. In: Proceedings of Interspeech 2017, 18th Annual Conference of the International Speech Communication Association (ISCA). Stockholm, Sweden; 20-24 Aug 2017. DOI: 10.21437/interspeech.2017-200 [Accessed: August 6, 2024]

[14] Etienne C, Fidanza G, Petrovskii A, Devillers L, Schmauch B. CNN+LSTM architecture for speech emotion recognition with data augmentation. 2018. arXiv:1802.05630. Available from: https://arxiv.org/abs/1802.05630 [Accessed: August 6, 2024]

[15] Chen M, He X, Yang J, Zhang H. 3-D convolutional recurrentneural networks with attention model for speech emotion recognition. IEEE Signal Processing Letter. 2018;**25**(10):1440-1444. DOI: 10.1109/LSP.2018.2860246 [Accessed: August 6, 2024]

[16] Zhao Z, Zhao Y, Bao Z, Wang H, Zhang Z, Li C. Deep spectrum feature representations for speech emotion recognition. In: Proceedings of the Joint Workshop of the 4th Workshop on Affective Social Multimedia Computing and the 1st Multi-Modal Affective Computing of Large-Scale Multimedia Data (ASMMC-MMAC'18). Seoul, Republic of Korea; 2018. pp. 27-33 [Accessed: August 6, 2024]

[17] Zhao Z, Bao Z, Zhang Z, Cummins N, Wang H, Schuller BW. Attention-enhanced connectionist temporal classification for discrete speech emotion recognition. In: Proceedings of Interspeech 2019, 20th Annual Conference of the International Speech Communication Association (ISCA). Graz, Austria: 2019. pp. 206-210. DOI: 10.21437/interspeech.2019-1649 [Accessed: August 6, 2024]

[18] Xiao T, Xu Y, Yang K, Zhang J, Peng Y, Zhang Z. The application of two-level attention models in deep convolutional neural network for fine-grained image classification. In: Proceedings of the IEEE Conference on Computer Vision and Pattern Recognition (CVPR). Vol. 2015. Boston, MA, USA: IEEE; 7-12 June 2015. pp. 842-850. DOI: 10.1109/CVPR.2015.7298685 [Accessed: August 6, 2024]

[19] Zhao B, Wu X, Feng J, Peng Q, Yan S. Diversified visual attention networks for fine-grained object classification. IEEE Transactions on Multimedia. 2017;**19**(6):1245-1256. DOI: 10.1109/tmm.2017.2648498 [Accessed: August 6, 2024]

[20] Lin Z, Feng M, Santos CND, Yu M, Xiang B, Zhou B, et al. A structured self-attentive sentence embedding. arXiv preprint; arXiv:1703.03130. 2017. DOI: 10.48550/arXiv.1703.03130 [Accessed: August 6, 2024]

[21] Rajpoot AS, Panicker MR. Subject independent emotion recognition using EEG signals employing attention driven neural networks. arXiv preprint;

arXiv:2106.03461. 2021. DOI: 10.1109/arXiv:2106.03461 [Accessed: August 9, 2024]

[22] Wöllmer M, Eyben F, Reiter S, Schuller B, Cox C, Douglas-Cowie E, Cowie R. Abandoning emotion classes – Towards continuous emotion recognition with modelling of long-range dependencies. In: Proceedings of Interspeech 2008, 9th Annual Conference of the International Speech Communication Association (ISCA). Brisbane, Australia: ISCA; 22-26 Sept 2008

[23] Keren G, Schuller B. Convolutional RNN: An enhanced model for extracting features from sequential data. In: Proceedings of the 2016 International Joint Conference on Neural Networks (IJCNN). Vol. 2016. Vancouver, Canada: IEEE; 24-29 July 2016. pp. 2785-2792. DOI: 10.1109/ijcnn.2016.7727636 [Accessed: August 9, 2024]

[24] Mirsamadi S, Barsoum E, Zhang C. Automatic speech emotion recognition using recurrent neural networks with local attention. In: Proceedings of the IEEE International Conference on Acoustics, Speech, and Signal Processing (ICASSP). New Orleans, Louisiana, USA: IEEE; 5-9 Mar 2017. pp. 2120-2124. DOI: 10.1109/icassp.2017.7952552 [Accessed: August 9, 2024]

[25] Wagner HL. On measuring performance in category judgment studies of nonverbal behavior. Journal of Nonverbal Behavior. 1993;**17**(1):3-28. DOI: 10.1007/bf00987006 [Accessed: August 9, 2024]

[26] Sultana S, Iqbal MZ, Selim MR, Rashid MM, Rahman MS. Bangla speech emotion recognition and cross-lingual study using deep CNN and BLSTM networks. IEEE Access. 2021;**10**:564-578. DOI: 10.1109/access.2021.3136251 [Accessed: August 9, 2024]

[27] Mustaqeem N, Kwon S. A CNN-assisted enhanced audio signal processing for speech emotion recognition. Sensors. 2019;**20**(1):183. DOI: 10.3390/s20010183 [Accessed: August 9, 2024]

Chapter 9

Application of Artificial Neural Networks in Economic and Financial Sciences

Roya Seifipour and Azadeh Mehrabian

Abstract

Neural networks excel in handling complex, non-linear relationships, making them suitable for predictions where traditional linear models fall short. Applications include forecasting exchange rates, stock prices, and bankruptcy risks, demonstrating superior accuracy compared to conventional methods. In the realm of economics, neural networks facilitate the integration of theories like the Kuznets curve with advanced modeling techniques, allowing for nuanced analyses of economic development and environmental impacts. They also play a critical role in identifying financial risks, enabling policymakers to respond effectively during economic crises. Furthermore, neural networks are instrumental in business and marketing, providing insights into consumer behavior and market demand. They enhance decision support systems, guiding strategic investments and financial decisions. By classifying data sets, they assist in predicting bankruptcy among various economic entities. Overall, the diverse applications of neural networks across disciplines underscore their significance in contemporary research and practical implementations, paving the way for future advancements in artificial intelligence and data analytics. Thus neural networks a type of machine learning, are increasingly used in economics and management due to their ability to analyze complex data and make predictions.

Keywords: artificial neural networks, forecasting, non-linear relationships, consumer behavior, bankruptcy prediction, stock price prediction

1. Introduction

Artificial neural networks are among the latest achievements resulting from rapid progress in science and knowledge. These networks are analytical and trainable tools designed to imitate the patterns of information processing in the human brain. In fact, an artificial neural network is a concept for information processing inspired by the nervous system, processing information similarly to how the brain does. Neural networks not only have the ability to learn, but they can also adapt themselves to the environment in order to maintain their performance by changing the environment.

In general, neural networks are computational models that can determine the relationship between the inputs and outputs of a physical system through a network of interconnected nodes. The activity level of each connection is influenced by past information. The learning process should be regulated, allowing the model to discover the rules that relate the inputs to the outputs. However, these relationships are complex and non-linear [1].

Artificial neural networks simulate the functioning of the human brain by using mathematical functions and processors and are able to model unknown and highly non-linear relationships. Therefore, they are considered powerful tools for analyzing data and formulating non-linear relationships. Neural networks consist of many interconnected non-linear information processing units (neurons or nodes) that are involved in learning. The role of neurons in the neural network is information processing, which is done through a mathematical process that is the same as the activation function. The activation function can be linear or non-linear, which is chosen by the designer based on the specific needs of the problem that is supposed to be solved by the neural network. New activation functions are used in parts of the network to make real use of the ability of neural networks. Nowadays, the use of intelligent systems and neural networks is so common that these tools can be classified in the line of basic mathematical operations and as general and common tools in different sciences. Therefore, neural networks are used in most sciences that require analysis, decision making, estimation, prediction, design, and construction. In this study of neural networks and their different models, the importance of these networks and the reasons for their use in different sciences are examined. Neural networks, a type of machine learning, are increasingly used in economics and management due to their ability to analyze complex data and make predictions. Also, the use of neural networks in economic, financial, and management sciences and the superiority of this method over other methods are discussed.

2. Different models of neural networks

In neural networks, there are different models for prediction, each of which, in some way, sets the brain as a model and tries to imitate the human mind's learning process by using computational methods to automate the knowledge acquisition process. These models aim to solve complex and large problems using samples or data. In these calculations, the normal or expert human brain is modeled.

2.1 Artificial neural network (ANN)

An artificial neural network (ANN) is composed of several perceptron-neurons in each layer. This network is also called a Feed Forward Neural Network because the inputs are processed only in the forward direction. An ANN consists of input, hidden, and output layers, with each layer taking a certain weight. In comparing the neural network model with regression models, it can be said that the inputs of the neural network are the independent variables, and the outputs are the dependent variables. The different weights of the network are similar to the parameters of the regression model, and the bias term is also the same as the intercept or constant term in the regression model. The main difference is that the understanding of the rules between input and output is considered by a linear function or similar form for all functions. This is while searching in the neural network to understand these rules both linearly and non-linearly. Especially in models that have more complications, there is a higher probability of non-linear relationships in them. Therefore, the search space for finding regularities between inputs and outputs in the neural network model is much larger than in simple linear regression models.

Figure 1 shows a simple picture of an artificial neural network. Neural networks usually consist of several layers. Input layer contains neurons that receive input data. Each neuron in this layer represents one of the input features. Hidden layers are located between the input layer and output layer and are responsible for processing information. Each hidden layer can contain several neurons that are connected to each other. These neurons process information using activation functions. Output layer produces the final result of network processing. The number of neurons will be equal to the number of classes. Weights are parameters that determine the importance of each connection between two neurons. Each connection between two neurons has a weight that indicates the influence of that neuron on the other neuron. During the training process, the weights are updated to improve the performance of the network. Larger weights indicate a greater influence of one neuron on another. While weights closer to zero indicate little or no influence [2].

These networks can be deep or shallow. Surface networks have one hidden layer (one layer between input and output), but deep networks have more layers.

The flow methodology of the artificial neural network model is depicted in **Figure 2**.

In a neural network, each neuron has a linear regression [3]. For example, if each neuron has three inputs and one output, the linear regression for each function is as follows:

$$Y = W_1X_1 + W_2X_2 + W_3X_3 + D \tag{1}$$

In Eq. (1), Y, output, X's, input, coefficients W, weight, and D, constant value are also called bias.

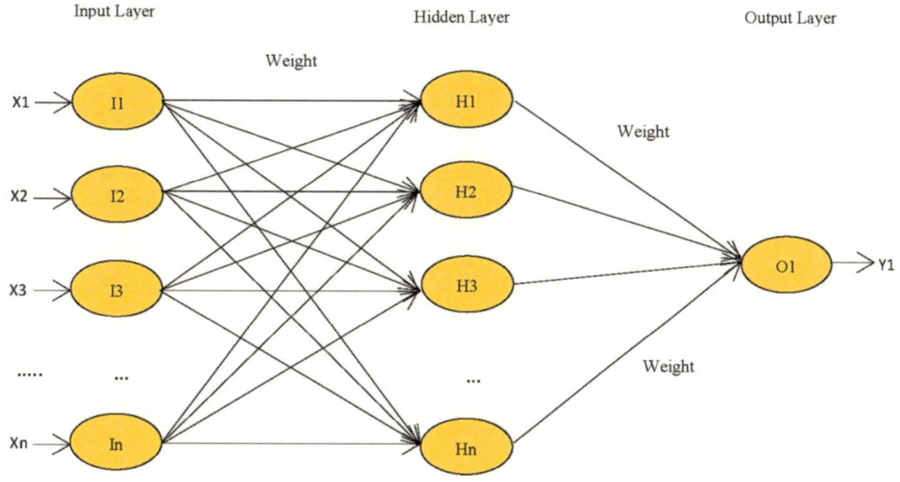

Figure 1.
A diagram of a simple artificial neural network.

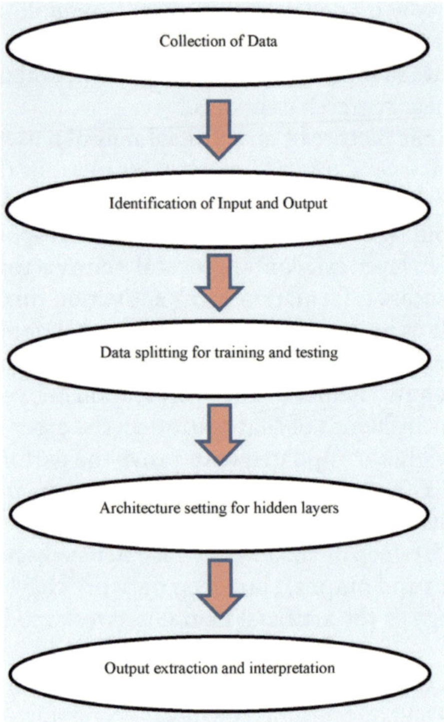

Figure 2.
Methodological flow of ANN model.

In neural networks, output would have desired parameters and the predicted error would be minimal. Let F: $x_t \in R^k \rightarrow y_t \in R^1$ be a projection assigning k-dimensional vector of inputs $x_t^T = (x_{1t}, x_{2t}, \ldots, x_{kt})$ one dimensional output y_t in specific time moment t. let G: $G(X_t, W_t) : X_t \in R^k_{train} \rightarrow y_t \in R^1_{train}$ be a restriction of F. The task is then to find the values of w_t so that functional values of G would be so close to known sample as it is possible. Let $E(w)$ is a function defined as:

$$E(w_t) = \sum_{x_t, y_t \in R^k_{train}} \left(G(x_t, w_t) - y_t \right) \qquad (2)$$

Eq. (2) will represent squares of deviations of function G from expecting values of function F. If a minimum is found, G is adapted for approximation of F. Training or adaptation is performed on the training set. Validation set is used for the validation of training network.

Neural networks can be used to solve problems related to tabular data, photo data, and text. These networks, which are data-oriented, have few initial assumptions when designing the model for the issue under study. This feature makes them valuable for many forecasting issues. These networks can obtain relationships and correlations between data, even if the law governing them is unknown and very complex.

Other advantages of this method are the storage of information in the entire network, the ability to work with incomplete knowledge, the ability to tolerate errors, not having too many assumptions, the ability to generalize, the high speed in processing information, and having distributed memory. However, depending on the hardware, inexplicable behavior of the network and determining the appropriate structure for the network are some of the disadvantages of this method.

2.2 Multi-layer perceptron neural networks (MLP)

One of the most common neural networks used in economic and financial sciences is the multi-layer perceptron neural network. A multi-layer perceptron is a standard combination of inputs, linear and non-linear neural units, and outputs. All processing units from each layer are connected to all processing units of the next layer. The processing units of the input layer are homogeneous and linear, while neurons with non-linear and continuously differentiable functions are used in the hidden layer [4].

2.3 Recurrent neural network (RNN)

A recurrent neural network (RNN) is a complex architecture designed to process data and information that are time series. In an RNN, due to its internal memory, past information and data are stored, allowing the network to utilize this memory to process a sequence of inputs. In these networks, the outputs from processing nodes are stored, and the results are returned to the model.

These types of networks do not transmit information in only one direction. Each node in this network functions like a memory cell, continuously calculating and executing operations. If the network makes an incorrect prediction, the system performs self-learning and adjusts its predictions during backpropagation. One of the disadvantages of this method is the difficulty associated with working with this network [5].

2.4 Dynamic neural networks

In dynamic networks, the output depends not only on the current input entering the network but also on the inputs, outputs, and current or previous states of the network. A dynamic network has memory; its response at any given time depends not only on the current input but also on the history of the input sequence. Time Delay Neural Networks (TNN) are an example of this type of network. The structure of the neural network with time delay was first introduced by Waibel et al. [6]. Additionally, Autoregressive Neural Networks with Exogenous Variables (NNARX) are another example of dynamic neural networks.

3. The reasons for using neural networks in different sciences

Due to their unique capabilities, neural networks have been widely used in various scientific fields. In many areas of science, artificial neural networks hold the potential to solve problems that are difficult or impossible to simulate through logic or other methods. Like the human brain, neural networks continuously learn and adapt to their environment. This means that if a small change occurs in existing conditions, they can account for it and remain effective under new circumstances. In a neural network, the malfunction of a part of the neurons does not lead to the complete failure of the system. Therefore, this method can provide logical answers for data under conditions of uncertainty, whether the data is incomplete or received in a fragmented manner.

In general, neural networks possess several advantages that have contributed to their widespread use in various scientific disciplines.

- Recognizing complex patterns and relationships: Neural networks excel at recognizing complex and non-linear patterns compared to traditional models and many competing approaches.
- Management of large data sets: Many scientific fields deal with vast amounts of information, variables, and data. Neural networks can effectively manage these datasets and extract meaningful patterns and results.
- Adaptive learning: Neural networks can learn from data and their past values, adjusting their parameters to improve prediction accuracy over time. This capability is particularly important in dynamic systems.
- Resilience, parallel processing, and extensive memory: Thanks to their parallel processing capabilities and extensive memory, neural networks exhibit high processing speeds. These features are significant advantages that have facilitated their adoption across various scientific domains.
- Feature extraction: Neural networks can automatically and quickly extract relevant features from data without requiring specialized expertise.
- Robustness to errors: Neural networks are generally insensitive to the presence of errors in the available statistics and information.

The significance of neural networks in human sciences can be illustrated as follows:

1. Social sciences: neural networks are employed to analyze social networks, understand social interactions, and predict behavioral patterns.
2. Political science: these networks are utilized for modeling political trends and predicting election outcomes.
3. Economic, financial, and management sciences: neural networks play a crucial role in these fields and have numerous applications, which will be discussed further.

4. Application of neural networks in economic, financial and management sciences

With many advances in fast information processing with computers and application software, the motivation to use and apply non-linear models in many sciences has increased. Since artificial neural networks can identify and justify patterns and non-linear relationships between variables, this method has found many applications in economic, financial, and management sciences and also provides great help in analyzing data and information in these courses. The use of artificial neural networks in economics and financial issues started in the late 80s with the study of White [7] on financial markets and forecasting the stock price of IBM. White's main goal was first to investigate the efficiency of the market, which then led to the prediction of the company's stock price. Although the results of this study showed that the minimization algorithms used in econometrics are better than the neural network algorithms, due to the simplicity of this network, different researchers used the results of this study a lot in their works. Therefore, after White, several studies were conducted in the field of using neural networks in predicting various economic variables. Neural networks can help economists by creating a series of economic and financial models to analyze the relationships between variables and predict them, which brings very useful results for them. With these models, you can gain better knowledge and understanding in relation to economic issues and make more informed and better decisions in this regard. Therefore, we will have a better and more successful future in economic and financial terms.

Below are some applications of artificial neural networks in economics, management, and financial issues.

4.1 Prediction in the future

The main and most important application of artificial neural network models in the fields of economics and financial management is the prediction of economic variables. With this method, good forecasts can be made for many economic issues in the branches of microeconomics and macroeconomics. Using methods for more accurate estimation of forecasts will help researchers and people who want to use these forecasts a lot. The use of advanced linear models sometimes provided good forecasts in the short- and medium-term periods. But in many cases, because the behavior of the investigated variable does not follow a linear model, therefore, linear models cannot accurately identify and predict this behavior. However, neural networks are one of the methods that have been successful in this field and have brought good results.

By learning from past experiences, this method predicts non-linear algorithms and provides images and numerical signals related to data. Due to the structure of the internal dynamic system of neural networks in forecasting, information error changes occur without the need for additional input data. As a result, the use of neural networks has become prevalent in various forecasting issues in economics and finance. A major problem in using neural networks as a prediction tool is the lack of objective guidelines for choosing the appropriate dimensions (i.e., the number of layers or hidden neurons) for the network. Neural network models predict numerous macroeconomic and microeconomic variables, such as economic growth, gross domestic product (GDP), exchange rates, inflation, stock price indices, total productivity of production factors, energy consumption, and more. These models have been applied in different countries around the world and have sometimes provided better and more acceptable results compared to other forecasting models.

4.1.1 Exchange rate forecast

In exchange rate forecasting, we can refer to the studies of Lisi and Schiavo [8] and Ince and Trafalis [9]. Bosarge [10] predicted various exchange rates and crude oil prices using neural networks, which were highly accurate. Kuan and Liu [11] also used Feed Forward Neural Network and Recurrent Neural Network (RNN) methods to predict different exchange rates and make more accurate predictions than traditional methods.

Wu and Gao [12] predicted the exchange rate with two combined methods of Support Vector Neural Network and Variational Mode Decomposition. With this method, they were able to correctly identify the high and irregular fluctuations of the exchange rate and predict the exchange rate with high accuracy.

Forecasting the exchange rate using the neural network method requires accurate selection of inputs in order to identify the factors affecting the exchange rate. These inputs and variables that can explain the behavior of the exchange rate and help predict this variable more accurately are determined according to the theoretical foundations related to the exchange rate in economic matters. In this part of the study, a number of important and effective variables on the exchange rate, according to the various studies that have been done in connection with this variable by authors in different countries, and also according to the theoretical foundations of the exchange rate, are introduced as follows:

1. Interest rate: the difference in interest rate between countries significantly affects the exchange rate. The higher the interest rates, the more foreign investment is attracted to that country, and as a result, the demand for currency increases.

2. Inflation rate: high inflation causes a decrease in the value of a country's currency.

3. Gross domestic product: the higher the gross domestic product and economic growth in a country, the stronger the country's currency value and affects the exchange rate.

4. Government debt: high bank debt causes financial instability in the country and potentially leads to a decrease in the value of the country's currency and affects the exchange rate.

5. Trade balance: if exports are more than imports and the current balance of a country is positive, the value of the country's currency increases and strengthens due to the increase in demand for it, and vice versa.

6. Any variable that leads to the creation of economic uncertainties in society, such as types of political instability (types of economic and political sanctions, civil wars, and types of international conflicts) and natural disasters (floods, earthquakes, etc.)) affects the exchange rate.

7. Central bank policies: the decisions of the central bank in relation to various types of monetary policies, such as interest rate changes or any foreign exchange interventions, directly affect the exchange rate.

4.1.2 Stock price prediction

In economics and financial management, there are various forecasts in different stock exchange companies related to stock prices, profit, bankruptcy, risk assessment and lending, portfolio and securities management, planning and registration of future contracts and customer classification in financial institutions. It has been done using the method of artificial neural networks, which have had higher prediction accuracy.

Therefore, the extent of the use of neural networks in financial markets is not hidden to anyone.

Olson and Mosman [13] used neural network in addition to predicting stock returns for financial market grouping and grouped companies based on their returns.

Forecasting the stock price index is important for economic policymakers due to the high dynamics of the market and its importance and its effect on most macroeconomic variables. Neural network models are one of the most efficient models in predicting stock market prices., Soni [14], Dase and Pawar [15], Jibendu et al. [16], Li and Liu [17], Mandziuk and Jaruszewicz [18], Thenmozhi [19], Yamashita et al. [20] and Phua et al. [21] forecasting the stock market in different countries using artificial neural network models and obtained accurate predictions in this connection, which showed the superiority of this method.

Sutheebanjard and Premchaiswad [22], Mehrara et al. [23] and Tong [24] have estimated stock prices by different methods of neural networks and obtained accurate predictions in this regard. Back Propagation Neural Network (BPNN), Group Method of Data Handling (GMDH), Multi Branch Artificial Neural Networks (MBNN), and Adaptive Neuro-Fuzzy Inference Systems (ANFIS) There are different models of neural networks that have been used in these studies, and in all these studies, the results obtained confirmed the high prediction accuracy of different neural network models.

By considering the appropriate inputs and choosing the right variables in the neural network model, valid and meaningful models can be obtained for it, which also have high predictive power. According to the history of studies related to the stock price and also according to the theoretical foundations in this regard, the most important factors affecting the stock price are introduced as the most important inputs as follows:

1. Stock price in the past: one of the most important effective factors in predicting the stock price is looking at the past trend of this variable.

2. Volume of transactions: the number of shares traded every day is an indication of the profit and loss situation in the market and price fluctuations. Therefore, it is considered as an effective factor on the stock price.

3. Macroeconomic indicators: interest rate, inflation, unemployment, economic growth, government policies, and economic and political uncertainties (such as embargo and international wars) are important factors that affect the stock price index.

4. Internal factors of listed companies: amount of assets.

5. Internal and internal factors of listed companies: the amount of assets, price-to-profit ratio, profitability, news and financial reports related to the company, liquidity, and development plans are important and effective factors on the stock price.

4.1.3 Prediction of bankruptcy

Bankruptcy prediction is one of the other topics that is done by different neural network models. Bredart [25] predicted the bankruptcy of companies using the neural network method, which had a very high accuracy.

With various types of financial and operational data, one can understand the health of a company and its potential to deal with financial issues and problems. Common input variables in neural networks to predict bankruptcy according to related theories are:

1. Ratios including liquidity ratios, leverage ratios (debt), activity ratios (functional), profitability ratios and valuation ratios (market).

2. Internal information about the company such as its competitive outlook, quality of management, corporate governance, and legal issues and regulations.

3. Macroeconomic conditions such as economic growth, interest rate, inflation, and market tension.

Due to the fact that predicting bankruptcy is a very complicated task, therefore, using the opinions of experts and experts in this field helps a lot in reaching accurate predictions.

4.1.4 Predicting the impact of per capita income on environmental pollution

Neural networks can predict the effect of per capita income on environmental pollution. Neural networks are capable of modeling non-linear relationships that can be useful in Kuznets curve analysis. Kuznets curve is an economic theory that describes the relationship between per capita income and environmental pollution. According to this theory, in the initial stages of economic development, pollution increases, but after reaching a certain level of income, pollution decreases. In the early stages of development, countries may experience more pollution due to rapid industrialization and lack of attention to environmental issues. With increasing income and economic development, social awareness of environmental issues increases and countries move toward using cleaner technologies. In the next stages, the government's policymaking may try to enact environmental laws that will help reduce pollution. Using past data of income and pollution, these networks can predict how changes in per capita income may affect pollution. Also, artificial networks can be used to analyze the sensitivity of different factors (such as environmental policies) on pollution.

Sah et al. [26] and Bennedsen et al. [27] conducted studies on the effect of per capita income of countries and the level of energy consumption on the level of environmental pollution using the neural network method, with significant results in this regard.

According to the background of the studies and theoretical foundations in order to model the Kuznets curve and its relationship with pollution (e.g., carbon dioxide in the air) in neural networks, different input variables can be used, some of which are as follows:

a. Economic factors

1. Per capita income: the main variable that shows the level of economic development of a country.

2. Economic growth rate: changes in Gross Domestic Product (GDP) as an indicator of economic development.

3. The level of industrialization: the percentage of industrial production to the total production, which can indicate the intensity of pollution.

4. Investment in clean technologies: amount of investment in renewable energies and green technologies.

5. The amount of energy consumption.

6. Amount of renewable energy consumption.

b. Social factors

1. Population: the number of population and its density that affects the pollution.

2. Transportation systems: type and quality of public and private transportation systems.

3. Health indicators: the rate of respiratory diseases that may be affected by air pollution.

c. Environmental factors

1. Environmental awareness: a set of indicators that show public awareness and environmental policies.

2. Natural resources: access to natural resources and how to manage them.

3. Environmental policies: existence or non-existence of environmental laws and regulations.

4.2 Identification of risks and dangers

With the method of artificial neural networks, it is possible to predict some of the economic and financial issues such as financial bubbles and financial risks and trace their existence. This will help the policymakers and give them time to prevent the deterioration of the economic conditions and show an appropriate response.

Wittkemper and Steiner [28] predicted the operational risk of stocks for 67 German companies using neural networks. Persio et al. [29] predicted the risk of investment strategies using recurrent neural networks (RNN). Lingzi [30] used neural networks for risk prediction along with financial management and obtained accurate results in this connection. Huangn et al. [31] investigated credit risk in China using neural network models.

In the investigation of credit risks and their prediction through neural networks, the input variables of the network in most studies are the amount of capital and the amount of purchases, the amount of bounced checks, the history of membership, and the number of members.

4.3 Understanding of consumers

Another application of artificial neural networks is the recognition of types of business by consumers and how to treat them. In general, neural networks are widely used in business and marketing to better understand consumers and get to know their preferences and needs. With these patterns, it is possible to know the market demand and the factors affecting it, and to predict the willingness of consumers to pay, as well as the amount of people's purchases in the market.

Kruzsztof et al. [32] predicted the amount of customer purchases according to the number of transactions made using the neural network method, which also had high accuracy. Hansi et al. [33] obtained consumer preferences using artificial neural networks.

A set of input variables in neural networks in relation to the recognition of consumers' behavior according to the studies conducted in these fields are as follows:

- Information about the type of purchase of goods and services by consumers in the market and identification of goods and services that were not welcomed by people and the producer could not sell them to consumers.

- The points earned by a product and the level of customer loyalty in buying that product.

- Internet search of consumers in relation to the product and its features.

- Comments and feedback from customers regarding the desired products.

In addition to these indicators, a set of personal information such as age, gender, education level, income, wealth, and lifestyle can also be taken into account; with these indicators, it is possible to understand consumer behavior and preferences.

A number of macroeconomic variables such as inflation, employment rate, and economic growth can also affect these preferences.

By combining these inputs and using the capabilities of the neural network method, a deeper understanding of consumer behavior in markets can be obtained.

4.4 Decision support systems

Artificial neural networks can provide valuable information for decision making in all economic aspects. They can help businesses choose the right investment, and policymakers can use the results to develop effective strategies. Also, people should make better financial choices by making appropriate decisions. Decision support systems are a suitable process for decision making. It is very important that decision support systems are meant to strengthen human decisions and not to replace them. According to the opinions of experts and experts, these systems are powerful tools in the final decision of the investor.

Ashwood [34], Shun and Lei [35], and Wei Zhou et al. [36] presented a suitable portfolio for investment using neural networks.

Fazlollahtabar [37] pointed out that one of the important issues in e-commerce and electronic marketing is determining optimal markets. Decision support systems are a suitable process for making decisions in these matters. In his study, he considered different markets using neural networks and introduced optimal markets according to consumer behavior and decisions made.

If we want to find an acceptable result in connection with a suitable investment portfolio or determine the optimal markets in business using the neural network method, the selection of suitable independent variables and correct inputs is very important. According to the studies conducted in these fields, stock prices in the past, volume of transactions, profit and loss of listed companies, risk tolerance, interest rate, inflation, unemployment, economic growth, exchange rate, economic and political uncertainties (such as sanctions and international wars), government policies are important inputs in neural networks for the purpose of making appropriate financial choices.

4.5 Classification of economic agents

One of the abilities of neural networks is to classify a set of data into different groups. Neural networks can replace a series of traditional methods such as logistic regression. One of the features of neural networks that distinguish them from traditional methods is their ability to classify data that cannot be separated linearly.

Most of the articles that use the neural network method for classification work in economics can be found in the field of predicting the bankruptcy of economic actors, mainly banks, production units, stock exchange companies, consumers, etc.

Most of the studies that have been conducted in this regard have been published in the early 1990s, the period when most bank failures occurred in the United States of America.

With this model, economic units can be classified economically and predict whether they are exposed to bankruptcy or not. Oldom and Sharda [38] and Rahimian et al. [39] used five financial ratios in their studies which were proposed and calculated by Altman [40]. Both papers used a two-layer neural network.

The approach is to use the financial ratios calculated from the company's balance sheet as input to the neural network to obtain an estimate for the probability of bankruptcy as output.

Tam [41] and Tam and Kiang [42] analyzed a neural network with 19 input neurons and using 19 financial ratios. In their studies, they compared a simple feed-forward network with a pull-layer network trained using the backpropagation method, and the performance of the second method was on average better than the first method. In general, the classification with both types of networks were better than the classifications in traditional methods.

Poddig [43], Salchenberger et al. [44], and Altman et al. [45] are other studies that obtained results similar to previous studies.

There have been many discussions related to classification features. Brockett et al. [46] for insurance companies and Marose [47] to examine the suitability of customers to obtain bank credits and their classification, Grudnitzki [48] to evaluate the characteristics of residence in San Diego, Jagielska and Jaworski [49] to predict The probability of credit card holders not being cashed, they used the neural network method. Martin and Serrona [50] also classified Spanish companies into more than one group using the neural network method in their study. In their study, Colman et al. [51] also integrated the neural network model with an expert system in such a way that measures can be taken to prevent bankruptcy.

Most of the studies that have been done regarding the classification of units using artificial networks have had acceptable results compared to other methods. These classifications will help consumers and production units to make the right decisions regarding their financial issues. In connection with the classification of economic units and consumers, according to several studies that have been conducted in this regard, a set of input data of neural networks are as follows:

A. Demographic information: age, gender, level of education, size of the household and place of residence of the person, occupation, age of the company, size of the company.

B. Financial information: level of income and wealth, amount of savings, financial transactions, consumption patterns, income status of the company, amount of profit and loss of the company.

4.6 Modeling bounded rational economic agents

Modeling limited logical economic factors with neural networks makes it possible to obtain human decisions with all the complexities related to economic issues. Many people's decisions are complex and certainly not rational, but neural networks are powerful tools that can simulate these complexities. Therefore, one of the applications of neural networks is that they can be used to model the learning process of rational economic units. With this method, complex relationships between variables can be found and non-linear relationships between variables can be extracted. In this application, neurons are divided into units that update their inference from the environment based on the received information. Then, their decisions (neuron output) affect the environment, which may be given feedback to the agent.

Sargent [52] used artificial neural networks in this field for the first time. Beltratti et al. [53] argued that neural networks are suitable for modeling human behavior because they can interpolate between learned patterns and introduce a degree of uncertainty in their responses. Luna [54] used neural networks to model economic institutions. These models allow us to model the interaction between the learning environment and information of institutions. Orsini [55] proposed a neural network model to model the consumption behavior of people whose expectations about group behavior play an important role on individual and group outcomes.

The types of inputs that may be used in the modeling of rational economic units in neural networks are as follows:

A set of information related to people and demographic characteristics such as age, gender, education level, income, wealth, risk-taking or risk-aversion of people, the way a person interacts in a social network, the goals of a person, etc., which each can influence people's preferences.

Information related to macroeconomic issues of the country that are effective in these modeling with neural networks such as inflation, interest rate, and exchange rate.

5. The superiority of the neural network method over other forecasting methods

There are various methods for predicting and modeling economic and financial variables in the form of time series. Among these, Auto Regressive (AR), Moving Average (MA), and Auto Regressive Moving Average (ARMA) processes are linear models that are widely used for forecasting numerous time series variables. These processes generate predictions based on the past values of the variables themselves. Due to their simplicity and reliance on historical data, these methods are of great interest to many experts and researchers in economic and financial sciences. However, many economic and financial variables exhibit non-linear behavior, which means that accurate predictions cannot be obtained using these linear methods alone.

To address the limitations of linear models, various non-linear models can be employed. Examples include Auto Regressive Conditional Heteroskedasticity (ARCH), Generalized Auto Regressive Conditional Heteroskedasticity (GARCH), as well as Bilinear and Threshold Auto Regressive (TAR) models. However, the application of these models is generally limited, as they are designed for specific non-linear patterns and may not effectively model other types of non-linear time series. In addition to these, Bayesian models and the Wiener Process are other examples of non-linear models used in time series forecasting.

Intelligent methods offer a promising alternative to traditional statistical methods for predicting complex and non-linear time series. These methods include neural networks, fuzzy inference systems, genetic algorithms, and their combined forms, such as the Adaptive Neuro-Fuzzy Inference System (ANFIS), Multi-Branch Artificial Neural Network (MBNN), and Back Propagation Neural Network (BPNN). These intelligent methods are increasingly utilized in economic studies and are considered suitable for forecasting due to their ability to handle complexity and non-linearity effectively.

6. Conclusion

Neural networks are among the most fundamental and widely used algorithms in the field of artificial intelligence. These networks are expanding rapidly and have established their place among data analysis methods. One of the most important features of neural networks is their ability to learn independently and improve through experience and data repetition. This capability has enabled them to solve complex problems and make accurate predictions, leading to their application in various fields and disciplines. Additionally, the management of models with many variables and high sample volumes, adaptive learning, parallel processing, and extensive memory are other notable features of these networks. Neural networks encompass different models that are utilized across various sciences, depending on the subject under study. Artificial neural networks, in particular, are among the most common types, capable of identifying relationships and correlations between data, even when the underlying laws governing them are unknown or highly complex.

Multi-layer perceptron neural networks, recurrent neural networks, and dynamic neural networks are other methods that have been used in various studies to predict and investigate the relationships between variables.

Neural networks have found a special place in various scientific disciplines, particularly in the human sciences. In the social sciences, they are widely used to analyze social networks, understand social interactions, and predict behavioral patterns. In political science, they are employed to model political trends and predict election results.

These networks are crucial and widely utilized in economic, managerial, and financial sciences, which are specifically addressed in this study.

One of the most important applications of the neural network model in these fields is prediction. In many cases, because the investigated variable does not follow a linear model, therefore, linear models were not effective, but neural networks were successful in this field and had high accuracy in prediction. Researchers have used these models to predict many variables such as exchange rate, stock price index, bankruptcy, etc., which have been highly accurate compared to other methods.

Also, one of the economic issues that can be achieved with neural networks is the combination of the Kuznets curve theory with the neural network technique, which can help in a deeper analysis of the relationship between economic development and environmental pollution, and effective tools for provide policy making in the field of environmental protection.

Another application of neural networks in economic and financial sciences is the identification of various risks, dangers, and uncertainties in economic markets. Financial bubbles, financial risks, etc., are examples of these studies that can be predicted and traced with the neural network method. This helps policymakers prevent the deterioration of economic conditions and show an appropriate response in times of crisis and uncertainty.

Neural networks are also widely used in business and marketing for a better understanding of consumers and familiarity with consumer preferences. With these patterns, it is possible to know the market demand and the factors affecting it and to predict the willingness of consumers to pay and the amount of people's purchases in the market.

Decision support systems are also one of the other subjects in which valuable information can be provided for decision making in all economic aspects by using artificial neural networks. For example, choosing the right investment in businesses that policy makers can use the results to develop their effective strategies. Or making appropriate decisions by people that lead to better financial choices.

Classifying a set of data into different groups is essential in predicting the bankruptcy of economic actors, including banks, production units, stock exchange companies, and consumers. Additionally, modeling rational economic units is another capability of neural networks. By considering appropriate inputs and selecting the right variables in the neural network model, valid and meaningful models can be obtained that possess high predictive power. Therefore, in this study, we introduce and propose the theoretical foundations of the required inputs in relation to the investigated variables to facilitate their separation.

In general, intelligent methods are superior alternatives to statistical methods for predicting complex and non-linear time series. Examples of these intelligent methods include neural networks, fuzzy inference systems, genetic algorithms, and their combined forms, such as Adaptive Neuro-Fuzzy Inference System (ANFIS), Multi-Branch Artificial Neural Network (MBNN), and Back Propagation Neural Network (BPNN). These methods are widely used in economic studies and are effective for forecasting.

Considering the advancements in artificial intelligence worldwide and the numerous methods available in this field, research and study in this area have gained significant importance across various disciplines. Each of the methods mentioned above offers unique opportunities for researchers to explore.

Author details

Roya Seifipour* and Azadeh Mehrabian
Islamic Azad University, Central Tehran Branch, Tehran, Iran

*Address all correspondence to: roy.seifipour@iauctb.ac.ir

IntechOpen

© 2025 The Author(s). Licensee IntechOpen. This chapter is distributed under the terms of the Creative Commons Attribution License (http://creativecommons.org/licenses/by/4.0), which permits unrestricted use, distribution, and reproduction in any medium, provided the original work is properly cited.

References

[1] Neural HS. Networks, A Comprehensives Foundation. New York: Macmillan College Publishing Company; 1994. 94 p

[2] Malekian A, Chitsaz N. Advances in Steam Flow Forecasting. Amsterdam, Netherlands: Elsevier; 2021. pp. 115-147. DOI: 10.1016/8978-0-12-820673-7.00003-2. Ch 4

[3] Park YS, Lek S. Developments in Environmental Modeling. Amsterdam, Netherlands: Elsevier; 2016. pp. 123-140. DOI: 10.106/8978-0-444-63623-2.00007-4. Ch 7

[4] Singh J, Banerjee R. A Study on single and multi-layer perceptron neural network. In: International Conference on Computing Methodologies and Communication (ICCMC); 27-29 March 2019. IEEE

[5] Yang X, Guan J, Ding L, et al. Research and applications of artificial neural network in pavement engineering: A state of the art review. Journal of Traffic and Transportation Engineering. 2021;**8**(6):1000-1021. DOI: 10.1016/j.jtte.2021.03.005

[6] Waibel A, Hanazawa T, Hinton G, Shikano K, Lang KJ. Phoneme recognition using time-delay neural networks. IEEE Transactions on Acoustics Speech and Signal Processing. 1989;**37**(3):328-339

[7] White H. Economic using neural networks: The case of IBM daily stock returns. In: IEEE (Institute of Electrical and Electronics Engineers) International Conference on Neural Networks. San Diego, California, USA; 1988. pp. 451-458

[8] Lisi F, Schiavo RA. A comparison between neural networks and chaotic models for exchange rate prediction. Computable Statistics & Data Analysis. 1999;**30**:87-102

[9] Ince H, Trafalis TB. A hybrid model for exchange rate prediction. Decesion Support System. 2006;**42**(2):1054-1062. DOI: 10.1016/j.dss.2005.09.001

[10] Bosarge WE. Adaptive processes to exploit the nonlinear structure of financial market. In: Trippi RR, Turban E, editors. Neural Networks in Finance and Investing. McGraw-Hill; 1993. 371-402 p

[11] Kuan C, Liu T. Forecasting exchange rates using feedforward and recurrent neural networks. Journal of Applied Econometrics. 1995;**10**(4):347-364

[12] Wu Y, Gao J. Application of support vector neural network with variational mode decomposition for exchange rate forecasting. Soft Computing. 2019;**23**(16):6995-7004. Available from: https://link.springer.com/article/10.1007/s00500-018-3336-1

[13] Olson D, Mossman C. Neural networks of Canadian stock returns using accounting ratios. International Journal of Forecasting. 2003;**19**:435-465. DOI: 10.1016/S0169-2070(02)00058-4

[14] Soni S. Applications of ANNs in stock market prediction: A survey. International Journal of Computer Science & Engineering Technology (IJCEST). 2011;**2**(3):71-83. ISSN: 2229-3345. Available from: https://api.semanticscholar.org/CorpusID:14409722

[15] Dase RK, Pawar DD. Application of artifical neural network for stock market prediction: A review of literature.

International Journal of Machine Intelligence. 2010;**2**(2)

[16] Jibendu K, Gahan P, Nayak B. Artifical neural networks- an application to stock market volatility. International Journal of Engineering Science and Technology. 2010;**2**(5):1451-1460

[17] Li F, Liu C. Application study of BP neural network on stock market prediction. In: Ninth International Conference on Hybrid Intelligent Systems; 12-14 August 2009; Shenyang. China. 2009. pp. 174-178. DOI: 10.1109/HIS.2009.248

[18] Mandziuk J, Jaruszewicz M. Neuro-evolutionary approach to stock market prediction. In: Proceedings of International Johnt Conference on neural Network; Orlando, Florida USA. 2007. pp. 12-17

[19] Thenmozhi M. Prediction stock index returns using artificial neural networks. Delhi Business Review X. 2006;7(2):59-69

[20] Yamshita T, Kotaro H, Jinglu H. Application of multi- branch artificial neural networks stock market prediction. In: Proceedings of International Joint Conference on Neural Networks; January 2005; Montreal, Canada. 2005. DOI: 10.1109/IJCNN.2005.1556303

[21] Phua PKH, Ming D, Lin W. Neural network with genetic algorithms for stocks prediction. In: Fifth Conference of the Association of Asian Pacific Operations Research Societies; 5-7 July 2000; Singapore

[22] Sutheebanjard P, Premchaiswad WI. Stock exchange of Thailand index prediction using back propagation neural networks. In: Second International Conference on Computer and Network Technology. Bangkok, Thailand: IEEE; 23 April 2010. pp. 377-380. DOI: 10.1109/ICCNT.2010.21

[23] Mehrara M, Moeini A, Ahrari M, Jafari A. Using technical analysis with neural network for prediction stock price index in Tehran stock exchange. In: Middle Eastern Finance and Economics. Euro Journals Publishing. Inc; 2010

[24] Tong-Seng Q. Using neural network for DJIA stock selection. Engineering Letters. 2007;**15**(1):15-31

[25] Bredart X. Bankruptcy prediction model using neural networks. Accounting and Finance Research. 2014;**3**(2):124. DOI: 10.5430/afr.v3n2p124

[26] Sah HK, Siasodia GS, Ahmed G, Rafiuddin A, Abidi N. The role of energy consumption and economic growth on carbon emission: Application of artificial neural network. International Journal of Energy Economics and Policy. 2023;**13**(6):591-596. DOI: 10.32479/ijeep.14666

[27] Bennedsen M, Hillebrand E, Jensen S. A neural network approach to the environmental Kuznets curve. Energy Economics. 2023:126. DOI: 10.1016/j.eneco.2023.106985

[28] Wittkemoer HG, Steiner M. Using neural networks to forecast the systematic risk of stocks. European Journal of Operational Research. 1996;**90**(3):577-588

[29] Presio L, Garbelli M, Mottaghi F, Wallbaum K. Volatility forecasting with hybrid neural networks methods for risk parity investment strategies. Expert Systems with Applications. 2023;**229**(1). DOI: 10.1016/j.eswa.2023.120418

[30] Lingzi G. Optimized backpropagation neural network for risk prediction in corporate

financial management. Scientific Reports. 2023;**13**:19330. DOI: 10.1038/s41598-023-46528-8

[31] Huangn X, Liu X, Ren Y. Enterprise credit risk evaluation based on neural network algorithm. Cognitive Systems Research. 2018;**52**(1):317-324. DOI: 10.1016/j.cogsys.2018.07.023

[32] Kruzsztof L et al. Prediction of customer purchases using LSTM deep neural network. In: Conference Paper, Emerging Challenges in Intelligent Management Information Systems. 2024. pp. 161-181

[33] Hansi C, Liu H, Chu X, Zhang L, Yan B. A two phased SEM neural network approach for consumer preference analysis. Advanced Engineering Informatics. 2020:46. DOI: 10.1016/j.aei.2020.101156

[34] Ashwood AJ. Portfolio selection using artificial intelligence [thesis]. Queensland University of Technology; 2016. Available from: http://eprints.qut.edu.au/66229/1/Andrew_Ashwood_Thesis.pdf

[35] Shun C, Lei G. A learning-based strategy for portfolio selection. International Review of Economics and Finance. 2021;**71**:936-942. DOI: 10.1016/j.iref.2020.07.010

[36] Wei Z, Zhao Y, Chen W, Liu Y, Yang R, Liu Z. Research on investment portfolio model based on neural network and genetic algorithm in big data area. EURASIP Journal on Wireless Communications and Networking. Open Access. 2020;**2020**. Article ID 1850. DOI: 10.1186/s13638-020-01850-x

[37] Fazlollahtabar H. A DSS-based dynamic programming for finding optimal markets using neural networks and pricing. Iranian Journals of Management Studies (IJMS). 2020;**14**(1):87-106. DOI: 10.22059/ijms.2020.269091.673397

[38] Oldom MD, Sharda R. A neural network model for bankruptcy prediction. In: Proceedings of the IEEE International Conference on Neural Networks; 17-21 June 1990; San Diago California. IEEE; 1990. pp. 163-168

[39] Rahimian E, Singh T, Thammachote V. Bankruptcy prediction by neural network. In: Trippi RR, Turban E, editors. Neural Networks in Finance and Investing. Probus Publishing. pp. 159-171

[40] Altman EL. Financial ratios, discriminant analysis and the prediction of corporate bankruptcy. Journal of Finance. 1968;**23**:589-609. DOI: 10.2307/2978933

[41] Tam KY. Neural network models and the prediction of bank bankruptcy. Omega, Elsevier. 1991;**19**(5):429-445

[42] Tam KY, Kiang M. Predicting bank failures: A neural network approach. Decision Sciences. 1992;**23**:926-947

[43] Poddig T. Bankruptcy prediction: A comparison with discriminant analysis. In: Refenes AP, editor. Neural Networks in the Capital Markets. John Wiley & Sons; 1995. pp. 311-323

[44] Salchenberger L et al. Neural networks: A new tool for predicting thrift failures. Management Faculty Research and Publications. Decision Sciences. 1992;**23**(4):899-916

[45] Altman EL, Marco G, Varetto F. Corporate distress diagnosis: Comparisions using linear discriminant analysis and neural networks. Journal of Banking and Finance. 1994;**18**:505-529. DOI: 1016/0378-4266(94)90007-8

[46] Brockett PL, Cooper WW, Golden LL, Pitaktong U. A neural network method for obtaining an early warning of insurer insolvency. The Journal of Risk and Insurance. 1994;**61**(3):402-424. DOI: 10.2307/253568

[47] Marose RA. A financial neural network application. In: AI Expert May. Armonk, New York, USA: M. E. Sharpe, Inc; 1990. pp. 50-53

[48] Grudnitzki G. Valuations of residential properties using a neural network. In: Handbook of Neural Computation. New York, USA: IEEE; 1997. pp. G6.4:1-G6.4:5

[49] Jagielska I, Javorski J. Neural network for predicting the performance of credit card accounts. Computational Economics. 1996;**9**(1):77-82. DOI: 10.1007/BF00115693

[50] Martin DB, Serrano C. Self-organizing neural networks: The financial state of Spanish companies. In: Refenes AP, editor. Neural Networks in the Capital Markets. Wiley; 1995. pp. 341-357

[51] Coleman KG, Graettinger TJ, Lawrence WF, Coleman KG. Neural networks for bankruptcy prediction: The power to solve financial problems. AI Review. 1991;**4**:48-50

[52] Sargent TJ. Bounded Rationality in Macroeconomics. Oxford: Clarendon Press; 1993

[53] Beltratti A, Margarita S, Terna P. Neural Networks for Economic and Financial Modelling. London: International Thomson Computers; 1996

[54] Luna F. Computable learning, neural networks and institutions. In: Computing in Economics and Finance _037. Society for Computational Economics. University of Venice (IT); 1996

[55] Orsini R. Esternalita locali, aspettative, comportamenti erratici: Un modello di consume con razionalita limitata. Rivista Internazional di scienze Economiche e Commerciali. 1996;**43**:981-1012

Section 4

Hardware and Control Systems

Chapter 10

Robust Flat Filtering DSP-Based Control of the Buck-Boost Power Converter

Jesús Linares-Flores, Arturo Hernández-Méndez, José Antonio Juárez-Abad, Gerardo Mino-Aguilar, José Fermi Guerrero-Castellanos, Germán Ardul Muñoz Hernández and Cesar Arriaga-Arriaga

Abstract

The chapter deals with designing and implementing a flat filter regulation digital controller for a buck-boost DC-DC power converter. A highly perturbed, switched buck-boost power converter circuit is shown to be efficiently controlled in a regulation task for its non-minimum phase output using a suitable linear filter, addressed to as a flat filter. The flat filter control method is calculated from a transfer function, as in adaptive filtering control theory. It uses integral reconstructors regarding the input and output and finally employs partial state dynamics. Flat filtering is a natural, robust version of generalized proportional integral control (GPIC), by which the effects of arbitrary time-varying exogenous disturbances, unknown endogenous nonlinearities, and unmodeled dynamics can be jointly attenuated in a conceptually similar fashion to observer-based active disturbance rejection control (ADRC) and algebraic identification-based model-free control (MFC) but: a) without using linear extended state observers and b) respecting the original system order in a time-varying simplified model, while avoiding algebraic estimation techniques. The proposed control technique is implemented on the TMS320F28335 digital signal processor chip, with tests employing realistic simulations and an experimental setup.

Keywords: flat filter controller, buck-boost power converter, differential flatness, active disturbance control, generalized proportional integral control, adaptive filtering control, partial state

1. Introduction

The DC-DC buck-boost converter is a classical power converter that provides a DC output voltage lower or higher than the DC input voltage [1]. It is essential to design a robust controller for the power converter so that the output voltage provided to the load is unaffected by significant endogenous and exogenous disturbances [2].

Additionally, the controller should improve the regulation performance and system dynamics, considering the control design's simplicity, applicability, and cost. Classical linear controllers developed using the linearized system model are less effective under extensive line and sudden load variations, mainly when the linearized system works far from the equilibrium point where it is linearized [3].

However, the buck-boost power converter is differentially flat [2, 4]. This critical feature generally alleviates and trivializes the control design problem in more aspects (exact linearization, trajectory planning, etc.), provided all endogenous nonlinearities are perfectly known. Our purpose is to propose a method which handles those cases of exogenously perturbed nature where the acting endogenous nonlinearities are primarily unknown or disregarded.

Flat filtering constitutes a reinterpretation of the Generalized Proportional Integral Controller (GPIC) [5] in the form of classical compensation networks (CCN). Roughly speaking, any linear controllable system whose output is Brunovski's output (Flat Output) can be output regulated with the help of a well-tuned proper linear filter and a suitable linear combination of the available internal states of such filter. Here, it is shown that such a classical tool is also capable of efficiently handling control tasks on perturbed linearizable nonlinear systems (i.e., flat systems [6, 7]), such as the boost converter, including unknown or neglected nonlinearities, exogenous disturbances, and unmodeled dynamics; in a fashion similar as these uncertainties are handled in ADRC schemes [8–15].

Our proposed flat filter control is more than just a theoretical concept within the context of adaptive filtering control [16–18]. It is a practical solution, calculated from a transfer function and employing state integral reconstructors in terms of the system's input and output [5]. The state partial approach [19] is used to find the state partial dynamics and then to estimate the unknown parameters to adapt the flat filter control in a closed loop [20–22]. Unlike other adaptive filtering controls [17, 18], the tuning of our FFC is realized through a Hurwitz polynomial [20, 21], eliminating the need for an optimization algorithm and instilling confidence in its practicality. However, this FFC technique is similar to adaptive filtering control in that the system adapts to a changing environment, especially under internal and external disturbance. It carries the output signal to a desired reference signal despite the disturbances.

The paper is organized as follows: Section 2 describes the background of physical interpretations based on a generalized proportional-integral controller and the partial state concept for the proposed flat filter controller. Section 3 presents the buck-boost power converter circuit design and the flat filter controller's performance in closed-loop for the buck-boost power converter. Section 4 shows the experimental setup and results of the flat filter controller's performance in closed-loop. Finally, Section 5 gives the conclusions of the proposed flat filter controller.

2. Background of physical interpretations

Our solution was centered on reviewing the polynomial criterion $z(s)a(s) + w(s)b(s) = 1$ for the coprimeness of $[a(s), b(s)]$. To better understand the physical significance of this condition, we note that $[b(s), a(s)]$ are not arbitrary polynomials but are related to the system input and output by

$$y(s) = \frac{b(s)}{a(s)}u(s) \tag{1}$$

Now, we can rewrite (1) as

$$y(s) = b(s)\xi(s), a(s)\xi(s) = u(s) \tag{2}$$

We should recall that the partial state $\xi(t)$ and its time derivatives entirely determine the state of any realization [19].

On the other hand, we expose the validity of flat filters or robust GPIC for handling simplified models of perturbed controllable systems [5, 20, 21]. We briefly illustrate this in the context of an output stabilization task for a pure integration, third-order system. Consider the linear time-invariant system:

$$\dddot{y}(t) = u(t) \tag{3}$$

Integrating the system expression once and again while purposefully neglecting the effects of the unknown initial conditions, one obtains two expressions for the unknowns $\hat{\ddot{y}}$ and $\hat{\dot{y}}$, which we subsequently address as the structural estimates: $\hat{\ddot{y}}$ and $\hat{\dot{y}}$ of those variables. These two variables, in terms of iterated integrals of inputs, are just given by

$$\hat{\ddot{y}} = \int_0^t u(\tau)d\tau, \hat{\dot{y}} = \int_0^t \int_0^\lambda u(\tau)d\tau d\lambda \tag{4}$$

These estimates, or integral reconstructors [5], of the phase variables, $\hat{\ddot{y}}$ and $\hat{\dot{y}}$, are off by a first-degree time polynomial and by a constant term depending on the unknown initial conditions. Using these faulty estimates in any stabilizing linear feedback scheme demands additive integral output compensation, including up to a double integral of the available output signal. A stabilizing controller proposed to be

$$u = \left[-\gamma_4 \hat{\ddot{y}} - \gamma_3 \hat{\dot{y}} - \gamma_2 y - \gamma_1 \left(\int y\right) - \gamma_0 \left(\int\int y\right)\right] \tag{5}$$

After substituting the expressions of the integral reconstructors for $\hat{\ddot{y}}$ and $\hat{\dot{y}}$, the following implicit expression for the controller is obtained.

$$u = \left[-\gamma_4 \int\int u - \gamma_3 \int u - \gamma_2 y - \gamma_1 \left(\int y\right) - \gamma_0 \left(\int\int y\right)\right] \tag{6}$$

Simple association of the iterated integrals leads to the following equivalent expressions, fully explaining the controller representation depicted in **Figure 1a**.

$$u + \gamma_4 \int\int u + \gamma_3 \int u = -\gamma_2 y - \gamma_1 \left(\int y\right) - \gamma_0 \left(\int\int y\right) \tag{7}$$

Applying Laplace transforms in the last expression and after rearrangement, it yields

$$u(s) = -\left[\frac{\gamma_2 s^2 + \gamma_1 s + \gamma_0}{s^2 + \gamma_4 s + \gamma_3}\right] y(s) \tag{8}$$

or

$$y(s) = -\left[\frac{s^2 + \gamma_4 s + \gamma_3}{\gamma_2 s^2 + \gamma_1 s + \gamma_0}\right] u(s) = -\left[\frac{b(s)}{a(s)}\right] u(s) \tag{9}$$

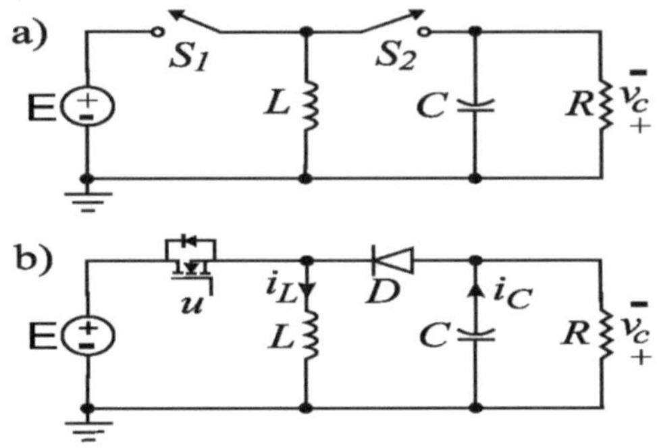

Figure 1.
Buck-boost converter. (a) Switch implementation. (b) Transistor diode implementation.

Employing the partial state approach (1) and (2), thus we have the following

$$y(s) = \left(s^2 + \gamma_4 s + \gamma_3\right)\xi(s) \tag{10}$$

Applying the inverse transforms of Laplace to (7) yields the following

$$y(t) = \ddot{\xi}(t) + \gamma_4\dot{\xi}(t) + \gamma_3\xi(t) \tag{11}$$

Therefore, we calculate the partial state dynamics as follows.

$$\begin{aligned} \dot{\xi}_1(t) &= \xi_2(t) \\ \dot{\xi}_2(t) &= -\gamma_3\xi_1(t) - \gamma_4\xi_2(t) + y(t) \end{aligned} \tag{12}$$

Substituting the partial state dynamics in (5) to calculate the input control, we have

$$u(s) = -\left[\gamma_2 s^2 + \gamma_1 s + \gamma_0\right]\xi(s) \tag{13}$$

Once again, applying the inverse transforms of Laplace to (11), we have

$$u(t) = -\gamma_2\ddot{\xi}(t) - \gamma_1\dot{\xi}(t) - \gamma_0\xi(t) \tag{14}$$

Employing the dynamics of (10) into (12), finally, we have the input control as

$$\begin{aligned} u(t) &= -\gamma_2\left[-\gamma_3\xi_1(t) - \gamma_4\xi_2(t) + y_\xi(t)\right] - \gamma_1[\xi_2(t)] - \gamma_0\xi_1(t) \\ &= (\gamma_2\gamma_3 - \gamma_0)\xi_1(t) + (\gamma_2\gamma_4 - \gamma_1)\xi_2(t) - \gamma_2 y(t) \end{aligned} \tag{15}$$

Notice that the partial state dynamics $\xi(t)$ helps filter the output, considering $y(t)$ as an input.

3. The buck-boost power converter circuit

Figure 2 illustrates the buck-boost converter, which can produce an output voltage lower than, equal to, or higher than the input voltage. Unlike the buck and boost

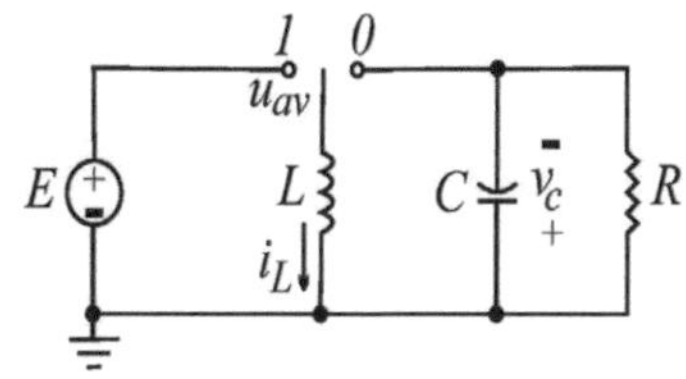

Figure 2.
Average model equivalent circuit of the buck-boost converter.

converters, this topology generates a negative output voltage when operating without isolation [1].

3.1 Continuous conduction mode

In the buck-boost converter's continuous conduction mode (CCM), the current through the inductor L never drops to zero. The operation is divided into two stages: when the switch S_1 is closed, the inductor is charged with the potential of the input source E, storing energy in its magnetic field while the switch S_2 is open. In the second stage, when the switch S_1 is open, the inductor attempts to maintain current continuity by releasing the stored energy *via* S_2, allowing energy transfer to the load. Remember, the output voltage can be either higher or lower than the input voltage but always has a negative polarity (see **Figure 1(a)**). Without loss of generality, we introduce a change in terminology and now define the inductor current as i_L, the supply voltage as E, the diode as D, the output voltage as v_C, the load as R, and the converter's duty cycle as u. Consequently, the equivalent transistor diode implementation is shown in **Figure 1(b)**. In that sense, the steady-state analysis assumptions for the buck and boost converter follow now: i_L is given by

$$i_L(t) = \frac{1}{L}E(t) + I_L(0) \tag{16}$$

where $I_L(0)$ represents the initial inductor current, corresponding to its minimum value, evaluating (16) at $t = uT$, the moment when the switch turns off, yields the maximum inductor current. This results in the following relationship:

$$I_{L\max} - I_{L\min} = \frac{1}{L}EuT \tag{17}$$

Similarly, in mode 2, the inductor current is given by

$$i_L(t) = -\frac{v_C}{L}(t - uT) + I_L(uT) \tag{18}$$

Evaluating (18) at $t = T$, and since we assume steady-state operation, we use $I_L(0) = I_L(T)$ to obtain the following

$$I_L(0) = -\frac{v_C}{L}(T - uT) + I_L(uT) \tag{19}$$

Thus, we have

$$I_{L\max} - I_{L\min} = \frac{v_C}{L}(1 - u)T \tag{20}$$

Equating (17) with (20), we obtain the following voltage conversion ratio:

$$\frac{v_C}{E} = \frac{u}{(1-u)} \tag{21}$$

The output voltage can be either smaller or more significant than the input voltage:
u > 0.5 Boost.
u < 0.5 Buck.
u = 0.5 Unity gain.
We calculate the average input current as follows.

$$I_{in} = \frac{(I_{L\max} + I_{L\min})u}{2} \tag{22}$$

and the average output current is given by

$$I_o = \frac{(I_{L\max} + I_{L\min})(1-u)}{2} \tag{23}$$

As we know that the power held, we use the following relation $I_{in}E = I_o v_C$ to obtain

$$\frac{I_{in}}{I_o} = \frac{v_C}{E} = \frac{u}{(1-u)} \tag{24}$$

To solve for $I_{L\max}$ and $I_{L\min}$ in terms of the converter components, we substitute for $I_o = v_C/R$. Hence, from (20) and (23) we obtain

$$I_{L\max} = E\left[\frac{u}{R(1-u)^2} + \frac{uT}{2L}\right] \tag{25}$$

while the minimum inductor current value is given by

$$I_{L\min} = E\left[\frac{u}{R(1-u)^2} - \frac{uT}{2L}\right] \tag{26}$$

In the above equation, the critical inductor value that keeps the buck-boost converter in the discontinuous conduction mode (DCM) mode can yield through $I_{L\min} = 0$.

$$L_{crit} = \frac{RT(1-u)^2}{2} = \frac{R(1-u)^2}{2f} \tag{27}$$

Notice that for the same frequency of operation and load resistance, the buck converter has the highest critical inductor limit compared to the boost and buck-boost one. In contrast, the boost converter has the smallest L_{crit}, resulting in a broader range of inductor designs.

3.1.1 Output voltage ripple

It shows that the capacitor current of the buck-boost converter is the same as that of the boost. Thus, the capacitor voltages are given by

$$\frac{\Delta v_c}{v_c} = \frac{uT}{RC} = \frac{u}{RCf} \tag{28}$$

3.1.2 Buck-boost nominal values

The value of the critical inductance from (27) is given by

$$L_{crit} = \frac{47(1-0.5)^2}{2(45 \times 10^3)} \approx 130\,\mu H \tag{29}$$

To have a small ripple in the input current, we choose the inductance value L as follows

$$L = 3.85 \times L_{crit} = 500\,\mu H \tag{30}$$

with this nominal value and employing (17), the input current error is

$$\Delta i_L = \frac{1}{L} EuT = \frac{(20 \times 0.5)}{(500 \times 10^{-6})(45 \times 10^3)} = 0.444A \tag{31}$$

On the other hand, the ripple level of the output voltage is calculated as:

$$\Delta v_c = \left(\frac{0.5}{47(470 \times 10^{-6})(45 \times 10^3)}\right) 20 = 10 \times 10^{-3} V \tag{32}$$

Table 1 shows all the nominal values of the buck-boost power converter. These values were calculated to work in continuous conduction mode (CCM). The next subsection will deal with the Flat Filter Controller design based on the buck-boost average model.

3.2 Average model of the buck-boost power converter

We designed the buck-boost power converter to work in continuous conduction mode (CCM) to guarantee that the buck-boost average model is always continuous. For this, we average the input control at the time interval fixed as follows

$$u_{av}(t) = \frac{1}{T}\int_0^T u(\tau)d\tau = \frac{1}{T}\left[\int_0^{\frac{T}{2}} u(\tau)d\tau + \int_{\frac{T}{2}}^T u(\tau)d\tau\right] \tag{33}$$

When we calculate the average value of the input control shown in **Figure 2**. Thus, we have the following

$$u_{av}(t) = \frac{1}{T}\left[\int_0^{\frac{T}{2}} 1 \times d\tau + \int_{\frac{T}{2}}^T 0 \times d\tau\right] = \frac{1}{T}\int_0^{\frac{T}{2}} 1 \times d\tau = \frac{1}{T}\frac{T}{2} = \frac{1}{2} \tag{34}$$

Employing the laws of Kirchhoff, we calculate the average dynamical model of the buck-boost power converter shown in **Figure 2**, which is described by

Parameter	Nominal value
L	500 μH
C	470 μH
R	47 Ω
E	20 V
f	45 kHz
Δi_L	0.444 A
Δv_c	10 mV

Table 1.
Buck-boost parameters.

$$L\frac{di_L}{dt} = (1 - u_{av})v_C + Eu_{av} \tag{35}$$

$$C\frac{dv_C}{dt} = -(1 - u_{av})i_L - \left(\frac{1}{R}\right)v_C \tag{36}$$

where v_C is the output capacitor voltage, i_L is the inductor current, E is a constant voltage value of the main power supply voltage, R is the load resistance, while L and C are the inductance and capacitance parameters of the power converter. The average control input u_{av} is the average value of the binary-valued switch position function $u \in \{0, 1\}$, which is defined in the closed-interval value $u_{av} \in [0, 1]$. Thus, we obtain a state average model of the buck-boost circuit, described in Ref. [1].

The buck-boost converter average model assumes that power-switching devices and converter components are lossless. Then, a precise average model is not required, which justifies the use of model-free control methods [8], such as Classical PID Control [5], Sliding Mode Control [4], and Active Disturbance Rejection Control (ADRC) such as the one proposed in the present paper [20, 21].

Then, the equilibrium points of the buck-boost power converters system (35)–(36) can be obtained in a parameterized form as a function of the corresponding output voltage equilibrium (constant desired reference), $\overline{v}_C = V_d < 0$, that is

$$\overline{u}_{av} = \frac{V_d}{V_d - E}, \quad \overline{\imath}_L = \frac{V_d(V_d - E)}{RE} \tag{37}$$

with $\overline{u}_{av} \in [0, 1]$. Note that if $\overline{u}_{av} = 0.5$, then $\overline{v}_C = E$. For $\overline{u}_{av} > 0.5$, then $\overline{v}_C > E$. Finally, if $\overline{u}_{av} < 0.5$, then $\overline{v}_C < E$. Consequently, the buck-boost power converter circuit has three modes of operation to regulate its output voltage. The zero-dynamics corresponding to the desired output voltage: $\overline{v}_C = V_d$, is given by the unstable differential equation for the average inductor current:

$$L\frac{di_L}{dt} = \frac{V_d}{LRi_L}(E - V_d) + \frac{E}{L} \tag{38}$$

thus, the output voltage is a non-minimum phase variable [2, 6]. The state average buck-boost power converter model is locally differentially flat, that is, feedback linearizable. The output function (flat output or linearizing output) leading to the state space exact linearization system is the following [2, 4]:

$$H(i_L, v_C) = \frac{1}{2}\left[Li_L^2 + C(E - v_C)^2\right] \tag{39}$$

we have then the following coordinate transformations:

$$\begin{bmatrix} x_1 \\ x_2 \end{bmatrix} = \phi(i_L, v_C) = \begin{bmatrix} \frac{1}{2}Li_L^2 + C(E - v_C)^2 \\ Ei_L + v_C\frac{1}{R}(E - v_C) \end{bmatrix} \tag{40}$$

According to **Proposition 2.1** [23] the Jacobian matrix at $x(0) = (0, 0)^T$ of the function (40) is nonsingular, hence $\phi(x)$ is a local diffeomorphism in an open subset $x \in R^n$ including x (0). The flat output H is, as it is easily verified, the relative degree $^{\circ}r = 2$. According to the coordinate transformation in (40), the original system (35)–(36) can be transformed into the following normal form:

$$\dot{x}_1 = x_2 \tag{41}$$

$$\dot{x}_2 = \alpha(x) + \beta(x)u_{av} \tag{42}$$

where, x_1 and x_2 are states, u_{av} is the average control input, and $y(t) = x_1$ is the Flat output. The variables $\alpha(x) := Ev_C/L + (2v_C - E)\left(\frac{v_C}{R^2C} + \frac{i_L}{RC}\right)$ and $\beta(x) := E(E - v_C)/L + \frac{i_L}{RC}(E - 2v_C)$ are the nonlinear scalar functions of x. The last equation, which involves the control variable u_{av} is nonlinear. We know $\beta(x) \neq 0$, considering that the relative degree $^{\circ}r$ is well-defined. The equilibrium of the average total stored energy, corresponding to an operating point $(\bar{\imath}_L, \bar{v}_C)$, is given, in terms of the voltage equilibrium value, $\bar{v}_C$, by:

$$\overline{H}(\bar{\imath}_L, \bar{v}_C) = \frac{1}{2}\left[L\bar{\imath}_L^2 + C(E - \bar{v}_C)^2\right] \tag{43}$$

where $\overline{H}$ is the constant desired reference of the Flat Output, which has a direct dependency on the desired output voltage V_d. Thus, we have

$$\overline{H} = \frac{1}{2}\left[\frac{LV_d^2(V_d - E)^2}{(RE)^2} + C(E - V_d)^2\right] \tag{44}$$

3.3 Flat filter controller design

We define the energy error as: $e_H = H - \overline{H}$, and instead of using the transformed canonical dynamics (40) and (41) in terms of $(x_1, x_2) = (H, \dot{H})$, for the total average stored energy dynamics, we examine the relation between the second-order time derivative of e_H and the average control input u_{av} in terms of the original average model state variables i_L and v_C. Thus, the energy error dynamics are given by

$$\ddot{e}_H(t) = \alpha(x) + \beta(x)u_{av} \tag{45}$$

Borrowing concepts from ADRC, which are intimately related also to the model-free controller (MFC), we intend to ignore the nonlinearities largely appearing in the total stored energy second derivative expression $\ddot{H}$. We simplify the model to a completely unstructured model. Consider the input channel modified dynamics with a state and dependent total perturbation term:

$$\begin{aligned} \ddot{e}_H(t) &= \xi(i_L, v_C, u_{av}) + ae_u \\ \xi(i_L, v_C, u_{av}) &= \alpha(x) + \beta(x)u_{av} - ae_u \end{aligned} \tag{46}$$

where $a \in R, a \neq 0$, the error of the input control is defined as: $e_u = u_{av} - \overline{u}_{av}$. The next crucial and controversial step has been recently rigorously justified in Refs. [8–14] in the context of ADRC and the work [20, 21] in the context of MFC. This consists of replacing the internal nonlinearity $\xi(i_L, v_C, u_{av}) = z_1$ by a low degree, unstructured time polynomial model represented as a local internal disturbance model (described by a corresponding low-order homogeneous linear state model) in the simplified dynamics. This is achieved by either letting: $\dot{z}_1 = 0$ in the zeroth degree polynomial model case. This step is performed disregarding the state and control input dependence of the additive nonlinearities in the additive term: $\xi(i_L, v_C, u_{av})$. The choice of the nonzero constant, a, replacing the nonlinear, state, and input-dependent gain, which turns out to be, more surprisingly, quite arbitrary [20, 21]; although educated guesses, or, alternatively, local algebraically-based parameter identification procedures may prove to be substantially effective [21]. The model to be controlled, using a first-order local homogeneous state model for the state and input-dependent nonlinearities, $\xi(i_L, v_C, u_{av}) = z_1$, is thus given by

$$\dddot{e}_H(t) = \dot{z}_1 + a\dot{e}_u \tag{47}$$

we calculate the integral reconstructors $\hat{\ddot{e}}_H$, and $\hat{\dot{e}}_H$ from (47) as follows

$$\hat{\ddot{e}}_H = ae_u, \hat{\dot{e}}_H = a\int_0^t e_u(\tau)d\tau \tag{48}$$

From (5), we propose a regulation controller in terms of the energy error

$$e_u = \left[-\gamma_4\hat{\ddot{e}}_H - \gamma_3\hat{\dot{e}}_H - \gamma_2 e_H - \gamma_1\left(\int_0^t e_H(\tau)d\tau\right) - \gamma_0\left(\int_0^t\int_0^\lambda e_H(\tau)d\tau d\lambda\right)\right] \tag{49}$$

Substituting (48) into (49) and combining common terms, we have the following

$$(1 + a\gamma_4)e_u + a\gamma_3\int_0^t e_u(\tau)d\tau = -\gamma_2 e_H - \gamma_1\left(\int_0^t e_H(\tau)d\tau\right) - \gamma_0\left(\int_0^t\int_0^\lambda e_H(\tau)d\tau d\lambda\right) \tag{50}$$

We calculate the time derivative twice to (50) and yield the following

$$(1 + a\gamma_4)\ddot{e}_u(t) + a\gamma_3\dot{e}_u(t) = -\gamma_2\ddot{e}_H(t) - \gamma_1\dot{e}_H - \gamma_0 e_H(t) \tag{51}$$

Applying the Laplace transform to (49) and after rearrangement,

$$e_H(s) = -\frac{(1 + a\gamma_4)s^2 + a\gamma_3 s}{(\gamma_2 s^2 + \gamma_1 s + \gamma_0)}e_u(s) \tag{52}$$

Employing the *partial state approach* to (52), thus we have the following

$$e_H(s) = \left[(1 + a\gamma_4)s^2 + a\gamma_3 s\right]\xi(s) \tag{53}$$

From (53), we calculate the partial state dynamics as follows:

$$\begin{aligned}\dot{\xi}_1(t) &= \xi_2(t)\\ \dot{\xi}_2(t) &= -\left[\frac{a\gamma_3}{(1 + a\gamma_4)}\right]\xi_2(t) + e_H(t)\end{aligned} \tag{54}$$

Therefore, the Flat Filter Controller (FFC) law is proposed from (8) as follows:

$$e_u(s) = -\left[\gamma_2 s^2 + \gamma_1 s + \gamma_0\right]\xi(s) = -\gamma_2 s^2\xi(s) - \gamma_1 s\xi(s) - \gamma_0\xi(s) \tag{55}$$

Applying the Laplace inverse transform to (55), we obtain the following:

$$e_u(t) = -\gamma_2\ddot{\xi}(t) - \gamma_1\dot{\xi}(t) - \gamma_0\xi(t) \tag{56}$$

Substituting the partial state dynamics (54) together with the input control nominal value in (56), finally, we have the FFC law

$$u_{av}(t) = \left(\frac{V_d}{V_d - E}\right) + \left(\frac{a\gamma_2\gamma_3}{1 + a\gamma_4} - \gamma_1\right)\xi_2(t) - \gamma_0\xi_1(t) - \left(\frac{\gamma_2}{1 + a\gamma_4}\right)e_H(t) \tag{57}$$

The Flat Filter Controller is based on the *partial state dynamics* (54), this approach of control constitutes a reinterpretation of GPIC [5] in the form of classical compensation networks (CCN). Roughly speaking, any linear controllable system whose output is Brunovski's output can be output regulated with the help of a well-tuned proper linear filter and a suitable linear combination of the available internal states of such filter. The characteristic polynomial of the normalized closed-loop system, ignoring the attenuated effects of the nonlinearities and disturbances, is given by

$$p_d(s) = \left(s^2 + 2\zeta\omega_n s + \omega_n^2\right)^2(s + \alpha) \tag{58}$$

with $\zeta = 0.707, \omega_n = \alpha = 10,\ a = 5$. Thus, the gains of the flat filter controller (FFC) are given by

$$\begin{aligned}\gamma_4 = \alpha + 4\zeta\omega_n, \gamma_3 = 4\alpha\zeta\omega_n + 2\omega_n^2 + 4\zeta^2\omega_n, \gamma_2 = 2\alpha\omega_n^2 + 4\alpha\zeta^2\omega_n + 4\zeta\omega_n^3,\\ \gamma_1 = \omega_n^4 + 4\zeta\alpha\omega_n^3, \gamma_0 = \alpha\omega_n^4\end{aligned} \tag{59}$$

3.4 Simulation results

This subsection compares two controllers: our FFC proposal and the digital predictor controller (DPC). We can observe that the DPC has a regulation error higher than the FFC. On the other hand, the response of the DPC inductor current presents a ripple current content longer than the FFC. FFC and DPC reach the desired constant value reference in a short time. Under the sudden output load changes, both controllers show a speedy recovery. **Figure 3** shows the simulation results for both controllers.

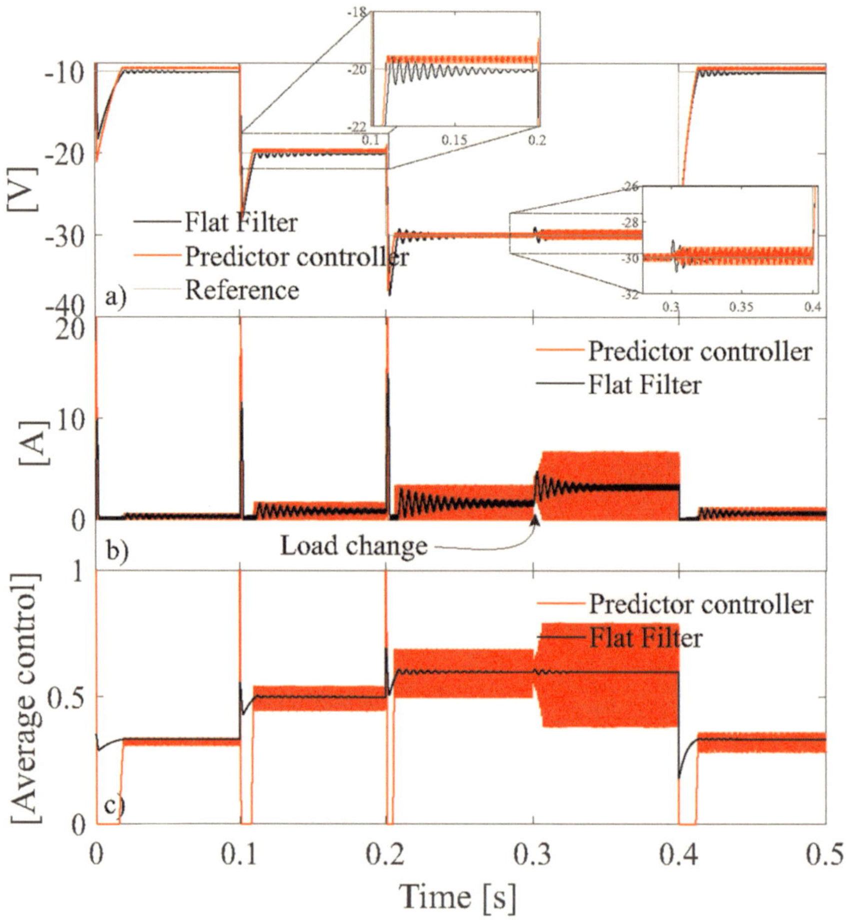

Figure 3.
Performance of the FFC versus DPC. (a) Output voltage responses. (b) Inductor current responses. (c) Input control responses.

4. Experimental results

The controller performance tests are performed using the experimental platform shown in **Figure 4** and the parameters shown in **Table 1**. The performance is studied based on changes in the output voltage reference, load resistance, and the converter supply voltage level variation.

In this sense, **Figure 5** shows the output voltage response when varying the reference voltage V_d between three levels: 10, 20, and 30 V. In this test, you also measure the current response in the inductor, and it is shown in **Figure 6**. The results show that the control scheme adequately follows the desired reference.

On the other hand, changes are made to the converter's output load resistance. The load resistance of the converter is 47Ω to which a resistor of the same value is connected in parallel for approximately 3 s. **Figure 7** shows the performance response of the control scheme at three different output voltages: 10, 20, and 30 V. **Figure 7(a)** shows the output voltage response, which remains regulated at the desired voltage during changes in load resistance, with minimal output voltage variations. **Figure 7(b)** shows the

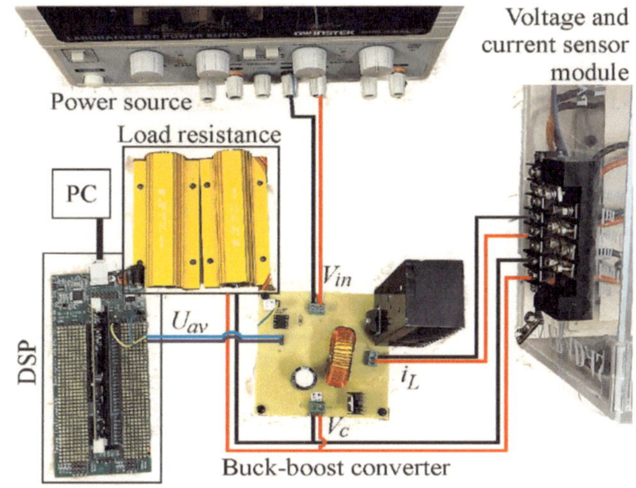

Figure 4.
Connecting the experimental platform.

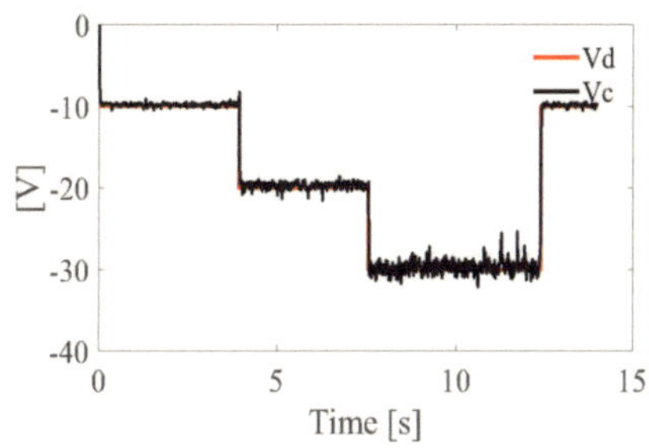

Figure 5.
Output voltage response to reference voltage variations.

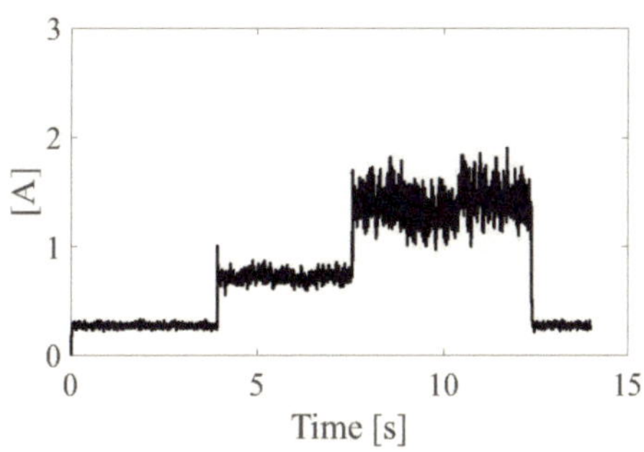

Figure 6.
Current response in the inductor during variations of the output voltage reference.

current response in the inductor, where it is observed that the current doubles during the time interval of the output resistance disturbance. **Figure 7(c)** shows the control maneuver to compensate for the load resistance disturbance.

Finally, tests are performed with variations in the supply voltage of the buck-boost converter. The supply voltage variation range goes from 15 to 25 V. **Figure 8(a)** shows

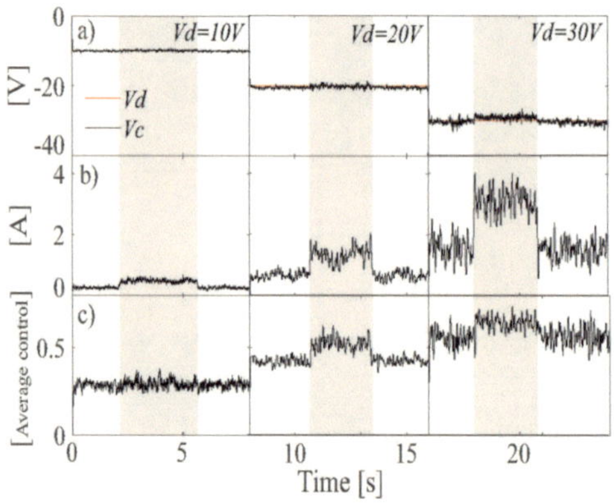

Figure 7.
Response of the buck-boost converter when changing the load resistance in the range marked with the shaded area: (a) output voltage response, (b) current response in the inductor, and (c) control input response.

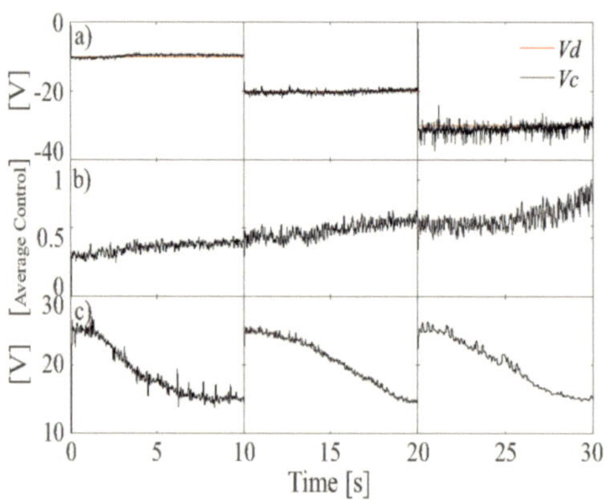

Figure 8.
Response of the buck-boost converter when varying the converter supply voltage level: (a) output voltage response, (b) inductor current response, and (c) supply voltage.

the response of the converter output voltage when the supply voltage level is varied. In this figure, the output voltage remains at the desired reference level. **Figure 8(b)** shows the compensation maneuver of the control input signal. The variation of the supply voltage level of the buck-boost converter is shown in **Figure 8(c)**.

5. Conclusions

The buck-boost power converter's flat filter controller design is robust to sudden output load changes and sudden voltage supply. The flat filter control methodology begins with the transfer function, after employing the integral reconstructors and finishes with the state partial to find the controller. FFC is easy to implement and tune, since a Hurwitz polynomial makes the tuning. The TMS320F28335 digital signal processor chip helped demonstrate the static and dynamic performance of FFC in closed-loop in the output voltage regulation of the Buck-boost power converter, even though the output voltage is a state variable of non-minimum phase.

Acknowledgements

Parts of this chapter were previously published in the article entitled Robust flat filtering DSP-based control of the boost converter, H. Sira-Ramirez, A. Hernández-Méndez, J. Linares-Flores, A. Luviano-Juárez, Control Theory Technology, Springer-Verlag, Vol. 14, No. 3, pp. 224–236, ISSN: 2095-6983, August 2016. DOI: 10.1007/s11768-016-6025-6.

Conflict of interest

The authors declare no conflict of interest.

Notes/thanks/other declarations

Thanks to Dr. Hebertt Sira-Ramirez for all his advice on the creation of this chapter.

Abbreviations

MFC	model-free control
GPIC	generalized proportional integral control
FFC	flat filter control
SMC	sliding mode control
PIDC	proportional integral derivative control
ADRC	active disturbance rejection control

Author details

Jesús Linares-Flores[1*], Arturo Hernández-Méndez[1], José Antonio Juárez-Abad[1], Gerardo Mino-Aguilar[2], José Fermi Guerrero-Castellanos[2], Germán Ardul Muñoz Hernández[1] and Cesar Arriaga-Arriaga[1]

1 Universidad Tecnologica de la Mixteca, Huajuapan de Leon, Oaxaca, Mexico

2 Benemerita Universidad Autonoma de Puebla, Puebla, Mexico

*Address all correspondence to: jlinares@mixteco.utm.mx

IntechOpen

© 2025 The Author(s). Licensee IntechOpen. This chapter is distributed under the terms of the Creative Commons Attribution License (http://creativecommons.org/licenses/by/4.0), which permits unrestricted use, distribution, and reproduction in any medium, provided the original work is properly cited.

References

[1] Batarseh I. Power Electronic Circuits. 1st ed. United States of America: John Wiley; 2004. ISBN 0-471-12662-4

[2] Linares-Flores J, Barahona-Avalos JL, Sira-Ramírez H, Contreras-Ordaz MA. Robust passivity based control of a buck–boost–converter/DC–motor system: An active disturbance rejection approach. IEEE Transactions on Industry Applications. 2012;**48**(6):2362-2371, ISSN: 0093-9994

[3] William Z-BE, Linares-Flores J, Guzmán-Ramírez E, Sira-Ramírez H. FPGA implementation of PID controller for the stabilization of a DC-DC Buck converter. Frontiers in Advanced Control Systems. 2012;**10**:215-230. ISBN 978-953-51-0677-7

[4] Linares-Flores J, Juarez-Abad JA, Hernandez-Mendez A, Castro-Heredia O, Guerrero-Castellanos JF, Heredia-Barba R, et al. Sliding mode control based on linear extended state observer for DC-to-DC Buck-boost power converter system with mismatched disturbances. IEEE Transactions on Industry Applications. 2022;**58**(1):940-950. DOI: 10.1109/TIA.2021.3130017

[5] Zurita-Bustamante EW, Linares-Flores J, Guzman-Ramirez EH, Sira-Ramirez H. A comparison between the GPI and the PID controllers for the stabilization of a DC-DC buck converter: A field programmable gate array implementation. IEEE Transactions on Industrial Electronics. 2011;**58**(11):5251-5262, ISSN: 0278-0046

[6] Sira-Ramirez H, Agrawal SK. Differentially Flat Systems. 1st ed. Marcel Dekker Inc.; 2004. ISBN 10-987-65432-1

[7] Levine J. Analysis and Control of Nonlinear Systems. 1st ed. Dordrecht Heidelberg London New York: Springer; 2009. ISBN 978-3-642-00838-2

[8] Kang J, Huang X, Xia C, Huang D, Wang F. Ultralocal model-free adaptive supertwisting nonsingular terminal sliding mode control for magnetic levitation system. IEEE Transactions on Industrial Electronics. 2024;**71**(5):5187-5194. DOI: 10.1109/TIE.2023.3285925

[9] Han J. From PID to active disturbance rejection control. IEEE Transactions on Industrial Electronics. 2009;**56**(3):900-906

[10] Zheng Q, Chen Z, Gao Z. A practical approach to disturbance decoupling control. Control Engineering Practice. 2009;**17**(9):1016-1025

[11] Zheng Q, Gao L, Gao Z. On validation of extended state observer through analysis and experimentation. ASME Journal of Dynamic Systems, Measurement and Control. 2012;**134**(2):1-6

[12] Guo B, Zhao Z. Weak convergence of nonlinear high-gain tracking differentiator. IEEE Transactions on Automatic Control. 2013;**58**(4):1074-1080

[13] Guo B, Zhao Z. On the convergence of an extended state observer for nonlinear systems with uncertainty. Systems Control Letters. 2011;**60**(6):420-430

[14] Guo B, Zhao Z. On the convergence of the nonlinear active disturbance rejection control for MIMO systems. SIAM Journal of Control and Optimization. 2013;**51**(2):1727-1757

[15] Madoński R, Herman P. Survey on methods of increasing the efficiency of extended state disturbance observers. ISA Transactions. 2014;**56**: 18-27

[16] Goodwin GC, Sin KS. Adaptive Filtering Prediction and Control. Mineola, N.Y.: United States of America Dover Publications, Inc.; 2014

[17] Algreer M, Armstrong M, Giaouris D. Adaptive PD+I control of a switch-mode DC–DC power converter using a recursive FIR predictor. IEEE Transactions on Industry Applications. 2011;**47**(5):2135-2144. DOI: 10.1109/TIA.2011.2161856

[18] Kelly A, Rinne K. A self-compensating adaptive digital regulator for switching converters based on linear prediction. In: Twenty-First Annual IEEE Applied Power Electronics Conference and Exposition, 2006. APEC '06, Dallas, TX, USA; 2006. p. 7. DOI: 10.1109/APEC.2006.1620617

[19] Kailath T. Linear Systems. 1st ed. Prentice-Hall, Inc.; 1980. ISBN 10-987-65432-1

[20] Zurita Bustamante EW, Sira-Ramírez H, Linares-Flores J. An equivalence between the ADRC and the flat filtering controllers: A case study in double buck converter. In: 2018 14th International Conference on Power Electronics (CIEP), Cholula, Puebla, Mexico. 2018. pp. 188-193. DOI: 10.1109/CIEP.2018.8573339

[21] Sira-Ramírez H, Zurita-Bustamante EW, Huang C. Equivalence among flat filters, dirty derivative-based PID controllers, ADRC, and integral reconstructor-based sliding mode control. IEEE Transactions on Control Systems Technology. 2020;**28**(5): 1696-1710. DOI: 10.1109/TCST.2019.2919822

[22] Sira-Ramirez H, Luviano-Juarez A, Ramirez-Neria M, Zurita-Bustamante E. Active Disturbance Rejection Control of Dynamic Systems: A Flatness-Based Approach. 1st ed. United Kingdom: Butterworth-Heinemann Elsevier; 2017. ISBN 978-0-12-849868-2

[23] Lu Q, Sun Y, Mei S. Nonlinear Control Systems and Power System Dynamics. First ed. United States of America: Kluwer Academic Publishers; 2010. ISBN 9-781441-948854